the ATOMIC BOMB

the ATOMIC BOMB

The Great Decision

Second Revised Edition
Edited by Paul R. Baker
New York University

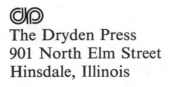
The Dryden Press
901 North Elm Street
Hinsdale, Illinois

Copyright © 1976 by The Dryden Press
A division of Holt, Rinehart and Winston
All rights reserved
Library of Congress Catalog Card Number: 75–36668
ISBN: 0–03–089873–0
Printed in the United States of America
6789 090 987654321

Cover illustration: A desert "flower" of colossal
proportions blossoms rapidly above the sandy floor at
Yucca Flat, Nevada, during A-bomb testing in May, 1952.
(United Press International)

Contents

Chronology   vii

Introduction   1

Part One   **Problems of Strategy to End the War**

1. *Henry L. Stimson*   The Decision to Use the Bomb   13

2. *Samuel Eliot Morison*   The Bomb and Concurrent Negotiations with Japan   29

3. *Hanson W. Baldwin*   The Strategic Need for the Bomb Questioned   41

4. *Herbert Feis*   The Great Decision: Pros and Cons   49

Part Two   **Diplomatic Fencing and the Cold War**

5. *P. M. S. Blackett*   A Check to the Soviet Union   61

6. *David Joel Horowitz*   The Bomb as a Cause of East-West Conflict   66

7. *Gar Alperovitz* A Demonstration of American Power to the Soviet Union   71

8. *Michael Amrine* "Believing the Unbelievable"   79

9. *Gabriel Kolko* A Question of Power   84

10. *Martin J. Sherwin* The Bomb and the Origins of the Cold War   92

Part Three **The Administrative Context**

11. *Kenneth M. Glazier* Administrative and Procedural Considerations   115

Part Four **The Moral Dimensions**

12. *Robert C. Batchelder* Changing Ethics in the Crucible of War   129

13. *Dwight Macdonald* The "Decline to Barbarism"   136

Part Five **The Bomb and the World Today**

14. *Richard H. Rovere* The Bomb: A Deterrent of War   147

15. *Carroll Quigley* Pervasive Consequences of Nuclear Stalemate   154

16. *Norbert Wiener* Moral and Social Aspects of Science and Technology   163

Part Six **A Summary View**

17. *Walter Smith Schoenberger* Decision of Destiny   173

Guide to Further Reading   186

Chronology—1945*

Feb. 4–11 At the Yalta Conference, Stalin promises to enter the war against Japan two or three months after Germany has surrendered.

Apr.   **7** Suzuki forms a new Japanese Cabinet which is to try to end the war.

Apr. 12 Franklin D. Roosevelt dies, and Harry S. Truman becomes President.

Apr. 25 The United Nations Conference opens in San Francisco.

May   **8** The war with Germany ends (V-E Day).

May   **9** The Interim Committee charged with advising the President on the development and use of atomic weapons meets for the first time.

May 31-June 1 The Interim Committee recommends use of the atomic bomb on a Japanese "dual target" as soon as possible and without prior warning.

June 12   The Franck Report is delivered to the office of the Secretary of War, and its substance is sent on to the Scientific Advisory Panel.

June 16   The Scientific Advisory Panel reports that it is unable to suggest an effective nonmilitary technical demonstration of the atomic bomb.

June 22   The Japanese Supreme War Strategy Council meets and approves a move to bring about a negotiated peace, seeking Soviet mediation.

July 12   Japanese Foreign Minister Togo instructs Ambassador Sato in Moscow to try to get Soviet mediation to end the war.

July 16   The first atomic explosion takes place at Alamogordo, N.M.

July 17-Aug. 2   The Potsdam Conference is held. On July 24, Truman casually informs Stalin that the United States has developed "a new weapon of unusual destructive force."

July 24   The results of the Chicago Metallurgical Laboratory poll of scientists on the use of the bomb are sent to General Groves and turned over to Stimson's office on August 1.

July 25   A directive, approved the previous day by Truman, is transmitted to General Carl Spaatz, Commanding General, U.S. Strategic Air Force, ordering the 509 Composite Group to "deliver its first special bomb as soon as weather will permit visual bombing after about 3, August, 1945"; with additional bombs to be delivered on selected targets "as soon as made ready."

July 26   The Potsdam Declaration, issued by Truman, Attlee, and Chiang Kai-shek, calls on the Japanese to surrender unconditionally or face "prompt and utter destruction." The Declaration does not mention the atomic bomb, and it does not give any assurance to the Japanese about retaining the emperor, though it assures the Japanese that they will ultimately be able to decide on their own form of government.

July 28   Suzuki calls the Potsdam Declaration "unworthy of public notice."

Aug. 6   A uranium atomic bomb ("Little Boy") is dropped on Hiroshima.

Aug. 8   The Soviet Union declares war on Japan and invades Manchuria the following day.

Aug. 9   A plutonium atomic bomb ("Fat Man") is dropped on Nagasaki.

Aug. 10   The Japanese Cabinet agrees to surrender on the Potsdam terms provided the sovereignty of the emperor may be retained.

Aug. 11   The U.S. replies to Japan, implicitly recognizing the emperor.

Aug. 14   Japan accepts the U.S. terms; the next day the Japanese people are first told that Japan has lost the war and surrendered.

Sept. 2   The instrument of surrender is signed in Tokyo Bay.

*Dates in local time.

theATUMIC BOMB

7

Introduction

Among the significant historical events of the twentieth century few surpass in dramatic impact and long-range importance the dropping of the two atomic bombs on Japan in the summer of 1945. The world at large was suddenly notified that a new era of human history had opened; with the testing of the first device at Alamogordo, New Mexico, in July 1945 and the destruction of Hiroshima and Nagasaki in August, the atomic age had begun. Man now had at his control a force capable both of bringing destruction and of doing work on an unprecedented scale. But with this new power, he soon became, to a degree, a creature of his own invention: the very existence of usable nuclear energy has been a fundamental determinant of the course of domestic and international relations since 1945.

The direct impetus for the program of atomic weapons development in the United States came in 1939. Late in the summer of that year, with the world on the verge of war, two Hungarian refugee scientists, Leo Szilard and Eugene

Wigner, became convinced of the need for systematic American investigation of the possible utilization of the power within the nucleus of the atom. Fearful of German research activity in this area, they persuaded Albert Einstein to sign a letter to President Roosevelt revealing that powerful new bombs might be developed and urging that American research be accelerated and given public support. Little action took place, however, until the end of 1941, when a substantial research and development program commenced. Subsequently, in August 1942, the Manhattan Engineer District, established under the War Department, set about to develop an atomic bomb. Directed by Brigadier General Leslie R. Groves, the Manhattan Project grew to a vast size; eventually some two billion dollars were spent and some 150,000 persons employed. Huge plants were built at Oak Ridge, Tennessee, and at Hanford, Washington, while laboratory research was carried on principally at the University of Chicago and at Los Alamos, New Mexico.

Even before July 16, 1945, when the new bomb was first tested secretly, controversy over use of the revolutionary device was building up within the scientific community. The project to develop the bomb had been instituted primarily out of fear that the Germans were attempting to develop such a weapon. Some of the scientists who had wanted it used against Germany were not, after the end of the war in Europe, so willing to have it employed against Japan. Moreover, as the strength and potentially greater power of the Soviet Union became evident during 1945, a few Americans who knew of the nuclear program considered the impact the new weapon would have on postwar international relations and began to warn that dropping the bomb on Japan would surely bring an arms race with the Soviet Union and might lead to an atomic war that could destroy civilization itself.

Szilard took the leading role in opposition to use of the as yet untested weapon. In April 1945 he arranged to send directly to President Roosevelt a memorandum setting forth his views as to why the bomb should not be employed, his fears as to its impact on American relations with the Soviet Union, and his suggestions as to the possibilities for control of atomic energy; but Roosevelt died before the memorandum could be given to him. When Szilard later tried to reach President Truman, he was referred to James F. Byrnes, who was soon to become Secretary of State. Szilard met with Byrnes in Spartanburg, South Carolina, but the meeting was not a success. Szilard and two fellow scientists failed to communicate their concern over an imminent arms race. Byrnes strongly believed that the United States must test, and if necessary use, the new weapon to show both the American and the Russian people the success of the project.

Many other scientists were also concerned about the implications of nuclear weapons. In April 1945, James Franck and Arthur H. Compton met with Secretary of Commerce Henry A. Wallace and gave him a memorandum detailing the ideas of the Chicago scientists on the political implications and the need for public awareness of the new force in the soon-to-arrive postwar world. This report stressed the danger of the complete annihilation of cities and peoples in atomic warfare, and urged the need for effective controls over the new weapon.

In the meantime, President Truman, on the advice of Secretary of War Henry L. Stimson, appointed a civilian advisory group known as the Interim Committee. Headed by Stimson and with Byrnes as the President's personal representative, this committee was charged with advising the President on the political, military, and scientific aspects of atomic energy. It was also to advise on the use of the atomic bomb—an underlying presumption was that it would be used—and to make recommendations for domestic and international controls of the new force.

On May 31 and June 1, 1945, the Interim Committee recommended to the President that the bomb be used against Japan as quickly as possible and without prior warning and that it be directed against a "dual target"—a military base or a war plant close to "houses and other buildings most susceptible to damage." One member of the committee, Undersecretary of the Navy Ralph Bard, later dissociated himself from these recommendations and urged instead a preliminary warning to the Japanese.

Scientific opposition continued and was crystallized in the so-called Franck Report. Scientists working at the Chicago Metallurgical Laboratory had formed a Committee on the Social and Political Implications of Atomic Energy with James Franck as chairman. Their report emphasized that the development of the new weapon could not long be kept secret and that its unexpected use would intensify the already present mistrust of the United States by the Soviet Union and surely lead to an arms race. Use of the weapon, it was also stressed, would endanger any possible future international control of atomic weapons, for the United States would have set an unfortunate precedent. The report recommended a demonstration on a desert or a barren island before representatives of the United Nations; if after this Japan still continued to reject an ultimatum to surrender, the weapon might be used. The Franck Report was routed to the Scientific Advisory Panel of the Interim Committee for consideration, but the panel members, all eminent scientists, were unable to make any suggestions for an effective test demonstration. There is no evidence that this fullest statement making a case against dropping the bomb was seen or directly discussed point by point by the full committee or the principal leaders for whom it had been intended.

Szilard continued his efforts to stop or delay use of the bomb and attempted to collect signatures among the scientists in Chicago who supported the Franck Report. When his petition was declared classified and its circulation forbidden, he sent around a new one protesting the use of the bomb on moral and humanitarian grounds and urging that the bomb not be dropped until Japan had been notified in detail of the terms to be imposed on her and given a chance to surrender. Another petition urging warnings to Japan and a nonmilitary demonstration of the bomb was sent to General Groves from Oak Ridge and a third came from another group at Chicago. At the same time, counterpetitions were being circulated among the scientists and signed by men opposed to the Szilard position. They supported the civilian and military leaders who planned to use the new weapon in the belief that it would save American lives by bringing a quick and conclusive victory over Japan.

Aware of the growing controversy, General Groves instructed Arthur Compton to supervise a poll of the atomic scientists. A formal poll was conducted among 150 scientists at Chicago, while J. Robert Oppenheimer at Los Alamos and Ernest Lawrence at Berkeley also made informal surveys of opinion. The Chicago poll indicated that 15 percent wanted the bomb used "in the manner that is from the military point of view most effective in bringing about prompt Japanese surrender"; 46 percent favored "a military demonstration in Japan to be followed by a renewed opportunity for surrender before full use of the weapon is employed," that is, limited use; 26 percent favored an experimental demonstration preceding military use; and 13 percent favored no military use. Groves and Compton both viewed this poll as support for prompt military use of the bomb.

The Interim Committee's recommendations of June 1 provided the basis for the ultimate decision as to how the new weapon would be employed against Japan, but specific military machinery for delivering the bombs had been set in motion many months earlier on the assumption that they would work and would be used. The military order from the office of the Chief of Staff to drop the atomic bombs on selected target cities was transmitted to General Carl Spaatz, Commanding General, United States Strategic Air Force, on July 25, the day before issuance of the final warning to Japan in the Potsdam Declaration. This ultimatum, which was released from Potsdam, Germany, where President Truman was meeting with the leaders of the Soviet Union and Great Britain, demanded "the unconditional surrender of all Japanese armed forces," threatening otherwise "prompt and utter destruction" of Japan. It did not mention the atomic bomb. President Truman later indicated that he gave final approval for use of the bomb from the high seas, on his return from the Potsdam Conference. Since no messages concerning this matter have been found, it is probable that this "final" decision was one not to change the existing plans. Decisions on the exact targets and timing of the bombs were made by the field commander.

The immediate public response in the United States to the dropping of the bombs is obscured by the rush of events in the days that followed and the rapid termination of the war. Perhaps jubilation that with the new weapon the war would soon be over was the prevalent feeling, though some Americans were obviously concerned by the morality of the wholesale slaughter. With the quick end to the war, those justifying the decision emphasized that the new atomic weapon had been a crucial factor in ending the conflict and thus in saving American and Japanese lives. As time has passed and as the complexities of the situation have unfolded, however, many negative judgments have been set forth.

Why has this issue contined to be disputed? Certainly many have felt that the position the United States Government took in 1945 was not well thought out, that the possible consequences of the act were not fully considered. While those defending the decision have generally stressed the strategic importance of the bomb in quickly ending the war, those opposed to it have dwelt more on the moral aspects of the problem. Many historians have dealt with the issue of the bombing of Nagasaki; was this second bomb really necessary to achieve American goals? Many historians have looked further into the diplomatic context of the decision to use the atomic weapon and have found implications that were not at first apparent. Some historians, particularly those on the political left, have stressed evidence supporting a view that the American use of the atomic bombs was an early step in the beginnings of the Cold War with the Soviet Union. Still other writers have studied the many ramifications of the act which bear on its ultimate historical significance. The present volume aims to show the full scope of the many arguments and interpretations involved with the several issues of the decision to use the atomic bomb in 1945.

The early historical discussion of the decision to use the bomb centered to a considerable extent about questions of strategy. Just how significant a factor had the atomic bombs actually been in bringing the war to a quick close? Was the bomb necessary to end the war? What was the precise nature of the decision as to its use? Could it have been utilized in a way that might have saved lives and prevented destruction? The first group of selections is generally concerned with problems of wartime strategy in the context of conditions during the final days of the war.

Henry L. Stimson's article reviews the development of the atomic energy program and shows that he and other officials up to 1945 considered the bomb as a military weapon that would be used as soon as it became available. When Truman became President in April 1945, Stimson, then Secretary of War, briefed him on the new weapon, about which Truman had previously known nothing. Is it possible that because Truman was new to office he did not exert the positive leadership in deciding what to do about the bomb that he might have provided if he had been more experienced? Is it possible that Stimson views the implications of the weapon too narrowly?

Samuel Eliot Morison focuses on the relation of the bomb to other historical elements that led to the ultimate step of Japan's surrender. The importance of the atomic bomb in bringing an end to the war must be viewed in light of pre-existing Japanese negotiation efforts, the strength of Japanese militarism, and the impact of the Soviet war declaration.

In the next article Hanson W. Baldwin, a military affairs analyst, taking direct issue with Stimson's position on the strategic importance of the bomb, denies that the new weapon significantly hastened victory or furthered the aims of the war. Like others who deplore the American course, Baldwin attacks the Potsdam ultimatum, the over-hastiness of American action, and the extension of unrestricted warfare to enemy civilians. How does Baldwin's estimate differ from that of Stimson on the importance of the factors that brought the war to a close?

In the final selection of this group, Herbert Feis, a diplomatic historian, sums up his views on the decision to drop the bombs. He attempts to show that use of the new weapon was not essential to bringing about a surrender on Allied terms, and he develops the question of the justification for the decision. Under the military conditions existing in 1945 and taking into account the historical pattern of warfare, Feis believes that the reasons for use of the bomb by the United States were valid, even though he questions some aspects of the American course of action. How does Feis's position relate to that of Stimson and of Baldwin?

A second major focus of discussion has been the diplomatic implications of the great decision. Selections in the next group set forth views that the United States utilized the atomic bomb not primarily to defeat Japan but rather to influence the Soviet Union. The main reason for use of the new force was thus diplomatic and not strategic. P. M. S. Blackett, a British physicist, analyzes the reasons for the haste in making use of the bomb, considering the date of the planned invasion of Japan, and believes that the United States wanted above all to keep the Soviet Army out of the war in the Far East, where it would readily overrun Manchuria, so that the Japanese would surrender to the American forces alone. In Blackett's view the bomb was used because of circumstances having "a very special character," which presaged the split between East and West; however, since such special circumstances are not likely to recur, he feels that the world is in little danger of atomic warfare.

In the next article of this group, David Joel Horowitz places use of the atomic bomb in the context of the origins of the Cold War with the Soviet Union. He views the American act as a principal factor in the breakup of the wartime coalition between the United States and the Soviet Union and leading to the beginnings of the Cold War. The United States must bear a good part of the onus for the East-West conflict.

Gar Alperovitz develops the thesis that use of the atomic bomb was closely connected with an attempt by the United States to strengthen its negotiating position vis à vis the Soviet Union: the bombs were dropped chiefly to demonstrate American power, with the hope that the display would move the Soviets to change their course of action in Central and Eastern Europe. Does this view satisfactorily explain why the United States did not negotiate with

Japan when the government first became aware of Japan's efforts in this direction? Although many critics accepted the Alperovitz thesis, the challenges to his position have been vigorous; his use of evidence has been attacked and his interpretation of various events has been condemned. In a review of Alperovitz' book *Atomic Diplomacy: Hiroshima and Potsdam*, Michael Amrine sets forth a case against the Alperovitz position.

In the next selection Gabriel Kolko, whose various writings have provided radical criticism of American political and economic life, stresses that the Soviets knew about the Manhattan Project some two years before the bomb was actually used and that the Americans realized the Russians were aware of the American work. United States officials never believed that they could surprise the Soviets with the powerful new weapon, and to the very end of the war they continued to want Soviet aid to defeat Japan on the Chinese mainland. The main question of the use of the bomb was not an issue of diplomacy directed against the Soviet Union but was one of maintaining American power.

The final selection in this group by Martin J. Sherwin provides a detailed analysis of atomic-energy policy in the Roosevelt and Truman administrations. American political leaders, he shows, were well aware of the potential diplomatic value of the bomb and these considerations early began to shape their wartime policies. Roosevelt's views, Sherwin believes, reflected his lack of confidence in the Soviet Union and his wish to take full advantage of the bomb as a postwar instrument of Anglo-American diplomacy and peace-keeping. Against the views of some of his advisers who believed that a postwar nuclear arms race could only be avoided by international control, F.D.R. rejected sharing atomic secrets with the Soviet Union. Harry S. Truman stepped into a situation in which his options were limited. The evidence is not absolutely clear that he wanted to use the bomb against Japan primarily as a warning to the Soviet Union. But it seemed to be assumed that wartime demonstration of the bomb would lead the Soviets to become more cooperative and surrender some of their political and diplomatic objectives. Bound up in their assumptions, American officials did not seriously consider alternative courses of action, and opportunities for possible cooperation were lost. The Cold War then began.

In the next section Kenneth M. Glazier discounts both the military strategic reasoning and the revisionist diplomatic explanation for use of the atomic bomb. Rather he views this action primarily in terms of the administrative-bureaucratic framework in which the new President found himself. The decision to use the atomic bomb was significantly affected by the fact that it was made in time of presidential transition and by the secrecy surrounding the project. From the start it was assumed that the bomb would be used, and the assumption was never seriously questioned because of administrative-bureaucratic conditions.

Another important interest of historians has been the moral dimensions of the decision to use the bomb. While most discussions of the 1945 events touch on moral concerns, the next selections focus directly on such issues. Robert C. Batchelder takes the general question of ethics in war and closely analyzes the morality of the great decision, weighing and attempting to compare possible alternative courses of action. He and other moral analysts show how a gradual change in American ethical attitudes toward the conduct of war came about during the course of World War II so that the way was paved for use of the new mass-destruction weapon. Dwight Macdonald, whose article reprinted here was published immediately after the bombs were dropped, discusses the complexities of assigning moral responsibility for the bomb and its use by an impersonal society of specialists, and praises those who refused to participate in the project.

This discussion of moral considerations raises some important questions. To what extent was the morality of using atomic weapons really considered before Hiroshima and Nagasaki? Is it possible actually to calculate the ethics of a course of public action? Where does the real responsiblity for the use of such weapons lie? Does the use of atomic weapons have moral dimensions other than those that figure in the use of more conventional weapons? What are the consequences of the changes that have occurred in the meaning of war in the twentieth century?

The controlled explosion of atomic energy, it is commonly agreed, was one of the great turning points in man's history, and in the years since 1945 ramifications of the use of nuclear energy in war have been felt in the realms of morality, nationalism, international diplomacy, and science and technology. Indeed, we are only beginning to understand how the modern world has been changed by the events of the World War II years. The next group of selections deals with the short-term and the long-term consequences of the use of the new weapon.

The aftereffects of the 1945 decision have been most fully evident in the field of post-World War II diplomatic relations. Building on the Alperovitz thesis, Richard H. Rovere focuses on some diplomatic consequences, viewing the dropping of the bombs as the principal preventative of a third major world holocaust. The new atomic powers of the postwar world have been so fully aware of the terrible dangers of nuclear weapons that they have time and again turned away from the use of force, despite repeated provocations. Hiroshima and Nagasaki have thus become sacrifices to the maintenance of world peace.

Carroll Quigley goes considerably further than Rovere in viewing the effects, both international and domestic, of the 1945 course of action. He believes that use of the bomb by the United States precipitated an international arms race that subsequently brought a nuclear stalemate, which has in turn led to such pervasive and grave consequences as the growth of a specialized war machine dangerous to political democracy, the development of increasingly planned national economic systems vastly limiting individual freedom, and the destruction of traditional concepts of international law and the old relationships of the community of nations.

Moral considerations pervade the reflections of Norbert Wiener, the mathematician, concerning the wartime decision, as he discusses changes stemming from it in the nature of war and in postatomic international relations, in the altering popular attitude toward science, and in the role of science in modern society. The student may find it interesting at this point to compare the frame of reference and the points of discussion of Stimson, the statesman, and Wiener, the scientist.

The final selection by Walter Smith Schoenberger sets forth a summary analysis of the American decision to use the atomic bomb. Schoenberger considers problems of administrative bureaucratic organization, the nature and position of the new president, foreign policy perspectives and diplomatic maneuvers, military calculations, and moral evaluations. In studying these several comments, the student should estimate how comprehensively this summary takes into account the various dimensions of the problem.

As the selections reveal, the decision in 1945 to use the atomic bomb was highly complex. In analyzing and evaluating the different aspects of the problem, the student should attempt to put himself in the position of the decision makers in 1945; he must try to be aware of the scope of their understanding, their frame of reference, and the pressures on them. To evaluate this decision, the student must seek an attitude of historical-mindedness. He should ask himself whether the many aspects of the decision were considered as fully as might reasonably have been expected at the time in the midst of war; and, ultimately, was the great decision a wise one?

Part One

PROBLEMS OF STRATEGY TO END THE WAR

Chapter 1   THE DECISION TO USE THE BOMB

HENRY L. STIMSON *(1867–1950)*, *Secretary of War
under President Roosevelt from July 1940 to April
1945 and under President Truman from April to
September 1945, was in overall charge of the
United States atomic development program. Before
this wartime period Stimson had already had a long
and distinguished career in public service, as a
United States Attorney, Secretary of War under Taft,
Governor-General of the Philippine Islands under
Coolidge, and Secretary of State under Hoover.
The following article, appearing in 1947, provided a
significant retrospective evaluation of the decision to
use the atomic bomb, and, in a sense, it set the
terms for subsequent discussion. What was the nature
of the administrative decision to use the atomic bomb?**

In recent months there has been much comment about the decision to use atomic bombs in attacks on the Japanese cities of Hiroshima and Nagasaki. This decision was one of the gravest made by our government in recent years, and it is entirely proper that it should be widely discussed. I have therefore decided to record for all who may be interested my understanding of the events which led up to the attack on Hiroshima on August 6, 1945, on Nagasaki on August 9, and the Japanese decision to surrender, on August 10. No single individual can

*"The Decision to Use the Atomic Bomb" by Henry L. Stimson as it appeared in *Harper's Magazine* (February, 1947), pp. 97–107, later incorporated in the chapter "The Atomic Bomb and the Surrender of Japan" from *On Active Service in Peace & War* by Henry L. Stimson and McGeorge Bundy. Copyright 1947 by Henry L. Stimson. Reprinted by permission of Harper & Row, Publishers, and Hutchinson Publishing Group, Ltd., British publishers. Footnotes omitted.

hope to know exactly what took place in the minds of all of those who had a share in these events, but what follows is an exact description of our thoughts and actions as I find them in the records and in my clear recollection.

Plans and Preparations, September 1941–June 1945

It was in the fall of 1941 that the question of atomic energy was first brought directly to my attention. At that time President Roosevelt appointed a committee consisting of Vice President Wallace, General Marshall, Dr. Vannevar Bush, Dr. James B. Conant, and myself. The function of this committee was to advise the President on questions of policy relating to the study of nuclear fission which was then proceeding both in this country and in Great Britain. For nearly four years thereafter I was directly connected with all major decisions of policy on the development and use of atomic energy, and from May 1, 1943, until my resignation as Secretary of War on September 21, 1945, I was directly responsible to the President for the administration of the entire undertaking; my chief advisers in this period were General Marshall, Dr. Bush, Dr. Conant, and Major General Leslie R. Groves, the officer in charge of the project. At the same time I was the President's senior adviser on the military employment of atomic energy.

The policy adopted and steadily pursued by President Roosevelt and his advisers was a simple one. It was to spare no effort in securing the earliest possible successful development of an atomic weapon. The reasons for this policy were equally simple. The original experimental achievement of atomic fission had occurred in Germany in 1938, and it was known that the Germans had continued their experiments. In 1941 and 1942 they were believed to be ahead of us, and it was vital that they should not be the first to bring atomic weapons into the field of battle. Furthermore, if we should be the first to develop the weapon, we should have a great new instrument for shortening the war and minimizing destruction. At no time, from 1941 to 1945, did I ever hear it suggested by the President, or by any other responsible member of the government, that atomic energy should not be used in the war. All of us of course understood the terrible responsibility involved in our attempt to unlock the doors to such a devastating weapon; President Roosevelt particularly spoke to me many times of his own awareness of the catastrophic potentialities of our work. But we were at war, and the work must be done. I therefore emphasize that it was our common objective, throughout the war, to be the first to produce an atomic weapon and use it. The possible atomic weapon was considered to be a new and tremendously powerful explosive, as legitimate as any other of the deadly explosive weapons of modern war. The entire purpose was the production of a military weapon; on no other ground could the wartime expenditure of so much time and money have been justified. The exact circumstances in which that weapon might be used were unknown to any of us until the middle of 1945, and when that time came, as we shall presently see, the military use of atomic energy was connected with larger questions of national policy.

The extraordinary story of the successful development of the atomic bomb has been well told elsewhere. As time went on it became clear that the weapon would not be available in time for use in the European Theater, and the war against Germany was successfully ended by the use of what are now called conventional means. But in the spring of 1945 it became evident that the climax of our prolonged atomic effort was at hand. By the nature of atomic chain reactions, it was impossible to state with certainty that we had succeeded until a bomb had actually exploded in a fullscale experiment; nevertheless it was considered exceedingly probable that we should by midsummer have successfully detonated the first atomic bomb. This was to be done at the Alamogordo Reservation in New Mexico. It was thus time for detailed consideration of our future plans. What had begun as a well-founded hope was now developing into a reality.

On March 15, 1945 I had my last talk with President Roosevelt. My diary record of this conversation gives a fairly clear picture of the state of our thinking at that time. I have removed the name of the distinguished public servant who was fearful lest the Manhattan (atomic) project be "a lemon"; it was an opinion common among those not fully informed.

The President . . . had suggested that I come over to lunch today. . . . First I took up with him a memorandum which he sent to me from————
who had been alarmed at the rumors of extravagance in the Manhattan project.————suggested that it might become disastrous and he suggested that we get a body of "outside" scientists to pass upon the project because rumors are going around that Vannevar Bush and Jim Conant have sold the President a lemon on the subject and ought to be checked up on. It was rather a jittery and nervous memorandum and rather silly, and I was prepared for it and I gave the President a list of the scientists who were actually engaged on it to show the very high standing of them and it comprised four Nobel Prize men, and also how practically every physicist of standing was engaged with us in the project. Then I outlined to him the future of it and when it was likely to come off and told him how important it was to get ready. I went over with him the two schools of thought that exist in respect to the future control after the war of this project, in case it is successful, one of them being the secret close-in attempted control of the project by those who control it now, and the other being the international control based upon freedom both of science and of access. I told him that those things must be settled before the first projectile is used and that he must be ready with a statement to come out to the people on it just as soon as that is done. He agreed to that. . . .

This conversation covered the three aspects of the question which were then uppermost in our minds. First, it was always necessary to suppress a lingering doubt that any such titanic undertaking could be successful. Second, we must consider the implications of success in terms of its long-range postwar effect. Third, we must face the problem that would be presented at the time of our first use of the weapon, for with that first use there must be some public statement.

I did not see Franklin Roosevelt again. The next time I went to the White House to discuss atomic energy was April 25, 1945, and I went to explain the nature of the problem to a man whose only previous knowledge of our activities was that of a Senator who had loyally accepted our assurance that the matter must be kept a secret from him. Now he was President and Commander-in-Chief, and the final responsibility in this as in so many other matters must be his. President Truman accepted this responsibility with the same fine spirit that Senator Truman had shown before in accepting our refusal to inform him.

I discussed with him the whole history of the project. We had with us General Groves, who explained in detail the progress which had been made and the probable future course of the work. I also discussed with President Truman the broader aspects of the subject, and the memorandum which I used in this discussion is again a fair sample of the state of our thinking at the time.

Memorandum Discussed with President Truman April 25, 1945

1. Within four months we shall in all probability have completed the most terrible weapon ever known in human history, one bomb of which could destroy a whole city.

2. Although we have shared itsdevelop ment with the U. K., physically the U.S. is at present in the position of controlling the resources with which to construct and use it and no other nation could reach this position for some years.

3. Nevertheless it is practically certain that we could not remain in this position indefinitely.

a. Various segments of its discovery and production are widely known among many scientists in many countries, although few scientists are now acquainted with the whole process which we have developed.

b. Although its construction under present methods requires great scientific and industrial effort and raw materials, which are temporarily mainly within the possession and knowledge of U.S. and U.K., it is extremely probable that much easier and cheaper methods of production will be discovered by scientists in the future, together with the use of materials of much wider distribution. As a result, it is extremely probable that the future will make it possible for atomic bombs to be constructed by smaller nations or even groups, or at least by a larger nation in a much shorter time.

4. As a result, it is indicated that the future may see a time when such a weapon may be constructed in secret and used suddenly and effectively with devastating power by a wilful nation or group against an unsuspecting nation or group of much greater size and material power. With its aid even a very powerful unsuspecting nation might be conquered within a very few days by a very much smaller one. . . .

5. The world in its present state of moral advancement compared with its technical development would be eventually at the mercy of such a weapon. In other words, modern civilization might be completely destroyed.

6. To approach any world peace organization of any pattern now likely to be considered, without an appreciation by the leaders of our country of the power of this new weapon, would seem to be unrealistic. No system of control heretofore considered would be adequate to control this menace. Both inside any particular country and between the nations of the world, the control of this weapon will undoubtedly be a matter of the greatest difficulty and would involve such thoroughgoing rights of inspection and internal controls as we have never heretofore contemplated.

7. Furthermore, in the light of our present position with reference to this weapon, the question of sharing it with other nations and, if so shared, upon what terms, becomes a primary question of our foreign relations. Also our leadership in the war and in the development of this weapon has placed a certain moral responsibility upon us which we cannot shirk without very serious responsibility for any disaster to civilization which it would further.

8. On the other hand, if the problem of the proper use of this weapon can be solved, we would have the opportunity to bring the world into a pattern in which the peace of the world and our civilization can be saved.

9. As stated in General Groves' report, steps are under way looking towards the establishment of a select committee of particular qualifications for recommending action to the executive and legislative branches of our government when secrecy is no longer in full effect. The committee would also recommend the actions to be taken by the War Department prior to that time in anticipation of the postwar problems. All recommendations would of course be first submitted to the President.

The next step in our preparations was the appointment of the committee referred to in paragraph (9) above. This committee, which was known as the Interim Committee, was charged with the function of advising the President on the various questions raised by our apparently imminent success in developing an atomic weapon. I was its chairman, but the principal labor of guiding its extended deliberations fell to George L. Harrison, who acted as chairman in my absence. It will be useful to consider the work of the committee in some detail. Its members were the following, in addition to Mr. Harrison and myself:

James F. Byrnes (then a private citizen) as personal representative of the President.

Ralph A. Bard, Under Secretary of the Navy.

William L. Clayton, Assistant Secretary of State.

Dr. Vannevar Bush, Director, Office of Scientific Research and Development, and president of the Carnegie Institution of Washington.

Dr. Karl T. Compton, Chief of the Office of Field Service in the Office of Scientific Research and Development, and president of the Massachusetts Institute of Technology.

Dr. James B. Conant, Chairman of the National Defense Research Committee, and president of Harvard University.

The discussions of the committee ranged over the whole field of atomic energy, in its political, military, and scientific aspects. That part of its work which particularly concerns us here relates to its recommendations for the use of atomic energy against Japan, but it should be borne in mind that these recommendations were not made in a vacuum. The committee's work included the drafting of the statements which were published immediately after the first bombs were dropped, the drafting of a bill for the domestic control of atomic energy, and recommendations looking toward the international control of atomic energy. The Interim Committee was assisted in its work by a Scientific Panel whose members were the following: Dr. A. H. Compton, Dr. Enrico Fermi, Dr. E. O. Lawrence, and Dr. J. R. Oppenheimer. All four were nuclear physicists of the first rank; all four had held positions of great importance in the atomic project from its inception. At a meeting with the Interim Committee and the Scientific Panel on May 31, 1945 I urged all those present to feel free to express themselves on any phase of the subject, scientific or political. Both General Marshall and I at this meeting expressed the view that atomic energy could not be considered simply in terms of military weapons but must also be considered in terms of a new relationship of man to the universe.

On June 1, after its discussions with the Scientific Panel, the Interim Committee unanimously adopted the following recommendations:

(1) The bomb should be used against Japan as soon as possible.

(2) It should be used on a dual target—that is, a military installation or war plant surrounded by or adjacent to houses and other buildings most susceptible to damage, and

(3) It should be used without prior warning [of the nature of the weapon]. One member of the committee, Mr. Bard, later changed his view and dissented from recommendation (3).

In reaching these conclusions the Interim Committee carefully considered such alternatives as a detailed advance warning or a demonstration in some uninhabited area. Both of these suggestions were discarded as impractical. They were not regarded as likely to be effective in compelling a surrender of Japan, and both of them involved serious risks. Even the New Mexico test would not give final proof that any given bomb was certain to explode when dropped from an airplane. Quite apart from the generally unfamiliar nature of atomic explosives, there was the whole problem of exploding a bomb at a predetermined height in the air by a complicated mechanism which could not be tested in the static test of New Mexico. Nothing would have been more damaging to our effort to obtain surrender than a warning or a demonstration followed by a dud—and this was a real possibility. Furthermore, we had no bombs to waste. It was vital that a sufficient effect be quickly obtained with the few we had.

The Interim Committee and the Scientific Panel also served as a channel through which suggestions from other scientists working on the atomic project forwarded to me and to the President. Among the suggestions thus forwarded was one memorandum which questioned using the bomb at all against the enemy. On June 16, 1945, after consideration of that memorandum, the Scientific Panel made a report, from which I quote the following paragraphs:

> The opinions of our scientific colleagues on the initial use of these weapons are not unanimous: they range from the proposal of a purely technical demonstration to that of the military application best designed to induce surrender. Those who advocate a purely technical demonstration would wish to outlaw the use of atomic weapons, and have feared that if we use the weapons now our position in future negotiations will be prejudiced. Others emphasize the opportunity of saving American lives by immediate military use, and believe that such use will improve the international prospects, in that they are more concerned with the prevention of war than with the elimination of this special weapon. We find ourselves closer to these latter views; *we can propose no technical demonstration likely to bring an end to the war; we see no acceptable alternative to direct military use.* [Italics mine]
>
> With regard to these general aspects of the use of atomic energy, it is clear that we, as scientific men, have no proprietary rights. It is true that we are among the few citizens who have had occasion to give thoughtful consideration to these problems during the past few years. We have thoughtful consideration to these problems during the past few years. We have, however, no claim to special competence in solving the political, social, and military problems which are presented by the advent of atomic power.

The foregoing discussion presents the reasoning of the Interim Committee and its advisers. I have discussed the work of these gentlemen at length in order to make it clear that we sought the best advice that we could find. The committee's function was, of course, entirely advisory. The ultimate responsibility for the recommendation to the President rested upon me, and I have no desire to veil it. The conclusions of the committee were similar to my own, although I reached mine independently. I felt that to extract a genuine surrender from the Emperor and his military advisers, they must be administered a tremendous shock which would carry convincing proof of our power to destroy the Empire. Such an effective shock would save many times the number of lives, both American and Japanese, that it would cost.

The facts upon which my reasoning was based and steps taken to carry it out now follow.

U.S. Policy toward Japan in July 1945

The principal political, social, and military objective of the United States in the summer of 1945 was the prompt and complete surrender of Japan. Only the complete destruction of her military power could open the way to lasting peace.

Japan, in July 1945, had been seriously weakened by our increasingly violent attacks. It was known to us that she had gone so far as to make tentative proposals to the Soviet government, hoping to use the Russians as mediators in a negotiated peace. These vague proposals contemplated the retention by Japan of important conquered areas and were therefore not considered seriously. There was as yet no indication of any weakening in the Japanese determination to fight rather than accept unconditional surrender. If she should persist in her fight to the end, she had still a great military force.

In the middle of July 1945, the intelligence section of the War Department General Staff estimated Japanese military strength as follows: in the home islands, slightly under 2,000,000; in Korea, Manchuria, China proper, and Formosa, slightly over 2,000,000; in French Indo-China, Thailand, and Burma, over 200,000; in the East Indies area, including the Philippines, over 500,000; in the by-passed Pacific islands, over 100,000. The total strength of the Japanese Army was estimated at about 5,000,000 men. These estimates later proved to be in very close agreement with official Japanese figures.

The Japanese Army was in much better conditon than the Japanese Navy and Air Force. The Navy had practically ceased to exist except as a harrying force against an invasion fleet. The Air Force had been reduced mainly to reliance upon Kamikaze, or suicide, attacks. These latter, however, had already inflicted serious damage on our seagoing forces, and their possible effectiveness in a last ditch fight was a matter of real concern to our naval leaders.

As we understood it in July, there was a very strong possibility that the Japanese government might determine upon resistance to the end, in all the areas of the Far East under its control. In such an event the Allies would be faced with the enormous task of destroying an armed force of five million men and five thousand suicide aircraft, belonging to a race which had already amply demonstrated its ability to fight literally to the death.

The strategic plans of our armed forces for the defeat of Japan, as they stood in July, had been prepared without reliance upon the atomic bomb, which had not yet been tested in New Mexico. We were planning an intensified sea and air blockade, and greatly intensified strategic air bombing, through the summer and early fall, to be followed on November 1 by an invasion of the southern island of Kyushu. This would be followed in turn by an invasion of the main island of Honshu in the spring of 1946. The total U.S. military and naval force involved in this grand design was of the order of 5,000,000 men; if all those indirectly concerned are included, it was larger still.

We estimated that if we should be forced to carry this plan to its conclusion, the major fighting would not end until the latter part of 1946, at the earliest. I was informed that such operations might be expected to cost over a million casualties to American forces alone. Additional large losses might be expected among our allies, and, of course, if our campaign were successful and if we could judge by previous experience, enemy casualties would be much larger than our own.

It was already clear in July that even before the invasion we should be able to inflict enormously severe damage on the Japanese homeland by the combined application of "conventional" sea and air power. The critical question was whether this kind of action would induce surrender. It therefore became necessary to consider very carefully the probable state of mind of the enemy, and to assess with accuracy the line of conduct which might end his will to resist.

With these considerations in mind, I wrote a memorandum for the President, on July 2, which I believe fairly represents the thinking of the American government as it finally took shape in action. This memorandum was prepared after discussion and general agreement with Joseph C. Grew, Acting Secretary of State, and Secretary of the Navy Forrestal, and when I discussed it with the President, he expressed his general approval.

Memorandum for the President, Proposed Program for Japan   **July 2, 1945**

1. The plans of operation up to and including the first landing have been authorized and the preparations for the operation are now actually going on. This situation was accepted by all members of your conference on Monday, June 18.

2. There is reason to believe that the operation for the occupation of Japan following the landing may be a very long, costly, and arduous struggle on our part. The terrain, much of which I have visited several times, has left the impression on my memory of being one which would be susceptible

to a last ditch defense such as has been made on Iwo Jima and Okinawa and which of course is very much larger than either of those two areas. According to my recollection it will be much more unfavorable with regard to tank maneuvering than either the Philippines or Germany.

3. If we once land on one of the main islands and begin a forceful occupation of Japan, we shall probably have cast the die of last ditch resistance. The Japanese are highly patriotic and certainly susceptible to calls for fanatical resistance to repel an invasion. Once started in actual invasion, we shall in my opinion have to go through with an even more bitter finish fight than in Germany. We shall incur the losses incident to such a war and we shall have to leave the Japanese islands even more thoroughly destroyed than was the case with Germany. This would be due both to the difference in the Japanese and German personal character and the differences in the size and character of the terrain through which the operations will take place.

4. A question then comes: Is there any alternative to such a forceful occupation of Japan which will secure for us the equivalent of an unconditional surrender of her forces and a permanent destruction of her power again to strike an aggressive blow at the "peace of the Pacific"? I am inclined to think that there is enough such chance to make it well worthwhile our giving them a warning of what is to come and a definite opportunity to capitulate. As above suggested, it should be tried before the actual forceful occupation of the homeland islands is begun and furthermore the warning should be given in ample time to permit a national reaction to set in.

We have the following enormously favorable factors on our side—factors much weightier than those we had against Germany:

Japan has no allies.

Her navy is nearly destroyed and she is vulnerable to a surface and underwater blockade which can deprive her of sufficient food and supplies for her population.

She is terribly vulnerable to our concentrated air attack upon her crowded cities, industrial and food resources.

She has against her not only the Anglo-American forces but the rising forces of China and the ominous threat of Russia.

We have inexhaustible and untouched industrial resources to bring to bear against her diminishing potential.

We have great moral superiority through being the victim of her first sneak attack.

The problem is to translate these advantages into prompt and economical achievement of our objectives. I believe Japan *is* susceptible to reason in such a crisis to a much greater extent than is indicated by our current press and other current comment. Japan is not a nation composed wholly of mad fanatics of an entirely different mentality from ours. On the contrary, she has within the past century shown herself to possess extremely intelligent people, capable in an unprecedentedly short time of adopting not only the complicated technique of Occidental civilization but to a substantial extent their culture and their political and social ideas. Her advance in all these respects during the short period of sixty or seventy years has been one of the most astounding feats of national progress in history—a leap from the isolated feudalism of centuries into the position of one of the six or seven great powers of the world. She has not only built up powerful armies and navies. She has maintained an honest and effective national finance and respected position in many of the sciences in which we pride ourselves. Prior to the forcible seizure of power over her government by the fanatical military group in 1931, she had for ten years lived a reasonably responsible and respectable international life.

My own opinion is in her favor on the two points involved in this question:

a. I think the Japanese nation has the mental intelligence and versatile capacity in such a crisis to recognize the folly of a fight to the finish and to accept the proffer of what will amount to an unconditional surrender; and

b. I think she has within her population enough liberal leaders (although now submerged by the terrorists) to be depended upon for her reconstruction as a responsible member of the family of nations. I think she is better in this last respect than Germany was. Her liberals yielded only at the point of the pistol and, so far as I am aware, their liberal attitude has not been personally subverted in the way which was so general in Germany.

On the other hand, I think that the attempt to exterminate her armies and her population by gunfire or other means will tend to produce a fusion of race solidity and antipathy which has no analogy in the case of Germany. We have a national interest in creating, if possible, a condition wherein the Japanese nation may live as a peaceful and useful member of the future Pacific community.

5. It is therefore my conclusion that a carefully timed warning be given to Japan by the chief representatives of the United States, Great Britain, China, and, if then a belligerent, Russia by calling upon Japan to surrender and permit the occupation of her country in order to insure its complete demilitarization for the sake of the future peace.

This warning should contain the following elements:

The varied and overwhelming character of the force we are about to bring to bear on the islands.

The inevitability and completeness of the destruction which the full application of this force will entail.

The determination of the Allies to destroy permanently all authority and influence of those who have deceived and misled the country into embarking on world conquest.

The determination of the Allies to limit Japanese sovereignty to her main islands and to render them powerless to mount and support another war.

The disavowal of any attempt to extirpate the Japanese as a race or to destroy them as a nation.

A statement of our readiness, once her economy is purged of its militaristic influence, to permit the Japanese to maintain such industries, particularly of a light consumer character, as offer no threat of aggression against their neighbors, but which can produce a sustaining economy, and provide a reasonable standard of living. The statement should indicate our willingness, for this purpose, to give Japan trade access to external raw materials, but no longer any control over the sources of supply outside her main islands. It should also indicate our willingness, in accordance with our now established foreign trade policy, in due course to enter into mutually advantageous trade relations with her.

The withdrawal from their country as soon as the above objectives of the Allies are accomplished, and as soon as there has been established a peacefully inclined government, of a character representative of the masses of the Japanese people. I personally think that if in saying this we should add that we do not exclude a constitutional monarchy under her present dynasty, it would substantially add to the chances of acceptance.

6. Success of course will depend on the potency of the warning which we give her. She has an extremely sensitive national pride and, as we are now seeing every day, when actually locked with the enemy will fight to the very death. For that reason the warning must be tendered before the actual invasion has occurred and while the impending destruction, though clear beyond peradventure, has not yet reduced her to fanatical despair. If Russia is a part of the threat, the Russian attack, if actual, must not have progressed too far. Our own bombing should be confined to military objectives as far as possible.

It is important to emphasize the double character of the suggested warning. It was designed to promise destruction if Japan resisted, and hope, if she surrendered.

It will be noted that the atomic bomb is not mentioned in this memorandum. On grounds of secrecy the bomb was never mentioned except when absolutely necessary, and furthermore, it had not yet been tested. It was of course well forward in our minds, as the memorandum was written and discussed, that the bomb would be the best possible sanction if our warning were rejected.

The Use of the Bomb

The adoption of the policy outlined in the memorandum of July 2 was a decision of high politics; once it was accepted by the President, the position of the atomic bomb in our planning became quite clear. I find that I stated in my diary, as early as June 19, that "the last chance warning . . . must be given before an actual landing of the ground forces in Japan, and fortunately the plans provide for enough time to bring in the sanctions to our warning in the shape of heavy ordinary bombing attack and an attack of S-1." S-1 was a code name for the atomic bomb.

There was much discussion in Washington about the timing of the warning to Japan. The controlling factor in the end was the date already set for the Potsdam meeting of the Big Three. It was President Truman's decision that such a warning should be solemnly issued by the U.S. and the U.K. from this meeting, with the concurrence of the head of the Chinese government, so that it would be plain that *all* of Japan's principal enemies were in entire unity. This was done, in the Potsdam ultimatum of July 26, which very closely followed the above memorandum of July 2, with the exception that it made no mention of the Japanese Emperor.

On July 28 the Premier of Japan, Suzuki, rejected the Potsdam ultimatum by announcing that it was "unworthy of public notice." In the face of this rejection we could only proceed to demonstrate that the ultimatum had meant exactly what it said when it stated that if the Japanese continued the war, "the full application of our military power, backed by our resolve, will mean the inevitable and complete destruction of the Japanese armed forces and just as inevitably the utter devastation of the Japanese homeland."

For such a purpose the atomic bomb was an eminently suitable weapon. The New Mexico test occurred while we were at Potsdam, on July 16. It was immediately clear that the power of the bomb measured up to our highest estimates. We had developed a weapon of such a revolutionary character that its use against the enemy might well be expected to produce exactly the kind of shock on the Japanese ruling oligarchy which we desired, strengthening the position of those who wished peace, and weakening that of the military party.

Because of the importance of the atomic mission against Japan, the detailed plans were brought to me by the military staff for approval. With President Truamn's warm support I struck off the list of suggested targets the city of Kyoto. Although it was a target of considerable military importance, it had been the ancient capital of Japan and was a shrine of Japanese art and culture. We determined that it should be spared. I approved four other targets including the cities of Hiroshima and Nagasaki.

Hiroshima was bombed on August 6, and Nagasaki on August 9. These two cities were active working parts of the Japanese war effort. One was an army center; the other was naval and industrial. Hiroshima was the headquarters of the Japanese Army defending southern Japan and was a major military storage and assembly point. Ngasaki wasa a major seaport and it contained several large industrial plants of great wartime importance. We believed that our attacks had struck cities which must certainly be important to the Japanese military leaders, both Army and Navy, and we waited for a result. We waited one day.

Many accounts have been written about the Japanese surrender. After a prolonged Japanese cabinet session in which the deadlock was broken by the Emperor himself, the offer to surrender was made on August 10. It was based on the Potsdam terms, with a reservation concerning the sovereignty of the Emperor. While the Allied reply made no promises other than those already given, it implicitly recognized the Emperor's position by prescribing that his power must be subject to the orders of the Allied Supreme Commander. These terms were accepted on August 14 by the Japanese, and the instrument of surrender was formally signed on September 2, in Tokyo Bay. Our great objective was thus achieved, and all the evidence I have seen indicates that the controlling factor in the final Japanese decision to accept our terms of surrender was the atomic bomb.

The two atomic bombs which we had dropped were the only ones we had ready, and our rate of production at the time was very small. Had the war continued until the projected invasion on Novemer 1, additional fire raids of B-29's would have been more destructive of life and property than the very limited number of atomic raids which we could have executed in the same period. But the atomic bomb was more than a weapon of terrible destruction; it was a psychological weapon. In March 1945 our Air Force had launched its first great incendiary raid on the Tokyo area. In this raid more damage was done and more casualties were inflicted than was the case at Hiroshima. Hundreds of bombers took part and hundreds of tons of incendiaries were dropped. Similar successive raids burned out a great part of the urban area of Japan, but the Japanese fought on. On August 6 one B-29 dropped a single atomic bomb on Hiroshima. Three days later a second bomb was dropped on Nagasaki and the war was over. So far as the Japanese could know, our ability to execute atomic attacks, if necessary by many planes at a time, was unlmited. As Dr. Karl Compton has said, "it was not one atomic bomb, or two, which brought surrender; it was the experience of what an atomic bomb will actually do to a community, *plus the dread of many more*, that was effective."

The bomb thus served exactly the purpose we intended. The peace party was able to take the path of surrender, and the whole weight of the Emperor's prestige was exerted in favor of peace. When the Emperor ordered surrender, and the small but dangerous group of fanatics who opposed him were brought under control, the Japanese became so subdued that the great undertaking of occupation and disarmament was completed with unprecedented ease.

A Personal Summary

In the foregoing pages I have tried to give an accurate account of my own personal observations of the circumstances which led up to the use of the atomic bomb and the reasons which underlay our use of it. To me they have always seemed compelling and clear, and I cannot see how any person vested with such responsibilities as mine could have taken any other course or given any other advice to his chiefs.

Two great nations were approaching contact in a fight to a finish which would begin on November 1, 1945. Our enemy, Japan, commanded forces of somewhat over 5,000,000 armed men. Men of these armies had already inflicted upon us, in our breakthrough of the outer perimeter of their defenses, over 300,000 battle casualties. Enemy armies still unbeaten had the strength to cost us a million more. *As long as the Japanese government refused to surrender*, we should be forced to take and hold the ground, and smash the Japanese ground armies, by close-in fighting of the same desperate and costly kind that we had faced in the Pacific islands for nearly four years.

In the light of the formidable problem which thus confronted us, I felt that every possible step should be taken to compel a surrender of the homelands, and a withdrawal of all Japanese troops from the Asiatic mainland and from other positions, before we had commenced an invasion. We held two cards to assist us in such as effort. One was the traditional veneration in which the Japanese Emperor was held by his subjects and the power which was thus vested in him over his loyal troops. It was for this reason that I suggested in my memorandum of July 2 that his dynasty should be continued. The second card was the use of the atomic bomb in the manner best calculated to persuade that Emperor and the counselors about him to submit to our demand for what was essentially unconditional surrender, placing his immense power over his people and his troops subject to our orders.

In order to end the war in the shortest possible time and to avoid the enormous losses of human life which otherwise confronted us, I felt that we must use the Emperor as our instrument to command and compel his people to cease fighting and subject themselves to our authority through him, and that to accomplish this we must give him and his controlling advisers a compelling reason to accede to our demands. This reason furthermore must be of such a nature that his people could understand his decision. The bomb seemed to me to furnish a unique instrument for that purpose.

My chief purpose was to end the war in victory with the least possible cost in the lives of the men in the armies which I had helped to raise. In the light of the alternatives which, on fair estimate, were open to us I believe that no man, in the position and subject to our responsibilities, holding in his hands a weapon of such possibilities for accomplishing this purpose and saving those lives, could have failed to use it and afterwards looked his countrymen in the face.

As I read over what I have written, I am aware that much of it, in this year of peace, may have a harsh and unfeeling sound. It would perhaps be possible to say the same things and say them more gently. But I do not think it would be wise. As I look back over the five years of my service as Secretary of War, I see too many stern and heartrending decisions to be willing to pretend that war is anything else than what it is. The face of war is the face of death; death is an inevitable part of every order that a wartime leader gives. The decision to use the atomic bomb was a decision that brought death to over a hundred thousand Japanese. No explanation can change that fact and I do not wish to gloss it over. But this deliberate, premeditated destruction was our least abhorrent choice. The destruction of Hiroshima and Nagasaki put an end to the Japanese war. It stopped the fire raids and the strangling blockade; it ended the ghastly specter of a clash of great land armies.

In this last great action of the Second World War we were given final proof that war is death. War in the twentieth century has grown steadily more barbarous, more destructive, more debased in all its aspects. Now, with the release of atomic energy, man's ability to destroy himself is very nearly complete. The bombs dropped on Hiroshima and Nagasaki ended a war. They also made it wholly clear that we must never have another war. This is the lesson men and leaders everywhere must learn, and I believe that when they learn it they will find a way to lasting peace. There is no other choice.

Chapter 2 THE BOMB AND CONCURRENT NEGOTIATIONS WITH JAPAN

*A Pulitzer Prize-winning historian, long-time
professor at Harvard University, and during
World War II rear admiral in the United States Navy,*
SAMUEL ELIOT MORISON *(1887–   ) wrote*
History of United States Naval Operations in World
War II *(15 vols., 1947–1962), from which the following
selection is taken. In this excerpt, Morison views the
use of the atomic bomb by the United States in relation
to the ending of the war in the Pacific. Delineating
the course of critical events in Japan during the late
summer of 1945, he presents a broad perspective
from which one can estimate the strategic
significance of the new weapon.**

The Japanese people were never told that their country was losing the war; even our capture of such key points as Saipan, Manila, and Okinawa was explained as a strategic retirement. Hence, anyone high in the government or armed forces who recognized the symptoms of defeat found himself in a cruel dilemma. Love of country impelled him to seek a way out of the war, but admission of defeat exposed him to disgrace or assassination. Even the Emperor, who had always wished to preserve the peace, found himself caught in the same trap. When General MacArthur after the war asked Hirohito why he did not earlier take a stand against it, he made a symbolic gesture of his throat's being cut.

*Samuel Eliot Morison, "Why Japan Surrendered," *The Atlantic Monthy*, CCVI (October, 1960), 41–47, taken from Chapter 21 of *Victory in the Pacific, 1945*, vol. XIV of *History of United States Naval Operations in World War II*, Boston, 1960, pp. 336–353. Copyright © 1960, by the Atlantic Monthly Company, Boston, Mass. 02116. Reprinted with permission.

Early in 1945, following the Allied invasion of Luzon, the Emperor began to play an active part in the peace movement. His intervention had to be done cautiously and discreetly, so as not to disturb the established tradition and machinery of government. In late January and early February he conferred individually with seven of the *jushin*, the "important subjects"—former Premiers and presidents of the Privy Council. He found their feeling to be like his, that an early peace was necessary. Prince Konoye, the former Premier, stated bluntly that Japan faced certain defeat and urged his cousin the Emperor to take positive action to end the war.

Fear of the powerful military clique was so pervasive that nothing could be done until early April, when the invasion of Okinawa, and Russia's denunciation of the Soviet-Japanese neutrality pact, precipitated a new crisis. When General Koiso resigned the premiership on 5 April 1945, the *jushin* provided his relief. These men now had the confidence of the Lord Keeper, Marquis Kido, closest adviser and personal friend of the Emperor, who gave his approval to a political deal. The new Premier, who took office on 7 April, was the octogenarian Baron Kantaro Suzuki, who as a junior naval officer, forty years earlier, had participated in the battle of Tsushima Straits. He was now a retired admiral and president of the Privy Council, and it was ironic that, on the very day he took office, the battleship *Yamato* was sunk. Shigenori Togo, also an advocate of peace, was appointed Foreign Minister.

The Army chiefs insisted, as their price for allowing Suzuki to form a cabinet, that he prosecute the war to a victorious finish. Consequently, the new Premier had to pretend to be doing just that. He knew that he was expected by the Emperor to bring the war to an end; but, as he held office at the Army's sufferance, he had to continue making die-hard public pronouncements.

Although it takes but one antagonist to start a war, at least two are required to conclude peace; so it is natural to inquire what, if anything, the United States and the other Allies were doing about it. The answer is, almost nothing, except to press the war more and more vigorously. It is possible that if President Roosevelt had lived six weeks longer, he would have taken the advice of Joseph C. Grew to give public assurance that if Japan surrendered "unconditionally," she could keep her Emperor. The Department of State had envisaged just that, even at the beginning of the war. Following this line, government agencies in propaganda for home consumption had consistently ignored Hirohito and directed popular rage and hatred against Tojo and his military clique. This attitude was due in part to knowledge by the insiders that Hirohito had never wanted war; partly to experience of World War I, in which the Kaiser was played up as principal culprit, and his removal led to a weak government which was overthrown by Hitler. The Imperial Palace had been conspicuously spared in the successive bombings of Tokyo; and owing to the Secretary of

War's insistence the Army Air Force had not bombed the two principal religious and artistic centers in Japan, Nikko and Kyoto.

Mr. Grew, an old schoolmate and personal friend of President Roosevelt's, had been American ambassador to Japan for several years before Pearl Harbor. Knowing Japanese personalities and politics as did no other American, he detected through the double talk of the Suzuki government a genuine desire to end the war. He knew that the one essential gesture to help the peace party in Japan was to promise as a condition of peace that the Emperor would not be deposed. From 20 December 1944, Mr. Grew was undersecretary of state. He found that many top people in the department did not share his views. A popular demand, "Hirohito must go," was being whipped up by a section of the American press and by certain columnists and radio commentators. Admiral Leahy observed that some of the civilians who had access to the President wanted Hirohito to be tried as a war criminal, and the nationalist press in China demanded that he be hanged. The Soviet government, of course, aimed to break up the imperial system, so that Communism could profit from the ensuing anarchy.

After hearing reports of the destructive bombing raids on Tokyo of 23 and 25 May 1945, Mr. Grew called on the President and begged him to make an explicit statement, in an address that he was planning to deliver on the thirty-first, that Hirohito could retain his throne if Japan surrendered. Harry Truman, who had been in the presidential office only six weeks, was sympathetic but felt unqualified to make so vital a policy pronouncement without military advice. At his request Mr. Grew consulted General Marshall and Secretaries Forrestal and Stimson. They, too, were sympathetic, but advised against making any such assurance at that time, because the Okinawa campaign had almost bogged down and the Japanese government would interpret any such statement as evidence of war weariness on our part. So this opportunity to proffer a friendly hand to Japanese advocates of peace was missed. It is very unlikely that it would have been accepted, since the Japanese military and naval chiefs were against concluding peace even after two atomic bombs had been dropped and explicit assurances about the Emperor had been given.

On 1 June the President's interim committee, composed of high officials and top atomic scientists, recommended that the new bomb be used against Japan, as soon as possible, without warning, and against a target that would reveal its "devastating strength." A well-considered alternative—to drop one bomb on a relatively uninhabited part of Japan, after due warning, in order to demonstrate the uselessness of further struggle—was rejected. It was feared that Japan would move in Allied prisoners of war as guinea pigs; and nobody could predict whether or not the bomb would work. If, after a warning, it proved a dud, the United States would be placed in a ridiculous position. And anyone who has followed our account of the senseless destruction and suffering inflicted by the kamikazes around Okinawa will appreciate the fact that compassion for Japan formed no factor in this decision.

Again, on 18 June, when Okinawa was almost secured, Mr. Grew urged the President to issue a proclamation on the subject of the Emperor. Again, the service chiefs asked for more time, and the President decided to refer the whole matter to Potsdam, where his conference with Churchill, Stalin, and the combined chiefs of staff was scheduled to open on 16 July.

On that very day the experimental atomic bomb was exploded in New Mexico. Churchill was told about it at Potsdam. "This is the Second Coming, in wrath," said he.

In Japan, in the meantime, responsible statesmen were groping and fiddling and getting exactly nowhere. After the news of Germany's surrender came through on 9 May, the more realistic Army chiefs realized that if Russia entered the war against them, a successful defense of the home islands would be impossible. The Suzuki cabinet agreed that every effort should be made to keep Stalin neutral and to seek his good offices to negotiate a favorable peace. Some halfhearted, unofficial feelers were put out to the Soviet ambassador in Tokyo, but nothing came of them. On 8 June the Supreme Council for the Direction of the War (S.C.D.W.), consisting mainly of the Premier, the War, Navy, and Foreign Ministers, and the Army and Navy Chiefs of Staff, approved a basic war policy that committed Japan to fight to the bitter end. Then, ten days later, they voted to propose peace through neutral powers, especially the Soviet Union.

Marquis Kido, who got wind of their first decision, prepared a plan, which the Emperor approved, to circumvent the S.C.D.W. He opened a series of personal and private negotiations with responsible government members. These dragged along for several days without result. The Emperor then summoned the S.C.D.W. to the palace (22 June) and supported Foreign Minister Togo in his determination to send a special envoy to Moscow, hoping to work out some means of ending the war through diplomatic negotiation.

By that time the Japanese government knew that Okinawa was lost; that the B-29s were capable of wiping out one Japanese city after another; that, in a word, the war was lost. But nothing was done to prepare the people for the inevitable. On the contrary, Premier Suzuki issued a statement that the loss of Okinawa "improved Japan's strategic position" and dealt America a "severe spiritual blow." "Peace agitators" were threatened in official broadcasts; efforts were made to increase war production; a program of building solid houses with underground shelters was announced to protect the people from air bombing, and one of stockpiling food to render them self-sufficient.

In the meantime, the Japanese ambassador in Moscow was being brushed off by Stalin, and the Soviet ambassador in Tokyo also refused to negotiate.

The Emperor, concerned by the delay, summoned Suzuki and proposed that a special envoy be sent to Moscow with a personal message from himself to Stalin. Togo jumped at the idea, and Prince Konoye consented to be the envoy. Permission had to be asked of the Soviet foreign office, and not until 18 July did the Soviet government send an evasive and discouraging reply. For Stalin had already decided to declare war on Japan.

Then, out of a clear sky, on a summer day of sweltering heat, came the Potsdam Declaration of 26 July by President Truman, Prime Minister Churchill, and Chiang Kai-shek, stating the conditions under which Japan would be called upon to surrender "unconditionally." The principal terms of the Potsdam Declaration were:

1. The authority and influence of the Japanese militarists "must be eliminated for all time."

2. Until a "new order of peace, security and justice" is established in Japan, Allied forces will occupy Japanese key points "to secure the achievement" of this basic objective.

3. Terms of the Cairo Declaration[1] will be carried out, and Japanese sovereignty will be limited to Hokkaido, Honshu, Kyushu, Shikoku, and adjacent smaller islands.

4. Japanese military forces, "after being completely disarmed, shall be permitted to return to their homes with the opportunity to lead peaceful and productive lives."

5. "We do not intend that the Japanese shall be enslaved as a race or destroyed as a nation, but stern justice shall be meted out to all war criminals. . . . Freedom of speech, of religion, and of thought, as well as respect for the fundamental human rights, shall be established."

6. Japan may retain such industries as will sustain her economy, but may not rearm; and she may look forward to "participation in world trade relations."

7. Occupation forces "shall be withdrawn from Japan as soon as these objectives have been accomplished and there has been established a peacefully inclined and responsible government."

8. The Japanese government is called upon "to proclaim now the unconditional surrender of all Japanese armed forces." The alternative is "prompt and utter destruction."

A broadcast of this declaration, received in Tokyo on 27 July, caused a flurry of discussion in high governmental circles as to how it should be handled. Foreign Minister Togo wished to play a waiting game and avoid any official statement. For (a typically Japanese condition), if any official declaration were

---

[1]The Cairo Declaration stated that Japan would be deprived of all conquests gained by aggression since the opening of Japan by Commodore Perry in 1853. Manchuria, Formosa, and the Pescadores would accordingly be restored to China; Korea would recover her independence; and the southern half of Sakhalin would be returned to Russia.

made, it would have to be a flat rejection, to please the military men in the cabinet. Unfortunately, Premier Suzuki upset the applecart when, at a press conference on 28 July, he indicated that the cabinet considered the Potsdam Declaration to be a mere rehash of the earlier and unacceptable Cairo Declaration, and as such unworthy of official notice. And, he added, the increase of aircraft production gave renewed hope of a Japanese victory.

No explicit assurance about the Emperor had issued from Potsdam; but (so Shigemitsu, Foreign Minister in the Koiso government, assured me in 1950) the reference in paragraph seven to withdrawing occupation forces after a "peacefully inclined and responsible government" had been set up indicated to the Japanese that they would be permitted to determine their own future.

If the Suzuki government could have made up its mind promptly to accept the Potsdam Declaration as a basis for peace, there would have been no explosion of an atomic bomb over Japan. Suzuki's bumbling statement to the press triggered it off.

Secretary of State Byrnes found the Premier's statement "disheartening." Both he and President Truman hoped that, before the Potsdam Conference broke up, the Japanese government would change its mind. The President had already decided to use the bomb if Japan did not accept the declaration and on 24 July had issued the necessary order to the Army Air Force to "deliver its first special bomb as soon as weather will permit visual bombing after about 3 August." But this could have been revoked, just as the Japanese strike on Pearl Harbor could have been recalled before 6 December 1941.

That was on 2 August, west longitude date. All parts and materials for assembling the bombs had arrived at Tinian before the first of the month. Weather on 3 and 4 August (east longitude dates) was unfavorable; but on the fourth, with a good forecast for the next two days, General LeMay decided to load the first bomb on 5 August and to drop it on the sixth.

The B-29 nicknamed "Enola Gay," commanded by Colonel Paul W. Tibbets, U.S.A., was chosen to carry the first atomic bomb. Captain William S. Parsons, a Navy ordnance specialist who had had charge of the ordnance aspects of the bomb and of its safety features, came along to assemble it and make the final adjustments en route.

At 0245 August 6 "Enola Gay" took off from North Field, Tinian, followed by two observation planes. Over Iwo Jima it began a slow climb to 30,000 feet. At 0730 Captain Parsons and his assistant made final adjustments on the bomb. Weather reconnaissance planes reported all clear over Hiroshima. The B-29 was over the city at 0911, when controls were passed to the bombardier, Major Thomas W. Ferebee, U.S.A., who at 0915 "toggled the bomb out" at an altitude of 31,600 feet and speed of 328 m.p.h. No enemy planes attacked "Enola Gay." She landed on Tinian at 1458.

Results were catastrophic. The bomb exploded right over a parade ground where the Japanese Second Army was doing calisthenics. The soldiers were wiped out almost to a man. Everything in the city within an area of over four square miles was razed or fused. An estimated 71,379 people, including the military, were killed; 19,691 were seriously injured; and about 171,000 rendered homeless. This seems, however, to have been an overestimate. A Japanese official notice of 31 July 1959 stated that the total number of deaths attributed to the bombing of Hiroshima, including all that had occurred in the nearly 14 years since it happened, was 60,175.

President Truman got the word at noon on 6 August (west longitude date) on board cruiser *Augusta* while crossing the Atlantic. He told the officers and men about it, saying, "This is the greatest thing in history."

Before sunrise 9 August the Russian declaration of war on Japan was known in Tokyo. At 1000 Marquis Kido conveyed to Premier Suzuki the Emperor's belief that it was urgent to accept the Potsdam Declaration immediately. The S.C.D.W., promptly summoned to the Imperial Palace, was already in session when the second atomic bomb exploded over Nagasaki, at 1101. All agreed to insist that the prerogatives of the imperial family be preserved, but beyond that there was no agreement. War Minister General Anami, Army Chief of Staff General Umezu, and Admiral Toyoda, the Navy Chief of Staff, insisted on three conditions: 1) the Japanese would disarm their own troops overseas, 2) war criminals would be prosecuted by Japanese courts, and 3) only a limited military occupation of Japan would be permitted. Togo pointed out that the Allies were certain to refuse such conditions, that all hope of Japanese victory had vanished, and that Japan must no longer delay seeking peace. But as Anami, Umezu, and Toyoda held out, nothing could be decided.

Nor could agreement be reached by the cabinet, at a meeting which opened at 1430, even after sitting for over seven hours and hearing more bad news from Hiroshima and Nagasaki. When that meeting broke up at 2230 August 9, Suzuki and Togo called on the Emperor and told him that, as neither cabinet nor S.C.D.W. could reach a decision, he must summon the council to meet with him. Hirohito agreed. The S.C.D.W. met with the Emperor in an underground air-raid shelter at the palace, at 1350 August 9.

This was what Togo, Shigemitsu, and Kido had been working toward for months. At the Imperial Conference, Suzuki took the floor and presented his arguments for immediate acceptance of the Potsdam Declaration. Togo and Navy Minister Yonai supported him. Generals Anami and Umezu and Admiral Toyoda argued for a resolute prosecution of the war, unless the Allies accepted the three above-mentioned conditions. There was a long discussion of possibilities, ably led by Baron Hiranuma. Suzuki requested an "imperial decision" to break the deadlock, an unprecedented step. The Emperor rose, said that ending the war was the only way to relieve Japan from unbearable distress, and left the room. Suzuki then declared: "His Majesty's decision should be made the decision of this conference as well," and the S.C.D.W. adjourned at 0230 August 10.

Since an Imperial Conference had no formal power to decide anything, a cabinet meeting was called at about 0300 August 10. There, the imperial decision was unanimously approved.

At 0700 August 10, a message was sent to the governments of the United States, Great Britain, the Soviet Union, and China, stating that Japan was ready to accept the terms of the Potsdam Declaration with the understanding that the prerogatives of the Emperor as a sovereign ruler were not prejudiced.

During that day the cabinet debated whether to announce this to the public. It was decided to make no announcement until after the publication of an imperial rescript accepting the Potsdam terms, because of the fear of a militarist coup d'état. That possibility was real indeed. On the morning of 10 August, War Minister Anami summoned all officers in Tokyo of the rank of lieutenant colonel and above, told them what had happened, and appealed to them to keep the Army quiet. Increasing restiveness at the war ministry during the day caused him to issue a warning against any overt effort to obstruct the government's decision. And Admiral Yonai issued a comparable warning to the Japanese Navy.

But the wireless waves and cables between Tokyo and Washington were working, via Switzerland. The message of 0700 August 10 accepting the Potsdam Declaration was received at about the same hour next day, 10 August, west longitude date. At Washington this created a flurry only less agitated than the one at Tokyo. Was it or was it not an acceptance of the Potsdam terms? At a conference in the White House between President Truman, Secretaries Byrnes, Stimson, and Forrestal, Admiral Leahy, and a few others, the question was threshed out. "Terrible political repercussions" were anticipated if a promise to keep the Emperor on his throne should backfire by encouraging the Japanese government to continue the war. The President decided, nevertheless, to take the risk, and Secretary Byrnes drafted a note in reply to the Japanese offer, which, after obtaining telegraphed approval from London, Moscow, and Chungking, he sent to Tokyo via Switzerland on 11 August (west longitude date) and immediately broadcast. The foreign office at Tokyo intercepted it at about noon the same day.

The Byrnes note of 11 August comprised five pertinent provisions:

1. "From the moment of surrender the authority of the Emperor and Japanese government . . . shall be subject to the Supreme Commander of the Allied Powers who will take such steps as he deems proper to effectuate the surrender terms."

2. The Emperor will authorize his government and Imperial General Headquarters to sign the surrender and shall command all his armed forces to lay down their arms.

3. Immediately upon the surrender the Japanese government shall transport

prisoners of war and interned civilians to places of safety where they can be embarked in Allied transports.

4. The ultimate form of the government of Japan shall be established by the free will of the Japanese people.

5. Allied occupation forces will remain in Japan "until the purposes set forth in the Potsdam Declaration are achieved."

The Byrnes note created new tensions and a fresh crisis in high circles at Tokyo. It left no doubt in anyone's mind that the Japanese would be permitted to retain the Emperor, and most of the cabinet were for accepting; but Anami, Umezu, and Toyoda were adamant, holding out for self-disarmament and a limited occupation or none. A fanatical coup d'état, with the purpose of continuing the war, was narrowly averted. Soon after receipt of the Allied reply, a group of young Army officers in the War Ministry approached Anami with a direct suggestion that the Army intervene to stop all peace moves. He succeeded in putting them off, but this powder-keg atmosphere persisted while the cabinet for two days longer remained deadlocked. Togo received support on 13 August in the form of a cablegram from the Japanese minister in Stockholm, reporting that the United States had resisted strong pressure from the Soviet Union and China to remove the Emperor.

On the eleventh, when the Byrnes note was dispatched, President Truman ordered all "strategic" air operations (the B-29s) by the Army Air Force to be suspended; but on the fourteenth, apparently with a view to helping the Japanese make up their minds, the bombers were ordered to resume. That order in turn was canceled after more than a thousand B-29s were in the air, but most of them were recalled before doing any further damage.

During the night of 13 to 14 August, seven B-29s dropped on Tokyo more than five million leaflets, containing the text of the Japanese note accepting the Potsdam Declaration and a Japanese translation of Secretary Byrnes's reply. This was the first intimation the people had of what was going on. At 0830 August 14, Marquis Kido brought one of these leaflets to the Emperor and urgently advised him to take prompt action, predicting that the leaflets would have a profound effect. Unless the Emperor declared immediately for peace, he might lose control of armed forces in the field. Shortly after, Premier Suzuki arrived at the palace. He and Marquis Kido, who had vainly endeavored to convert General Anami to reason, urged the Emperor to convoke an Imperial Conference (the S.C.D.W. in the "presence") on his own initiative. This was unprecedented. By Japanese constitutional procedure, an Imperial Conference could be convoked only after the Premier and chiefs of staff had agreed on the agenda. The Emperor, before taking so drastic a step, requested several senior Army and Navy officers to take measures to secure the obedience of all armed forces to his orders to cease fire. He then summoned the S.C.D.W. to the palace.

The meeting opened at 1100 August 14 in the air-raid shelter. Suzuki reported that most of those present favored an immediate acceptance of the Byrnes note but suggested that the Emperor hear the objectors before making his decision. In a highly emotional atmosphere, Anami, Umezu, and Toyoda repeated their earlier arguments for continuing to fight. The Emperor then spoke the thoughts that he had long firmly held. Continuing the war, he said, will merely result in additional destruction. The whole nation will be reduced to ashes. The Allied reply is a virtually complete acknowledgment of the position of his note of 0700 August 10 and evidence "of the peaceful and friendly intentions of the enemy." It is the imperial desire that his ministers of state accept it. They will at once prepare an imperial rescript broadcasting this decision directly to the people.

The deed was done. At 1449 August 14 Radio Tokyo flashed the Emperor's decision around the world. The cabinet was already making a final draft of the rescript, which had been in preparation since 10 August. At 2100 it was completed and taken to the Emperor, who signed it at 2250 August 14. Ten minutes later it was officially proclaimed that Japan would accept the Allied terms, and a note to that effect was sent to the Allied governments through a neutral country. This important news reached President Truman at 1550 August 14, west longitude date. He announced it from the White House at 1900 the same day and declared a two-day holiday of jubilation.

Despite every care to prevent incidents, the situation in Tokyo almost got out of hand. Hotheads in the war ministry and on the general staff were still planning a military coup. During the night of 14 to 15 August (east longitude date) they called on Lieutenant General Takeshi Mori, commanding the Imperial Guards Division, to demand that he order his men to disobey the surrender order. Mori refused and was then assassinated. With the connivance of two officers of his staff, orders were prepared, over his forged seal, to isolate the palace and the Emperor and impound the tape recording of the surrender message that was to be broadcast at noon next day. When General Tanaka of the Eastern District Area Army heard of this plot, he proceeded to the palace, took personal command of the Imperial Guards, countermanded the forged orders, and by 0800 August 15 had suppressed the nascent insurrection.

In the course of the day attempts were made to assassinate Premier Suzuki, Marquis Kido, and Baron Hiranuma. General Anami, who knew what was going on but either dared not or cared not to do anything about it, felt that the only honorable way out was to commit hara-kiri and did so. His example was followed by four of the principal conspirators and by General Tanaka, whose prompt action had defeated their plans, and (most appropriately) by Vice Admiral Takijiro Onishi, father of the Kamikaze Corps.

Throughout the morning of 15 August, Japanese radios announced that a most important broadcast would be made at noon. When listeners were told that the next voice would be that of the Emperor, which they had never before been permitted to hear, they anticipated something tremendous and generally assumed that it would be a plea for resistance to the bitter end. On the contrary, Hirohito reviewed the course of the war, announced that he had accepted the terms of the Allies, appealed to the people to rebuild the country, and ended: "We charge you, Our loyal subjects, to carry out faithfully Our will." The word "surrender" was carefully omitted from the text, but almost every listener realized that his ruler was announcing the end of the war on Allied terms. The people were stupefied by this revelation, and still appeared stunned when the first occupation troops arrived two weeks later.

The Japanese note of 2300 August 14 (east longitude date) was promptly acknowledged by Secretary Byrnes, together with an order that the Japanese cease hostilities at once, as our forces had already been ordered to do. This was received in Tokyo early 16 August (east longitude date), and the Emperor's definite order to cease fire went out at 1600 that day. The United States Navy had stopped all offensive operations 34 hours earlier, at 0615 August 15. The Emperor's order to his armed forces to surrender was not issued until after the signing of the surrender document on the *Missouri* on 2 September.

It was the Emperor who cut governmental red tape and made the great decision. This required courage. The Army chiefs and Admiral Toyoda were not greatly moved by the atomic explosions. They argued that the two bombs were probably all that the United States had, and if more were made, we would not dare use them when invading Japan; that there was a fair chance of defeating the invasion by massed kamikaze attacks; and that, in any event, national honor demanded a last battle on Japanese soil. All the fighting hitherto had been little more than peripheral skirmishes; the way to victory was to "lure" the Americans ashore and "annihilate" them, as had been done by the original kamikaze "divine wind" to the hordes of Kublai Khan in 1281 A.D. Such had been the propaganda line given to the Japanese people to explain the series of defeats; they had no idea that Japan was really beaten. Nothing less than an assertion of the imperial will could have overcome these arguments and objections.

An intelligent and patriotic French banker, M. Jacques Bardac, who was interned at Peiping through the entire war and cut off from all news and propaganda except Japanese, told me that it was so well done as to convince him up to the very last that Japan was winning. The older Japanese on Oahu, who could not understand English, believed even after the end of the war that Japan had won, and scores of them assembled one day on Aiea Heights to see the victorious Imperial Fleet enter Pearl Harbor.

On the Allied side, it has been argued that the maritime blockade, virtually complete by mid-August, would have strangled Japanese economy and that the B-29s and naval gunfire ships would have destroyed its principal cities and forced a surrender before long, without the aid of the atomic bombs or of invasion. Fleet Admirals King and Leahy lent their distinguished advocacy to tihs view.

Whether or not they were correct, not even time can tell. But of some things, one can be sure. The stepped-up B-29 bombings and naval bombardments, had they been continued after 15 August, would have cost the Japanese loss and suffering far, far greater than those inflicted by the two atomic bombs. And the probable effects of the projected invasions of Kyushu and Honshu in the fall and winter of 1945 to 1946 and of a desperate place-to-place defense of Japan stagger the imagination. It is simply not true that Japan had no military capability left in mid-August. Although 2550 kamikaze planes had been expended, there were 5350 of them still left, together with as many ready for orthodox use and some 7000 under repair or in storage; and 5000 young men were training for the Kamikaze Corps. The plan was to disperse all aircraft on small grass strips in Kyushu, Shikoku, and western Honshu and in underground hangars and caves and to conserve them for kamikaze crashes on the Allied amphibious forces invading the home islands. Considering the number of planes, pilots, and potential targets, all within a short distance of principal airfields, it requires little imagination to depict the horrible losses that would have been inflicted on the invading forces, even before they got ashore. After the landing, there would have been protracted battles on Japanese soil which would have cost each side very many more lives and created a bitterness which even time could hardly have healed. Japan had plenty of ammunition left; the U.S. Army after the war found thousands of tons holed up in Hokkaido alone. And, as Russia would have been a full partner in this final campaign, there is a fair chance that Japan would have been divided like Germany and Korea, if not delivered completely to the mercy of the Communists.

We must also point out that, even after two atomic bombs had been dropped, the Potsdam Declaration clarified, the guards' insurrection defeated, and the Emperor's will made known, it was touch and go whether the Japanese actually would surrender. Hirohito had to send members of the imperial family to the principal Army commands to ensure compliance. His younger brother, Prince Takamatsu, was just in time to make the Atsugi airfield available for the first occupation forces on 26 August and to keep the kamikaze boys grounded. They were boasting that they would crash the *Missouri* when she entered Tokyo Bay. If these elements had had their way, the war would have been resumed, with the Allies feeling that the Japanese were hopelessly treacherous and with a savagery on both sides that is painful to contemplate.

When these facts and events of the Japanese surrender are known and weighed, it will become evident that the atomic bomb was the keystone of a very fragile arch.

Chapter 3   THE STRATEGIC NEED FOR THE BOMB QUESTIONED

Providing a direct reply to Stimson's position,
HANSON W. BALDWIN *(1903–   ), a military*
affairs analyst, disputes the strategic necessity for
the atomic bomb. A graduate of the United States
Naval Academy, Baldwin became associated with The
New York Times *in 1929 and for many years was military*
editor of that newspaper. He has contributed
widely to various journals and has written
several volumes on naval and military affairs. In
Great Mistakes of the War *(1950), Baldwin views*
some major decisions of World War II on which, he
believes, the Allies erred; the use of the atomic
bomb against Japan was one such crucial mistake.
Can you accept Baldwin's conclusion that the
decision was an expedient one?*

The utilization of the atomic bomb against a prostrate and defeated Japan in the closing days of the war exemplifies . . . the narrow, astigmatic concentration of our planners upon one goal, and one alone: victory.

Nowhere in all of Mr. Stimson's forceful and eloquent apologia for the leveling of Hiroshima and Nagasaki is there any evidence of an ulterior vision; indeed, the entire effort of his famous Harper's article, reprinted and rearranged in his book, *On Active Service*, is focused on proving that the bomb hastened the end of the war. But at what cost!

To accept the Stimson thesis that the atomic bomb should have been used as it was used, it is necessary first to accept the contention that the atomic bomb achieved or hastened victory, and second, and more important, that it helped to

*Hanson W. Baldwin, *Great Mistakes of the War* (New York, 1950), pp. 88–107. Reprinted by permission of Curtis Brown Ltd.—Collins-Knowlton-Wing, Inc. Copyright © 1949, 1950 by Hanson W. Baldwin. Footnotes omitted.

consolidate the peace or to further the political aims for which war was fought.

History can accept neither contention.

Let us examine the first. The atomic bomb was dropped in August. Long before that month started our forces were securely based in Okinawa, the Marianas and Iwo Jima; Germany had been defeated; our fleet had been cruising off the Japanese coast with impunity bombarding the shoreline; our submarines were operating in the Sea of Japan; even inter-island ferries had been attacked and sunk. Bombing, which started slowly in June, 1944, from China bases and from the Marianas in November, 1944, had been increased materially in 1945, and by August, 1945, more than 16,000 tons of bombs had ravaged Japanese cities. Food was short; mines and submarines and surface vessels and planes clamped an iron blockade around the main islands; raw materials were scarce. Blockade, bombing, and unsuccessful attempts at dispersion had reduced Japanese production capacity from 20 to 60 per cent. The enemy, in a military sense, was in a hopeless strategic position by the time the Potsdam demand for unconditional surrender was made on July 26.

Such, then, was the situation when we wiped out Hiroshima and Nagasaki.

Need we have done it? No one can, of course, be positive, but the answer is almost certainly negative.

The invasion of Japan, which Admiral Leahy had opposed as too wasteful of American blood, and in any case unnecessary, was scheduled (for the southern island of Kyushu) for Nov. 1, 1945, to be followed if necessary, in the spring of 1946, by a major landing on the main island of Honshu. We dropped the two atomic bombs in early August, almost two months before our first D-Day. The decision to drop them, after the Japanese rejection of the Potsdam ultimatum, was a pretty hasty one. It followed the recommendations of Secretary Stimson and an "Interim Committee" of distinguished officials and scientists, who had found "no acceptable alternative to direct military use."

But the weakness of this statement is inherent, for none was tried and "military use" of the bomb was undertaken despite strong opposition to this course by numerous scientists and Japanese experts, including former Ambassador Joseph Grew. Not only was the Potsdam ultimatum merely a restatement of the politically impossible—unconditional surrender—but it could hardly be construed as a direct warning of the atomic bomb and was not taken as such by anyone who did not know the bomb had been created. A technical demonstration of the bomb's power may well have been unfeasible, but certainly a far more definite warning could have been given; and it is hard to believe that a target objective in Japan with but sparse population could not have been found. The truth is we did not try; we gave no specific warning. There were almost two months before our scheduled invasion of Kyushu, in which American ingenuity could have found ways to bring home to the Japanese the impossibility of their position and the horrors of the weapon being held over them; yet we rushed to use the bomb as soon as unconditional surrender was rejected. Had we devised some demonstration or given a more specific warning than the Potsdam ultimatum, and had the Japanese still persisted in continued resistance after some weeks of our psychological offensive, we should perhaps have been justified in the bomb's use; at least, our hands would have been more clean.

But, in fact, our only warning to a Japan already militarily defeated, and in a hopeless situation, was the Potsdam demand for unconditional surrender issued on July 26, when we knew Japanese surrender attempts had started. Yet when the Japanese surrender was negotiated about two weeks later, after the bomb was dropped, our unconditional surrender demand was made conditional and we agreed, as Stimson had originally proposed we should do, to continuation of the Emperor upon his imperial throne.

We were, therefore, twice guilty. We dropped the bomb at a time when Japan already was negotiating for an end of the war but before those negotiations could come to fruition. We demanded unconditional surrender, then dropped the bomb and accepted conditional surrender, a sequence which indicates pretty clearly that the Japanese would have surrendered, even if the bomb had not been dropped, had the Potsdam Declaration included our promise to permit the Emperor to remain on his imperial throne.

What we now know of the condition of Japan, and of the days preceding her final surrender on Aug. 15, verifies these conclusions. It is clear, in retrospect, (and was understood by some, notably Admiral Leahy, at the time) that Japan was militarily on her last legs. Yet our intelligence estimates greatly overstated her strength.

The background for surrender had been sketched in fully, well before the bombs were dropped, and the Strategic Bombing Survey declares that "interrogation of the highest Japanese officials, following V-J Day, indicated that Japan would have surrendered . . . even . . . if the atomic bombs had not been dropped." "Even before the large-scale bombing of Japan was initiated, the raw material base of Japanese industry was effectively undermined. An accelerated decline of armament production was inevitable."

Admiral Chester W. Nimitz, in a talk to the National Geographic Society on January 25, 1946, declared, "I am convinced that the complete impunity with which the Pacific Fleet pounded Japan at pointblank range was the decisive factor in forcing the Japanese to ask the Russians to approach us for peace proposals in July.

"Meanwhile, aircraft from our new fields in the Okinawa group were daily shuttling back and forth over Kyushu and Shokoku and B-29's of the Twentieth Air Force were fire-bombing major Japanese cities. The pace and the fury were mounting and the government of Japan, as its official spokesmen have now admitted, were looking for a way to end the war. At this point the Potsdam Ultimatum was delivered and the Japanese knew their choice.

"They were debating that choice when the atomic bomb fell on Hiroshima. They were debating that choice when our ships shelled installations within less than 100 miles of Tokyo. . . .

"The atomic bomb merely hastened a process already reaching an inevitable conclusion. . . ."

There can be no doubt that this conclusion of Admiral Nimitz will be the verdict of history. Militarily we "killed" Japan in many different ways: by crushing defeats at sea and on land; by the strangulation of the blockade of which the principal instrument was the submarine; by bombing with conventional bombs. After the seizure of Okinawa—probably even before that—the blockade alone could have defeated Japan; was, indeed, defeating her. Admiral Leahy was right; invasion was not necessary. . . .

In the words of a well known Japanese correspondent, Masuo Kato, who was in Washington for the Domei News Agency when the war started: "The thunderous arrival of the first atomic bomb at Hiroshima was only a *coup de grâce* for an empire already struggling in particularly agonizing death throes. The world's newest and most devastating of weapons had floated out of the summer sky to destroy a city at a stroke, but its arrival had small effect on the outcome of the war between Japan and the United Nations."

It is therefore clear today—and was clear to many even as early as the spring of 1945—that the military defeat of Japan was certain; the atomic bomb was not needed.

But if the bomb did not procure victory, did it hasten it?

This question cannot be answered with equal precision, particularly since the full story of the Japanese surrender attempts has not been compiled. But a brief chronology of known events indicates that the atomic bomb may have shortened the war by a few days—not more.

The day before Christmas, 1944 (two months *before* the Yalta conference), U.S. intelligence authorities in Washington received a report from a confidential agent in Japan that a peace party was emerging and that the Koiso cabinet would soon be succeeded by a cabinet headed by Admiral Baron Suzuki who would initiate surrender proceedings.

The Koiso cabinet *was* succeeded by a new government headed by Suzuki in early April, 1945, but even prior to this significant change, the Japanese—in February, 1945—had approached the Russians with a request that they act as intermediary in arranging a peace with the Western powers. The Russian Ambassador, Malik, in Tokyo, was the channel of the approach. The Russians, however, set their price of mediation so high that the Japanese temporarily dropped the matter. The United States was not officially informed of this approach until after the end of the war.

Prior to, coincident with, and after this February attempt, ill-defined peace approaches were made through the Japanese Ambassadors in Stockholm and

Moscow, particularly Moscow. These approaches were so informal, and to some extent represented to such a degree the personal initiative of the two Ambassadors concerned, that they never came to a head.

But after a meeting with Stalin in Moscow on May 27, before the trial A-bomb was even tested in New Mexico, Harry Hopkins cabled President Truman that:

"1. Japan is doomed and the Japanese know it.

"2. Peace feelers are being put out by certain elements in Japan. . . . "

In April, 1945, as the United States was establishing a foothold on Okinawa, the Russians in effect denounced their neutrality agreement with Japan, and from then until July 12, the new cabinet was moving rapidly toward surrender attempts.

On July 12, fourteen days before we issued the Potsdam Proclamation, these attempts reached a clearly defined point. Prince Konoye was received by the Emperor on that day and ordered to Moscow as a peace plenipotentiary to "secure peace at any price." On July 13, Moscow was notified officially by the Japanese foreign office that the "Emperor was desirous of peace."

It was hoped that Moscow would inform the United States and Britain at the Potsdam conference of Japan's desire to discuss peace. But instead of an answer from the "Big Three," Ambassador Sato in Moscow was told by Molotov on August 8 of Russia's entry into the war against Japan, effective immediately.

However, since early May—well before this disappointing denouement to the most definite peace attempts the Japanese had yet made—the six-man Supreme War Direction Council in Japan had been discussing peace. On June 20, the Emperor told the (Supreme War Direction) Council that it "was necessary to have a plan to close the war at once as well as a plan to defend the home islands."

The Council was deadlocked three to three, and Premier Suzuki, to break the deadlock, had decided to summon a Gozenkaigi (a meeting of "Elder Statesmen," summoned only in hours of crises) at which the Emperor himself could make the decision for peace or further war. Suzuki knew his Emperor's mind; Hirohito had been convinced for some weeks that peace was the only answer to Japan's ordeal.

The first atomic bomb was dropped on Hiroshima on August 6; Russia entered the war on August 8; and the second atomic bomb was dropped on Nagasaki on August 9. The dropping of the first bomb, and the Russian entry into the war, gave Suzuki additional arguments for again putting the issue before the Supreme War Direction Council, and, on August 9, he won their approval for the Gozenkaigi. But neither the people of Japan nor their leaders were as impressed with the atomic bomb as were we. The public did not know until after the war what had happened to Hiroshima; and even so, they had endured fire raids against Tokyo which had caused more casualties than the atomic bomb and had devastated a greater area than that destroyed at Hiroshima. The Supreme War Direction Council was initially told that a fragment of the Hiroshima bomb indicated that it was made in Germany (!), that it appeared to be a conventional explosive of great power, and that there was only one bomb available. When the Gozenkaigi actually was held on August 14, five days after the second bomb was dropped, War Minister Anami and the chiefs of the Army and Navy General Staff—three members of the War Council who had been adamant for continuation of the war—were still in favor of continuing it; those who had wanted peace still wanted it. In other words, the bomb changed no opinions; the Emperor himself, who had already favored peace, broke the deadlock.

"If nobody else has any opinion to express," Hirohito said, "we would express our own. We demand that you will agree to it. We see only one way left for Japan to save herself. That is the reason we have made this determination to endure the unendurable and suffer the insufferable."

. . . It is quite possible that the atomic bombs shortened the war by a day, a week, or a month or two—not more.

But at what a price! For whether or not the atomic bomb hastened victory, it is quite clear it has not won the peace.

Some may point to the comparative tranquility of Japan under MacArthur in the postwar period as due in part to the terror of American arms created by the bomb. This is scarcely so; Japan's seeming tranquility is a surface one which has been furthered by a single occupation authority and the nature of the Japanese people. But I venture to estimate that those who suffered at Hiroshima and Nagasaki will never forget it, and that we sowed there a whirlwind of hate which we shall someday reap.

In estimating the effect of the use of the bomb upon the peace, we must remember, first, that we used the bomb for one purpose, and one only; not to secure a more equable peace, but to hasten victory. By using the bomb we have become identified, rightfully or wrongly, as inheritors of the mantle of Genghis Khan and all those of past history who have justified the use of utter ruthlessness in war.

It may well be argued, of course, that war—least of all modern war—knows no humanity, no rules, and no limitations, and that death by the atomic bomb is no worse than death by fire bombs or high explosives or gas or flame throwers. It is, of course, true that the atomic bomb is no worse qualitatively than other lethal weapons; it is merely quantitatively more powerful; other weapons cause death in fearful ways; the atomic bomb caused more deaths. We already had utilized fire raids, mass bombardment of cities, and flame throwers in the name of expediency and victory prior to August 6, even though many of our people had recoiled from such practices.

Even as late as June 1, 1945, Stimson "had sternly questioned his Air Forces leader, wanting to know whether the apparently indiscriminate bombings of Tokyo were absolutely necessary. Perhaps, as he [Stimson] later said, he was misled by the constant talk of 'precision bombing,' but he had believed that even air power could be limited in its use by the old concept of 'legitimate military targets.' Now in the conflagration bombings by massed B-29's, he was permitting a kind of total war he had always hated, and in recommending the use of the atomic bomb he was implicitly confessing that there could be no significant limits to the horror of modern war."

If we accept this confession—that there can be no limits set to modern war —we must also accept the bitter inheritance of Genghis Khan and the mantles of all the other ruthless despoilers of the past.

In reality, we took up where these great conquerors left off long before we dropped the atomic bomb. Americans, in their own eyes, are a naively idealistic people, with none of the crass ruthlessness so often exhibited by other nations. Yet in the eyes of others our record is very far from clean, nor can objective history palliate it. Rarely have we been found on the side of restricting horror; too often we have failed to support the feeble hands of those who would limit war. We did not ratify the Hague convention of 1899, outlawing the use of dumdum (expanding) bullets in war. We never ratified the Geneva Protocol of 1925, outlawing the use of biological agents and gas in war. At the time the war in the Pacific ended, pressure for the use of gas against Japanese island positions had reached the open discussion stage, and rationalization was leading surely to justification, an expedient justification since we had air superiority and the means to deluge the enemy with gas, while he had no similar way to reply. We condemned the Japanese for their alleged use of biological agents against the Chinese, yet in July and August, 1945, a shipload of U.S. biological agents for use in destruction of the Japanese rice crop was en route to the Marianas. And even before the war, our fundamental theory of air war, like the Trenchard school of Britain, coincided, or stemmed from the Douhet doctrine of destructiveness: the bombardment of enemy cities and peoples.

Yet surely these methods—particularly the extension of unrestricted warfare to enemy civilians—defeated any peace aims we might have had, and had little appreciable effect in hastening military victory. For in any totalitarian state, the leaders rather than the peoples must be convinced of defeat, and the indiscriminate use of mass or area weapons, like biological agents and the atomic bomb, strike at the people, not the rulers. We cannot succeed, therefore, by such methods, in drawing that fine line between ruler and ruled that ought to be drawn in every war; we cannot hasten military victory by slaughtering the led; such methods only serve to bind the led closer to their leaders. Moreover, unrestricted warfare can never lay the groundwork for a more stable peace. Its heritage may be the salt-sown fields of Carthage, or the rubble and ruin of a

Berlin or Tokyo or Hiroshima; but neither economically nor psychologically can unrestricted warfare—atomic warfare or biological warfare—lead anywhere save to eventual disaster.

During the last conflict we brought new horror to the meaning of war; the ruins of Germany and Japan, the flame-scarred tissues of the war-wounded attest our efficiency. And on August 6, 1945, that blinding flash above Hiroshima wrote a climax to an era of American expediency. On that date we joined the list of those who had introduced new and horrible weapons for the extermination of man; we joined the Germans who had first utilized gas, the Japanese with their biological agents, the Huns and the Mongols who had made destruction a fine art.

It is my contention that in the eyes of the world the atomic bomb has cost us dearly; we have lost morally; we no longer are the world's moral leader as in the days of the Wilsonian Fourteen Points. It is my contention that the unlimited destruction caused by our unlimited methods of waging war has caused us heavy economic losses in the forms of American tax subsidies to Germany and Japan. It is my contention that unrestricted warfare and unlimited aims cost us politically the winning of the peace.

But it is not only—and perhaps not chiefly—in public opinion or in the public pocketbook or even in public stability that we have suffered, but in our own souls. The American public is tending to accept the nefarious doctrine that the ends justify the means, the doctrine of exigency. . . .

The use of the atomic bomb, therefore, cost us dearly; we are now branded with the mark of the beast. Its use may have hastened victory—though by very little—but it has cost us in peace the pre-eminent moral position we once occupied. Japan's economic troubles are in some degree the result of unnecessary devastation. We have embarked upon Total War with a vengeance; we have done our best to make it far more total. If we do not soon reverse this trend, if we do not cast about for means to limit and control war, if we do not abandon the doctrine of expediency, of unconditional surrender, of total victory, we shall someday ourselves become the victims of our own theories and practices.

Chapter 4 THE GREAT DECISION: PROS AND CONS

The leading American historian of the diplomacy of World War II and after, HERBERT FEIS *(1893–1972) served in the 1930s as an economic adviser to the Department of State and from 1944 to 1946 as special consultant to the Secretary of War. He was a member of the State Department Policy Planning Staff in 1950–1951. He received widespread recognition for his studies in diplomatic relations, including* The Road to Pearl Harbor *(1950),* The China Tangle *(1953),* Churchill-Roosevelt-Stalin *(1957), and* Between War and Peace: The Potsdam Conference *(1960). In 1960, Feis was awarded the Pulitzer Prize in history. In the following selection from* The Atomic Bomb and the End of World War II *(1966), he weighed what he felt were the primary considerations involved in the decision to use the bomb and to use it without warning.**

At the time of the event, only some contributing scientists protested the use of the atomic bomb against a vulnerable live target. The peoples fighting Japan looked upon its employment against the enemy as a natural act of war, and rejoiced at the swift ending it brought about. Any qualms they might have had over the cruel suffering of the victims were routed by the thought that if Germans or Japanese had developed this weapon they would surely have used it. Subsequently, however, as the blast and radiation effects of this new projectile were more fully appreciated, and as more and more powerful kinds were spawned, the precedent act has been regarded by many with rue.

*Herbert Feis, *The Atomic Bomb and the End of World War II* (Princeton, N.J. 1966), revised edition of *Japan Subdued: The Atomic Bomb and the End of the War in the Pacific* (1961). Reprinted by permission of Princeton University Press. Copyright © 1961, 1966, by Princeton University Press (Princeton Paperback, 1970), pp. 190–201. Footnotes omitted.

Whether, if the United States had pledged itself as soon as the war ended to destroy the other bombs it had and dismantle the factories in which they were made other countries would have been willing to join with it in a trust-worthy system of control of atomic energy, must remain forever a provocation to the speculative historian. But most probably the dismal failure to reach any restraining agreement was an inexpugnable accompaniment to the suspicions, animosities, fears and hatred that have been so rampant after the war. Unable to arrive at genuine peace with each other through mutal good will, respect and understanding, they live under the common canopy of mutual terror. Little wonder then that foreboding dominates the memory of the laboratory triumphs of the physicists, the achievements of the engineers, the test at Alamogordo and the display at Hiroshima.

In the evolving discussion about the decision to use the bomb, several related but separable questions have been commingled. One of these, and by far the easiest to answer conclusively, is whether it was *essential* to do so in order to compel Japan to surrender on our terms before it was invaded.

Some of the decision-makers were confident that the invasion of the main islands of Japan would not be necessary to compel surrender quickly and un-conditionally. Japan's ability to fend off our tremendous naval and air assaults was shattered. It seemed to them that the Japanese people, crowded in their small islands, with insufficient and destructible supplies of food and oil, would have to give in soon—unless bent on national suicide. Among those were Secretary of the Navy Forrestal and Under-Secretary Bard and Admiral Leahy and General Spaatz, the Commander of our Strategic Air Force.

But others, especially those in the Army, remained convinced that final victory on our own terms could only be achieved on land, as it had been in the Philip-pines, Iwo Jima, Okinawa. Had not their military histories taught them that a hopelessly beaten Confederate Army had battled on? Had they not witnessed the refusal of the Germans under the fanatic Hitler to give up long after any chance of winning was gone, and how that people rallied from the shattering air attacks on their cities? Would the war in Europe continue many months longer, they argued, except for the combined crushing assaults of large land armies from the East, the West, the South?

To the historian, taught by the accumulated records and testimony, the answer is obvious. There cannot be a well-grounded dissent from the conclusion reached as early as 1945 by members of the U.S. Strategic Bombing Survey. After inspection of the condition to which Japan was reduced, by studies of the mil-itary position and the trend of Japanese popular and official opinion, they esti-mated ". . . that certainly prior to 31 December 1945, and in all probability prior to 1 November 1945, Japan would have surrendered even if the atomic bombs had not been dropped, even if Russia had not entered the war, and even if no invasion had been planned or contemplated."[1]

If then the use of the bomb was not essential, was it justified—justified, that is, as the surest way in combination with other measures to bring about the earliest surrender? That is a harder question to answer, and a more troubling one than it was thought to be at the time of decision.

It may be contended with the grim support by history that no exceptional justification for the use of the bomb need be sought or given. For the prevalent rule of nations—except when "knighthood was in flower"—has allowed the use of any and all weapons in war except any banned by explicit agreement; and this was the prevailing view at the time, qualified only by revulsion against use of weapons and methods deemed needlessly inhumane such as poisoning of wells and torture. Did not, it should be borne in mind, every one of the contending nations strive its utmost to invent and produce more deadly weapons, faster planes of greater bomb capacity, new types of mines, rockets and buzz-bombs? And was not each and every improved sort of killing weapon brought into action without ado or reproach? For this reason alone, almost all professional military men, and those in uniform in 1945, would then have denied that any special justification for the use of the bomb was needed, and would still dispose of the subject in this way.

The more thoughtful might add that the decision to use the bomb was not really important; that the measures of permanent significance to mankind had been taken when physicists learned how to split the atom, and when scientists and engineers and builders succeeded in encasing the energy of the fissured atom in a bomb; and that after these were achieved, it made little or no difference if this novel weapon was used against Japan, since it would certainly be used in the future time unless nations renounced war. Or if it were not, other equally dreadful threats would remain; chemical and biological ways of bringing death; and these were already in the secret arsenals of nations.

The source of restraint lies in fear of consequences; fear of the fact that the enemy will use the same terrible weapon. This was, for example, why neither side used poison gas in the war. When humane feeling is allied to such fear, it may command respect, and even those striving to win a war may recognize that "virtue it is to abstain even from that which is lawful."

These considerations seem to me conclusive defenses of our right, legal and historical, for the use of the atomic bomb against Japan. Those who made the decision took them for granted. They thus felt free to make it without scruples on these scores.

[1] A well-qualified group sent to Japan right after the war to ascertain and appraise the performance of the U.S. air assaults and their effectiveness.

Their reckoning, I believe the record clearly indicates, was governed by one reason deemed paramount: that by using the bomb the agony of war might be ended most quickly and lives be saved. It was believed with deep apprehension that many thousands, probably tens of thousands, of lives of Allied combatants would have to be spent in the continuation of our air and sea bombardment and blockade, victims mainly of Japanese suicide planes. In spite of its confidence in ultimate success, our assailant naval force felt vulnerable, because of grim and agonizing experience. Since the desperate kamikaze attacks began, suicide planes had sunk 34 American ships, including 3 aircraft carriers, and damaged 285 (including 36 carriers of all sizes and sorts, 15 battleships, 15 cruisers and 87 destroyers). During the Okinawa campaign alone, 16 of our ships had been sunk and 185 damaged (including 7 carriers, 10 battleships and 5 cruisers).

It was reliably known that the Japanese were assembling thousands of planes, of all kinds and conditions, to fling against the invasion fleet and the troop-carrying ships. Thus, should it prove necessary to carry out the plans for invasion, not only of Kyushu but also of the Tokyo Plain, it was feared by Stimson and Marshall that the American casualties alone might mount to hundreds of thousands. Our allies, it was reckoned, would suffer corresponding losses.

But the people who would have suffered most, had the war gone on much longer and their country been invaded, were the Japanese. One American incendiary air raid on the Tokyo area in March 1945 did more damage and killed and injured more Japanese than the bomb on Hiroshima. Even greater groups of American bombing planes would have hovered over Japan, consuming the land, its people and its food, with blast and fire, leaving them no place to hide, no chance to rest, no hope of reprieve. A glance at the chart kept in the Headquarters of the U.S. Strategic Air Force at Guam, with its steeply ascending record of bombing flights during the summer of 1945 and scheduled for the next month or two, leaves visions of horror of which Hiroshima is only a local illustration. Observation of the plight of the country and its people made soon after the war ended left me appalled at what those would have had to endure had the war gone on.

But the same official forecasts of what it was thought would occur if we had to fight on, gave sharper shape to the impelling reason for the development of the bomb—to end the war victoriously. Thus the decision to use the bomb seemed to be the natural culminating act for the achievement of a settled purpose as attested by its leading sponsors:

General Groves: "My mission as given to me by Secretary of War Stimson [in October 1942] was to produce this [the atomic bomb] at the earliest possible date so as to bring the war to a conclusion."

Truman: "I regarded the bomb as a military weapon and never had any doubt that it should be used."

Churchill: "The historic fact remains . . . that the decision whether or not to use the atomic bomb to compel the surrender of Japan was never even an issue. There was unanimous, automatic, unquestioned agreement around our table; nor did I ever hear the slightest suggestion that we should do otherwise."

Stimson: "Stimson believed, both at the time and later, that the dominant fact of 1945 was war, and that therefore, necessarily, the dominant objective was victory. If victory could be speeded by using the bomb, it should be used; if victory must be delayed in order to use the bomb, it should *not* be used. So far as he knew, this general view was fully shared by the President and all his associates."

Some of those men who concurred in the decision to use the bomb discerned other advantages and justifications. It is likely that Churchill, and probably also Truman, conceived that besides bringing the war to a quick end, it would improve the chances of arranging a satisfactory peace both in Europe and in the Far East. Stimson and Byrnes certainly had that thought in mind. For would not the same dramatic proof of western power that shocked Japan into surrender impress the Russians also? Might it not influence them to be more restrained? Might it not make more effective the resistance of the western allies to excessive Soviet pretensions and ventures, such as the Soviet bid for a military base in the Black Sea Straits, and a foreseen demand for a part in the occupation and control of Japan akin to that which it had in Germany? In short, the bomb, it may have been thought or hoped, would not only subdue the Japanese aggressors, but perhaps also monitor Russian behavior.

Recognition of this element in official thinking must not be distorted into an accusation that the American government engaged in what Soviet propagandists and historians have called "atomic blackmail." To the contrary, even after the American government knew that it would have the supreme weapon, it keenly sought to preserve the friendly connection with the Soviet Union. It rebuffed Churchill's proposals that the Western allies face down the Soviet government in some climactic confrontation over the outward thrust of Soviet power. After the testing of the bomb, at the Potsdam Conference, it patiently sought compromise solutions for situations in dispute. While knowledge of the successful test may have somewhat stiffened Truman's resistance to some of the furthest-reaching Soviet wishes, it did not cause him to alter American aims or terms as previously defined. In brief, and obviously, the men who determined American policy strove to achieve a stable international order by peaceful ways. They were not swayed by an excited wish to impose our will on the rest of the world by keeping atomic bombs poised over their lives. Even as the American government proceeded to use the bomb against Japan, it was brewing proposals for controlling its production and banning its use, except possibly as an international measure to enforce peace.

Had—the query continues to haunt the historian—the American government, *before* using the bomb, informed Stalin candidly of its nature and potential, and solicited his cooperation in some system of international control, might the Soviet government have reacted differently? Might it have been deflected from making the utmost effort to master the task of producing like weapons and accumulating them as a national atomic force. It is highly improbable, I think, considering Stalin's determination, as evidenced at Potsdam, to wear down Western resistance to Soviet claims, his suspicions and soaring assurance, and his belief that nations respected only strength. It would have been like him, in fact, to regard our confidential briefing as a subtle way of threatening the Soviet government, of trying to frighten it to accede to our wishes.

My best surmise is that while openness would have disarmed some foreign critics and improved the reception abroad of our later proposals for control, it would not really have influenced the Soviet policy. Nevertheless, it is regrettable that we did not take Stalin into at least the outer regions of our confidence, thereby indicating to the world that we were not intent on keeping unto ourselves a secret means of domination. After all, our secrecy and our elaborate security measures in the end were ineffectual and suffused the atmosphere with the scent of enmity. . . .

There were those who believed all these purposes would be better served if the bomb was introduced in some other way. They urged that before using it against Japan its immense destructive power should be displayed to the world by dropping it in some remote, uninhabited or emptied spot—an isolated island perhaps, or over a dense forest area, or on a mountain top, or in the sea near land. All suggestions of this sort were judged impractical, ineffective and/or risky.

A genuine fear of failure persisted despite accumulated evidence that the weapon was going to bear out the scientists' prediction . . . . As early as December 1944, Groves had been sure enough that one of the two types of bomb being produced (the type that was dropped on Hiroshima) would work satisfactorily, to report to Stimson that he and presumably his technical advisers did not think a preliminary full test essential. This confidence mounted as the effort neared fruition. The physicist, Smyth, who wrote up the authorized explanation of the undertaking, entered in his notes that "the end of June [1945] finds us expecting from day to day to hear of the explosion of the first atomic bomb devised by man. All the problems are believed to have been solved at least well enough to make a bomb practicable. A sustained neutron chain reaction resulting from nuclear fission has been demonstrated; the conditions necessary to cause such a reaction to occur explosively have been established and can be achieved."

But the responsible officials and military men still had nervous fears of failure. As recalled summarily by Stimson, in explanation of the decision not to warn Japan in advance of the nature and destructive power of the weapon, "Even the

New Mexico test would not give final proof that any given bomb was certain to explode when dropped from an airplane. Quite apart from the generally unfamiliar nature of atomic explosives, there was the whole problem of exploding a bomb at a predetermined height in the air by a complicated mechanism which could not be tested in the static test of New Mexico."

This uncertainty remained despite the numerous varied trials that had been made in flight with a simulated bomb casing and components. For many precautions had been conceived and taken against each and every one of these hazards; many rehearsals to enable trained mechanics and bombing crews to detect any causes of failure beforehand and to correct them.

Then there were chances of human error or accident. What if the heavily laden plane carrying the bomb and fuel needed for the long flight to the point selected for the demonstration crashed? What if the individuals entrusted with the task of turning the containing tube (in the U-235 gun type bomb that was first available for use in Japan) into an atomic weapon, faulted?

Then, also, there were chances of physical defects. Some part of the mechanism of any single specimen might turn out to be defective and malfunction.

Still another opposed reason was that the American government had so few of the new bombs. One would be consumed by the New Mexico test; another (of a different type) was promised in time for use after July 31; and it was reckoned a third by August 6th; and no others according to the schedule given to the decision-makers in June, until about August 20th. By using all—two or three—with utmost effectiveness, the desired quick end of the war might well be brought about. If one of these was misspent in a demonstration that went awry for any reason, could the trial be justified to the men in uniform whose lives were in hazard every day the war went on?

Suppose an announced demonstration had failed. Would the consequences have been serious? Stimson, and even more decidedly Byrnes and Groves, thought so. They believed that if it did not come off "as advertised," the Japanese would take fresh heart and fight on harder and longer. They feared, also, that an uproar would ensue in Congress if the demonstration fizzled or failed to budge the Japanese. They had accepted the unavoidable risks of condemnation if the project on which such vast sums had been spent turned out to be a mistaken venture. But they were not willing to widen the margin of exposure for any other purpose. They tried to dismiss their worries as did the experienced construction engineer whom Robert Patterson, the Under Secretary of War, asked to size up the operation at Oak Ridge. On his return he assured Patterson, "You have really nothing to worry about. If the project succeeds, no one will investigate what was done, and if it does not succeed, every one will investigate nothing else the rest of your life."

Such were the grave apprehensions of the decision-makers of the consequences of a failure in an attempted demonstration. I cannot refrain from remarking that

I do not think they would have been as upsetting or harmful as imagined. The stimulant to Japanese military morale would have been very brief. In the United States, criticism would have faded as soon as the bomb was successfully proven —leaving admiration for a noble purpose.

However, speculation on this subject may be regarded as a professional indulgence. For, in fact, even if the decision-makers had not feared a possible failure in demonstration, they would not have tried it. For they deemed it most unlikely that a demonstration could end the war as quickly and surely as hurling the bomb on Japan; and that was their duty as they saw it. No matter what the place and setting for the demonstration, they were sure it would not give an adequate impression of its appalling destructive power, would not register its full meaning in human lives. The desired explosive impression on the Japanese, it was concluded, could be produced only by the actual awful experience. Such precursory opinion was in accord with Stimson's subsequent interpretation of why its use was so effective.

"But the atomic bomb was more than a weapon of terrible destruction; it was a psychological weapon. In March, 1945, our Air Force had launched the first incendiary raid on the Tokyo area. In this raid more damage was done and more casualties were inflicted than was the case at Hiroshima. Hundreds of bombers took part and hundreds of tons of incendiaries were dropped. Similar successive raids burned out a great part of the urban areas of Japan, but the Japanese fought on. On August 6th a B-29 dropped a single atomic bomb on Hiroshima. Three days later a second bomb was dropped on Nagasaki and the war was over."

It has since been contended and with perseverance, that even if the drop on Hiroshima was justified by its purpose and results, that the second drop on Nagasaki was not. For the exponents of this opinion think that if right after Hiroshima the American government had made it clear, as they did later, that the Japanese authorities could retain the Emperor, they would have surrendered; and hence the destruction of Nagasaki was unnecessary.

This is a tenable judgment. But the records of happenings within Japanese ruling circles during the few days between Hiroshima and Nagasaki foster the impression that if the second bomb had not been dropped, the Japanese rulers would have delayed, perhaps for some weeks, the response which was preliminary to capitulation. The military heads would have been so firm in opposition that the Emperor would probably have waited until the situation became more hopeless before overruling them.

The first reports which the military investigating group that the Japanese Chief of Staff hurried to Hiroshima gave out minimized the awfulness of the effects of the bomb, describing the burns suffered from the blast by persons clothed in white and those in shelters as relatively light. Military headquarters started to issue announcements of counter measures which could be effective against the new bomb. The truth about its nature and effects, as estimated by a group of physicists after their inspection, was only made known to the Cabinet on the morning of the 9th while the mushroom cloud was over Nagasaki. Even thereafter, the Army heads accepted the decision to surrender only because the Emperor's openly declared conclusion relieved them of shame and humiliation, and lessened their fear of disobedience by their subordinates.

Thus . . . it is probable that by intensifying the dread of the new weapon—of which, so far as the Japanese knew, we might have many more—the strike against Nagasaki hastened the surrender. But whether merely by a few days or few weeks is not to be known.

In summary it can be concluded that the decision to drop the bombs upon Hiroshima and Nagasaki ought not to be censured. The reasons were—under the circumstances of the time—weighty and valid enough. But a cluster of worrisome queries remain which the passage of time has coated with greater political, ethical and historical interest.

One of these is whether or not the desired quick surrender could have been induced if the American government had been more explicit in its explanations of how the Japanese people and Emperor would fare after surrender. . . .

Another, which has often been asked, is why ten days were allowed to pass between the receipt of information regarding the results of the test of the bomb and the issuance of our final warning. I think the delay was due to an intent to be sure that if the warning was at first unheeded, it could be driven quickly and deeply home by the bombs. Thus we waited until we knew all was in readiness to drop them. These tactics worked. But I wonder whether it might not have been wiser to issue the warning sooner, and thus to have allowed the Japanese author-ities more time to ponder its meaning and acceptability. I think it not out of the question that if allowed, say, another fortnight, the Emperor might have im-posed his final decision before the bomb was set for use. However, because of the blinding fury and pride of the fighting men, it is unlikely. He hardly would have dared to do so until the explosion of the atomic bomb destroyed the argu-ment that Japan could secure a better peace if it continued to refuse to surrender unconditionally.

But what if the American government had fully revealed the results of the New Mexico test to the Japanese (and the whole world)? Could that have in-duced the desired quick surrender? The most promising time for such revelations would have been in connection with the issuance of the Potsdam Declaration; for by then the American air assaults and naval bombardments were spreading havoc everywhere, and most Japanese were aware they had no way of countering them, no good idea of how to survive them. Suppose, to be more precise, the American government had published the reports on the test which were sent by

General Groves to Potsdam for Stimson and the President, such photographs of the explosion and of the mushroom cloud and the testimony of scientists about the destructive power of the weapon that were available. Might not that broadcast knowledge, prefaced by an explanation that one of our purposes was to spare the Japanese, have had enough shock effect to cause the Emperor to overrule the resistant Japanese military leaders?

Perhaps. But in order to make the disclosure as impressive as possible, it might have been necessary to postpone the issuance of the final warning— perhaps until the end of the Potsdam Conference. The test was July 16th; it would have taken time to assemble convincing accounts and photographs, and explanation. This postponement might have prolonged slightly the period of combat.

However, in retrospect, I believe that the risk should have been taken and the cost endured; for by so doing this we might have been spared the need to introduce atomic weapons into war. In the likely event that the Japanese would not have been swayed by this explicit warning of what would happen to them if they rejected our ultimatum, we as a people would be freer of any regret—I will not say remorse—at the necessity of enrolling Hiroshima and Nagasaki in the annals of history.

But the mind, circling upon itself, returns to the point of wondering whether, if the exterminating power of the bomb had not been actually displayed, the nations would have been impelled to make even as faltering an effort as they have to agree on measures to save themselves from mutual extinction by this ultimate weapon. In a novel published in 1914, H. G. Wells prophesied that nations would not recognize the impossibility of war "until the atomic bomb burst in their fumbling hands." Now, two great wars later, it remains entirely uncertain whether they will bow before its imperative.

Part Two

DIPLOMATIC FENCING AND THE COLD WAR

Chapter 5 A CHECK TO THE SOVIET UNION

*For many historians, interest in the use of the
new atomic weapon has centered around the
diplomatic implications of the event in 1945.* P. M. S.
BLACKETT *(1897–1974), a British physicist, viewed
the decision of the United States as primarily
directed against the Soviet Union. As a scientist,
educator, and scientific administrator, he played a
prominent role in the development of nuclear and
atomic physics in Great Britain, and he received
the Nobel Prize for physics in 1947. In* Fear, War and
the Bomb *(1949), published in Britain as* The
Military and Political Consequences of Atomic Energy,
*Blackett considered the use of atomic weapons in
the context of the diplomatic maneuvering of
mid-1945. How effectively does this selection counter the
arguments of Stimson?**

Why this necessity for speed? What was it in the war plans of the Allies which necessitated rapid action? Mr. Stimson's article makes it clear that there was nothing in the American-British military plan of campaign against Japan which demanded speed in dropping the bombs in early August, 1945. . . .

Since the next major United States move was not to be until November 1, clearly there was nothing in the Allied plan of campaign to make urgent the dropping of the first bomb on August 6 rather than at any time in the next two months. Mr. Stimson himself makes clear that, had the bombs not been dropped, the intervening period of eleven weeks between August 6 and the invasion planned for November 1 would have been used to make further fire raids with

*P. M. S. Blackett, *Fear, War and the Bomb* (New York, 1949), pp. 130–131, 132, 134–135, 137–140, 142–143. Reprinted by permission of Turnstile Press Limited. Copyright 1948, 1949 by P. M. S. Blackett. Footnotes omitted.

B-29's on Japan. Under conditions of Japanese air defense at that time, these raids would certainly have led to very small losses of American air personnel.

Mr. Stimson's hurry becomes still more peculiar since the Japanese had already initiated peace negotiations. . . .

A plausible solution of this puzzle of the overwhelming reasons for urgency in the dropping of the bomb is not, however, hard to find. It is, in fact, to be found in the omissions from both Dr. Compton's and Mr. Stimson's articles.[1] Both give a detailed account of the future plans for the American assault on Japan planned for the autumn of 1945, and the spring of 1946. But neither makes any reference in detail to the other part of the Allied plan for defeating Japan; that is, the long-planned Russian campaign in Manchuria. . . .[2]

The European war ended on May 8, so the Soviet offensive was due to start on August 8. This fact is not mentioned either by Mr. Stimson or Dr. Compton in their articles. . . . The first atomic bomb was dropped on August 6 and the second on August 9. The Japanese accepted the Potsdam terms on August 14.

The U.S.S.R. declared war on Japan on August 8, and their offensive started early on August 9. On August 24, the Soviet High Command announced that the whole of Manchuria, Southern Sakhalin, etc., had been captured and that the Japanese Manchurian army had surrendered. No doubt the capitulation of the home government on August 14 reduced the fighting spirit of the Japanese forces. If it had not taken place, the Soviet campaign might well have been more expensive; but it would have been equally decisive. If the saving of American lives had been the main objective, surely the bombs would have been held back until (a) it was certain that the Japanese peace proposals made through Russia were not acceptable, and (b) the Russian offensive, which had for months been part of the Allied strategic plan, and which Americans had previously demanded, had run its course. . . .

As far as our analysis has taken us we have found no compelling military reason for the clearly very hurried decision to drop the first atomic bomb on August 6, rather than on any day in the next six weeks or so. But a most compelling diplomatic reason, relating to the balance of power in the post-war world, is clearly discernible.

Let us consider the situation as it must have appeared in Washington at the end of July, 1945. After a brilliant, but bitterly-fought campaign, American forces were in occupation of a large number of Japanese islands. They had destroyed the Japanese Navy and Merchant Marine and largely destroyed their Air Force and many divisions of their Army: but they had still not come to grips with a large part of the Japanese land forces. Supposing the bombs had not been

---

[1]See Stimson article above and Karl T. Compton, "If the Atomic Bomb Had Not Been Used," *The Atlantic Monthly*, CLXXVIII (December 1946), 54–56.—*Ed.*

[2]Stalin had given assurances at Yalta that within three months from the end of the war in Europe, he would enter the war against Japan.—*Ed.*

dropped, the planned Soviet offensive in Manchuria, so long demanded and, when it took place, so gladly welcomed (officially), would have achieved its objective according to plan. This must have been clearly foreseen by the Allied High Command, who knew well the great superiority of the Soviet forces in armor, artillery and aircraft, and who could draw on the experience of the European war to gauge the probable success of such a well-prepared offensive. If the bombs had not been dropped, America would have seen the Soviet Armies engaging a major part of Japanese land forces in battle, overrunning Manchuria and taking half a million prisoners. And all this would have occurred while American land forces would have been no nearer Japan than Iwo Jima and Okinawa. One can sympathize with the chagrin with which such an outcome would have been regarded. Most poignantly, informed military opinion could in no way blame Russia for these expected events. Russia's policy of not entering the Japanese war till Germany was defeated was not only military common sense but part of the agreed Allied plan.

In this dilemma, the successful explosion of the first atomic bomb in New Mexico, on July 16, must have come as a welcome aid. One can imagine the hurry with which the two bombs—the only two existing—were whisked across the Pacific to be dropped on Hiroshima and Nagasaki just in time, but only just, to insure that the Japanese Government surrendered to American forces alone. The long-demanded Soviet offensive took its planned victorious course, almost unheralded in the world sensation caused by the dropping of the bombs. . . .

Two other theories of the timing of the dropping of the bomb are worth a brief notice. The first is that it was purely coincidental that the first bomb was dropped two days before the Soviet offensive was due to start. This view explains Mr. Stimson's statement, "It was vital that a sufficient effort be quickly obtained with the few we had," as referring to the universal and praiseworthy desire to finish the war as soon as possible. Another variant of this interpretation is that which emphasizes the compulsion felt by many Americans to make immediate use of any new gadget, irrespective of the consequences. The difficulty about this view is that it makes the timing of the dropping a supreme diplomatic blunder. For it must have been perfectly clear that the timing of the dropping of the bombs, two days before the start of the Soviet offensive, would be assumed by the Soviet Government to have the significance which we have assumed that it, in fact, did have. If it was not intended to have this significance, then the timing was an error of tact, before which all the subsequent "tactlessness" of Soviet diplomacy in relation to the control of atomic energy pales into insignificance. That the timing was not an unintentional blunder is made likely by the fact that no subsequent steps were taken to mitigate its effects.

The second view relates, not to the timing, but to the choice of an unwarned and densely populated city as target. This view admits that there was no convincing military reason for the use of the bombs, but holds that it was a political necessity to justify to Congress and to the American people the expenditure of the huge sum of two billion dollars. It is scarcely credible that such an explanation should be seriously put forward by Americans, but so it seems to have been, and rather widely. Those who espouse this theory do not seem to have realized its implications. If the United States Government had been influenced in the summer of 1945 by this view, then perhaps at some future date, when another two billion dollars had been spent, it might feel impelled to stage another Roman holiday with some other country's citizens, rather than 120,000 victims of Hiroshima and Nagasaki, as the chosen victims. The wit of man could hardly devise a theory of the dropping of the bomb, both more insulting to the American people, or more likely to lead to an energetically pursued Soviet defense policy.

Let us sum up the three possible explanations of the decision to drop the bombs and of its timing. The first, that it was a clever and highly successful move in the field of power politics, is almost certainly correct; the second, that the timing was coincidental, convicts the American Government of a hardly credible tactlessness; and the third, the Roman holiday theory, convicts them of an equally incredible irresponsibility. The prevalence in some circles of the last two theories seems to originate in a curious preference to be considered irresponsible, tactless, even brutal, but at all costs not clever.

There is one further aspect of the dropping of the bomb which must be mentioned. There were undoubtedly, among the nuclear physicists working on the project, many who regarded the dropping of the bombs as a victory for the progressively minded among the military and political authorities. What they feared was that the bombs would *not* be dropped in the war against Japan, but that the attempt would be made to keep their existence secret and that a stock pile would be built up for an eventual war with Russia. To those who feared intensely this latter possible outcome, the dropping of the bombs, and the publicity that resulted appeared, not unplausibly, as far the lesser evil. Probably those whose thoughts were on these lines did not reckon that the bombs would be dropped on crowded cities.

The motive behind the choice of targets remains obscure. President Truman stated on August 9, 1945: "The world will note that the first atomic bomb was dropped on Hiroshima, a military base. That was because we wished in the first instance to avoid, in so far as possible, the killing of civilians." On the other hand, in the official Bombing Survey Report we read: "Hiroshima and Nagasaki were chosen as targets because of their concentration of activities and population." There seem here signs of a lack of departmental coordination.

So we may conclude that the dropping of the atomic bombs was not so much the last military act of the second World War, as the first major operation of the cold diplomatic war with Russia now in progress. The fact, however, that the realistic objectives in the field of *Macht-Politik*, so well achieved by the timing of the bomb, did not square with the advertised objective of saving "untold numbers" of American lives, produced an intense inner psychological conflict in the minds of many English and American people who knew, or suspected, some of the real facts. This conflict was particularly intense in the minds of the atomic scientists themselves, who rightly felt a deep responsibility at seeing their brilliant scientific work used in this way. The realization that their work had been used to achieve a diplomatic victory in relation to the power politics of the post-war world, rather than to save American lives, was clearly too disturbing to many of them to be consciously admitted. To allay their own doubts, many came to believe that the dropping of the bombs had in fact saved a million lives. It thus came about that those people who possessed the strongest emotional drive to save the world from the results of future atomic bombs, had in general a very distorted view of the actual circumstances of their first use. . . .

The story behind the decision to drop the two atomic bombs on Hiroshima and Nagasaki, as far as it is possible to unravel it from the available published material, has been told in this chapter not with the intention of impugning motives of individuals or of nations, but for a much more practical reason. This is to attempt to offset as far as possible some of the disastrous consequences resulting from the promulgation of the official story that the bombs were dropped from vital military necessity and did, in fact, save a huge number of American lives. For this story is not believed by well-informed people who therefore have to seek some other explanation. Since they reject the hypothesis that they were dropped to win a diplomatic victory as being too morally repugnant to be entertained, the only remaining resort is to maintain that such things just happen, and that they are the "essence of total war." Believing therefore that America dropped atomic bombs on Japan for *no compelling military or diplomatic reason*, the belief comes easily that other countries will, when they can, drop atomic bombs on America with equal lack of reason, military or diplomatic. This is a belief that provides the breeding ground for hysteria.

In decisive contrast are the consequences of believing what the writer holds to be the truth, that is, that the bombs were dropped for very real and compelling reasons—but diplomatic rather than military ones. For though the circumstances did then exist in which a great diplomatic victory could be won by annihilating the population of two cities, these circumstances were of a very special character and *are not very likely to recur*. If they did recur, few nations would perhaps resist the temptation to employ these means to attain such an end. But if we are right in supposing that a repetition of such special circumstances is unlikely, then the world is less in danger of more Hiroshimas than is generally believed.

Chapter 6 THE BOMB AS A CAUSE OF EAST-WEST CONFLICT

DAVID JOEL HOROWITZ *(1939–   ), director of research and publications of the Bertrand Russell Peace Foundation, is author of* The Free World Colossus *(1965, rev. ed., 1971), a detailed study of United States diplomacy in the Cold War period, and* Empire and Revolution: A Radical Interpretation of Contemporary History *(1969). In the following article he develops the position that use of the atomic bomb by the United States was a significant step in the origin of the Cold War with the Soviet Union.**

It is now exactly twenty years since the Yalta Conference (February 4th–11th, 1945) and we are still only beginning to understand what happened in the immediately ensuing period to shatter the unity of the wartime allies and to initiate the cold-war conflict which has dominated world politics ever since. New light was recently shed on these developments, however, by former Secretary of State James F. Byrnes in the course of a television documentary *The Decision to Drop the Bomb*, shown on January 5th.

In discussing the policy decisions surrounding the use of the atomic bomb, Byrnes admitted for the first time that President Truman had deliberately not informed Stalin of the nature of the bomb, when they met at Potsdam, because

*David Joel Horowitz, "Hiroshima and the Cold War." Reprinted from *Liberation* magazine for September 1965. Copyright by *Liberation*, 339 Lafayette St., New York, N.Y. 10012, pp. 26–27.

the United States did not want the Russians to join the war against Japan. The implications of this admission are far-reaching, but their significance is apparent only if the specific historical context is recalled.

Until the Potsdam conference in July, 1945, Russia and the United States had been collaborating, together with England, in the wartime alliance against the axis powers. Within this alliance, the brunt of the fighting in the European war had been borne by Russia, while in the Pacific War, towards which Russia was still neutral, the main burden of the fighting rested with the United States. From the American point of view the chief practical result of the Yalta conference had been *the agreement of Russia to enter the Japanese War as soon as was feasible after the defeat of Germany* (Stalin actually pledged to do it within three months). In fact, the principal impetus behind the famous "concessions" made to the Russians by Roosevelt was the pressure exerted on him by his military chiefs (who disbelieved in the success of the scientists' new bomb) to secure Russia's aid in the brutal war with Japan.

When the European War ended on May 8, 1945, the Russians, in accord with the agreement, began to move their troops from central Europe to eastern Siberia to be ready to engage the two million man Japanese army in Manchuria by August 8th. On July 16th, however, the first atomic bomb test at Alamogordo was successful. "We were in the presence of a new factor in human affairs," remarked Churchill a month later, "we possessed powers which were irresistible . . . our outlook on the future was transformed."

This transformation in outlook, as a result of the bomb, was manifested immediately at the Potsdam conference, which opened a day later on July 17th. The Americans vigorously attacked Russian machinations in occupied Rumania and Bulgaria, while at the same time ignoring parallel maneuvers by the British in Greece, and took a stand of opposition to Russian reparation demands against defeated Germany. Then, on July 26th, two weeks before the Russians were to enter the Japanese War, the United States, Britain and China, without informing or consulting Russia, issued an ultimatum to Japan to surrender. The significance of this ultimatum was made clear to the Japanese (and to the Russians) on August 6th, when an atomic bomb was dropped on Hiroshima. Two days later Russia declared war on Japan. This was right on schedule and in accord with the Yalta agreement, but it appeared in a very bad public light at the time, as it looked for all intents and purposes merely like an attempt to reap some of the spoils from an already defeated power. On August 9th, another atomic bomb was dropped on Nagasaki and on August 14th, Japan surrendered.

It has long been maintained by P.M.S. Blackett and others, that the dropping of the two bombs was intelligible only as part of a diplomatic blow directed against Russia and not as a military strategy to save American lives. The heart of Blackett's argument is that since no invasion of the home islands was planned prior to November 1st, 1945, the only justification for the timing of the bomb attack was the imminence of Russia's entry into the war. One effect of Byrnes' recent admission is to make it virtually impossible to doubt any longer the validity of Blackett's thesis. But the implications of Byrnes' statement go even further.

Prior to Potsdam, the cohesion of the wartime alliance had been based on mutual necessity, namely, the need to repulse the German attack. It was only by virtue of this necessity that the two normally hostile powers had found it possible to sink their differences and really cooperate in a difficult wartime venture. The big question as the war drew to a close, therefore, was whether this cooperation could outlast victory and the removal of the external, unifying threat. The answer was that it couldn't, and the "Grand Alliance" soon gave way, in Deutscher's phrase, to the "Great Enmity."

It is the immediate source of this failure, and thus of the cold-war conflict, which has remained puzzling and it is on this question that Byrnes' admission throws the most revealing light. For the orthodox Western view of these events is that it was Russia who abandoned the wartime road of cooperation once the military threat faded. Ambassador Stevenson expressed this view in the United Nations on October 23rd, 1962: "As soon as the Soviet government saw no further military need for the wartime coalition, it set out on its expansionist adventures . . . abandoned the policy of wartime cooperation to which it had turned for self-protection. . . . " The West was then forced to take measures in its own self-defense.

Several insurmountable difficulties confront this version of events, however. In the first place, it is virtually impossible to square with the well-established conservatism of Stalin's foreign policy. Secondly, the weakness of Russia itself entailed compelling reasons of self-interest, *whatever her long-range intentions*, for continuing the wartime alliance beyond Germany's defeat. For cooperation with the United States was bound to be a one-sided and highly advantageous affair for war-devastated Russia. Self-interest alone would have dictated to the Red rulers a policy of caution in the early post-war years.

But Stevenson's orthodox view fails to be convincing on more specific grounds than these. For in June 1945, after the defeat of Germany, the Russians were still cooperating on major decisions with the West. They agreed, for example, to broaden the Polish government—which was then recognized by the Western powers on July 5th. They were keeping their commitment to open a second front in the Pacific War. In the following fall, they permitted a free election in Hungary, which the Communists lost. In Czechoslovakia, a democratic government existed until 1948. Only in the Nazi satellites, Bulgaria and Rumania, were puppet régimes in the process of being established in July 1945, which might correspond to Stevenson's "expansionist adventures."

But these steps were taken in accord with the secret Churchill-Stalin agreements of October 1944, which gave the British prerogative to do the same in

Greece. It is Byrnes who provides the key to the real attitudes of the wartime partners in this period and thus provides us with a plausible explanation of events. For if Byrnes' admission that the United States deliberately did not bring the Russians into the bomb secret, because they did not want to *encourage* the Russians to enter the war against Japan, is taken in the context of the Yalta agreement, then it is obvious that the real meaning of Byrnes' admission is that the United States wanted to *prevent* the Russians from entering the Japanese War (and the Japanese peace), a fact confirmed as we have noted by the dropping of the atomic bombs. In other words, once the atomic bomb had been proven to be a practical "super" weapon, the United States not only no longer needed the wartime coalition and Russian cooperation, but no longer *wanted* it! This period, in fact, marked the end of the alliance (Potsdam being the last meeting of the Big Three) and there can no longer be any question as to who bore the onus for its demise.

The steps from the end of the coalition to the inception of the Cold War itself, were swift. On August 18th, in the wake of Hiroshima and Nagasaki, Byrnes publicly attacked the rigging of elections in Bulgaria despite the fact that he was aware of the Churchill-Stalin agreement under which the rigging took place. In the fall, Truman reneged on his pledge that no territory would be taken as a result of American victories, and the United States proceeded to occupy the network of Japanese military bases off the coast of Siberia.

Russia's normally suspicious rulers were not likely to miss the strategic significance of these moves. The United States was setting about unilaterally to arrange its own "security" zone off the coast of Siberia, and throughout the Pacific, including Japan, while at the same time adopting a vigorous stand against any Soviet attempts to organize a "security" zone in Eastern Europe. Taken in conjunction with America's decision to "outdistance" Russia in the nuclear race (which, according to Byrnes, was arrived at by July 1945 and was certainly obvious to the Russians by the first post-war atomic test in July 1946) and with America's failure to take up Soviet requests for a six billion dollar credit for Soviet reconstruction, the Kremlin rulers could only have been confirmed in their inbred fears of a new capitalist encirclement. (Even so, according to Tito, Stalin's decision to bring East Europe fully under Soviet control as a "defensive measure," was taken only after Truman had proclaimed an ideological crusade against the Soviet Union in March 1947.)

That the new front against Russia was to be climaxed by invasion, as the Red rulers seemed to fear, was unlikely. It was more probably designed to increase the strains on the Soviet system and to lead to the break-up of Soviet power, as Kennan had virtually recommended. Indeed, this long-range goal of Soviet capitulation in Europe was abandoned only after the launching of Sputnik and the passing of John Foster Dulles from the American policy scene. As William Appleman Williams wrote of these years, *"The assumption that the United States has the power to force the Soviet Union to capitulate to American terms is the fundamental weakness in America's conception of itself and the world."* (*The Nation*, Nov. 2nd, 1957.)

This weakness in America's conceptions was very much connected with America's early unilateral possession of the atomic bomb. For what P. M. S. Blackett has called the almost mystical American belief in what technology can achieve, made American leaders think that with the atomic bomb in hand, there was no necessity for them to continue to "coexist" and cooperate with Communist Russia or to work out a postwar arrangement in Europe based on compromise and a recognition of Russia's power status and her legitimate security interests in the area. It was, in fact, the desire of the United States to "go it alone" in organizing the post-war world, conceding nothing to Russian interest, that led directly to the intense period of cold-war conflict.

The lesson provided by this insight into the origins of conflict in post-war Europe has a special contemporary relevance in Asia, where another great power is encircled, blockaded and denied its prerogatives by a temporarily predominant United States, while both time and technology run out.

Chapter 7 A DEMONSTRATION OF AMERICAN POWER TO THE SOVIET UNION

Another interpretation of the diplomatic meaning of the decision to use the atomic bomb has been set forth by GAR ALPEROVITZ *(1937–   ), who was educated at the universities of Wisconsin and California and at Cambridge University, where he became a fellow of Kings College. He subsequently served as a Congressional staff member and in the Department of State. He is presently associated with the Institute of Policy Studies, Harvard University. He is the author of* Cold War Essays *(1970). The following selection from* Atomic Diplomacy: Hiroshima and Potsdam *(1965) sets forth a view that adds another dimension to the question and may make more understandable some of the events connected with the decision.**

In the weeks preceding Potsdam . . . it became increasingly evident that the Japanese were seeking an early end to the hostilities. American intercepts of cables between Tokyo and the Japanese ambassador in Moscow confirmed the "real evidence" that the Emperor—the one person all agreed could end the war —had now taken an active hand in the matter. In the week before Potsdam, formal decisions of the Imperial Conference to stop the fighting were revealed in the cables, and the Japanese ambassador begged for an interview with Molotov to discuss a special mission to be headed by Prince Konoye "carrying with him the personal letter of His Majesty stating the Imperial wish to end

---

*Gar Alperovitz, *Atomic Diplomacy: Hiroshima and Potsdam* (New York: Simon & Schuster, Inc., 1965), pp. 176–181, 236–242. Copyright, © 1965, by Gar Alperovitz. Reprinted by permission of Simon and Shuster, Inc., and Laurence Pollinger Limited. Footnotes omitted (except for footnotes 1 and 2); all quotations and factual references can be found cited in the original.

the war." Molotov, however, refused an interview, and the ambassador was forced to carry his message to a subordinate official. He was then told that a response would undoubtedly be delayed because of the impending Big Three meeting.

On July 17, the day of the first plenary session, another intercepted Japanese message showed that although the government felt that the unconditional-surrender formula involved too great a dishonor, it was convinced that "the demands of the times" made Soviet mediation to terminate the war absolutely essential. Further cables indicated that the one condition the Japanese asked was preservation of "our form of government." A message of July 25 revealed instructions to the ambassador in Moscow to go anywhere to meet with Molotov during the recess of the Potsdam meeting (caused by the British elections) so as to "impress them with the sincerity of our desire" to terminate the war. He was told to make it clear that "we should like to communicate to the other party through appropriate channels that we have no objection to a peace based on the Atlantic Charter." The only "difficult point is the . . . formality of uncon-ditional surrender."

With the interception of these messages there could no longer be any real doubt as to Japanese intentions; the maneuvers were overt and explicit and, most of all, official acts. As Eisenhower told Stimson, "Japan was, at that very moment, seeking some way to surrender with a minimum loss of face!" Even the covert, devious, and unofficial maneuvers made in Germany a few months earlier had been recognized as important opportunities to secure a surrender and had been rapidly exploited by American officials. To be sure, the Japanese proposals had not yet been made in detail, and the unconditional-surrender formula would require some modification, but Truman had already determined that, if necessary, he would be quite prepared to modify the formula so as to allow the Japanese to maintain their Imperial institutions, and he reaffirmed this intention during the Potsdam Conference.

Thus, the cables showed not only the Japanese desire to end the war, but the fact that the Japanese and American governments were not very far apart in their conception of final surrender terms. Most important, however, the cables also confirmed that the last frail hopes of the Japanese were now unmistakably focused upon the as yet indeterminate position of the Soviet Union. The in-sistent attempts to see Molotov were such obvious evidence of Japanese anxiety that at one point the ambassador in Moscow had to caution the foreign minister in Tokyo against moves "which would only result in exposing our uneasy emo-tion and would be of no benefit to us."

Despite this advice and the continual reports that there was little reason for optimism concerning Russian intentions, the Japanese government continued to cling to the belief that so long as Stalin remained uncommitted it might be pos-sible to hope for Soviet mediation, or at least Soviet neutrality. Undoubtedly, the Soviet enigma gave pause to even the most ardent Japanese peace advocates. The combination of uncertainty and hope precluded open peace maneuvers within governing circles, for as long as Soviet mediation was a possibility, no government could assume the dishonor and disadvantage of suing for peace on unconditional terms.

Throughout the summer, the American government had recognized how this situation greatly enhanced the shock value of a Soviet declaration of war—it would eliminate the last hope and was likely to force capitulation. Now the point was even more obvious. On July 16, Stimson advised the President that "the impending threat of Russia's participation" and "the recent news of attempted approaches on the part of Japan to Russia" had produced "the psychological moment" to attempt to warn Japan into surrender. On July 18, Secretary Byrnes also noted the dependence of the Japanese on Soviet actions, commenting that the recent Japanese maneuvers were quite evidently inspired by a fear of what Russia might do.

This confirmation of earlier estimates of the crucial psychological and political role played by the Soviet Union was matched, at Potsdam, by renewed proof of Stalin's intentions. Since mid-May, American policy makers had been convinced that the Soviet Premier would enter the war, as pledged, as soon as the Soong negotiations were completed.[1] Now, on July 17, Stalin once more reaffirmed his plans in a private talk with Truman and Byrnes; the Red Army would be prepared to cross the Manchurian border by mid-August and would do so as soon as the Chinese treaty was initialed. On July 21, the Joint Chiefs of Staff informed the American commanders in the Pacific that they could expect a Russian declaration of war on or about August 15.

Thus the alternatives which had emerged during the summer of delay were confirmed at the Potsdam Conference; if all that appeared necessary to force Japanese capitulation was a "tremendous shock," the United States could choose to accomplish the objective with either a Soviet declaration of war or the atomic bomb. Additionally, there was the possibility of a negotiated settlement involving guarantees for the Emperor.

Truman did not hesitate. He had no wish to test the judgment that a Soviet declaration of war would probably force capitulation. Nor was he interested in attempts to negotiate. Instead, he simply followed through on earlier plans to use the atomic weapons as soon as possible. "The atomic bomb was no 'great decision,' " he later recalled, ". . . not any decision that you had to worry about"; and he has confirmed on numerous occasions that he "never had any doubt that it should be used." Once the cables announcing the tremendous success of the New Mexico test began to flow into Potsdam, Truman was concerned only

[1]T. V. Soong, the Chinese Foreign Minister, arrived in Moscow on June 30 to conclude an agreement on the postwar rights of the Soviet Union in China and Manchuria, based on the secret Yalta accords of February 1945—*Ed.*

with operational details. Formal British agreement to use the weapon had already been recorded on July 4, and Churchill confirms: "The historic fact remains, and must be judged in the after-time, that the decision whether or not to use the atomic bomb . . . was never even an issue."

Secretary of War Stimson records only that on July 22 the President "was intensely pleased" with word that the weapons might be delivered somewhat earlier than had been expected. When more detailed information arrived stating "operation may be possible any time from August 1," Truman "said that was just what he wanted, that he was highly delighted." And on July 25, the formal order to use the weapon in combat was issued by the Secretary of War. As the President later recalled, "I . . . instructed Stimson that the order would stand unless I notified him that the Japanese reply to our ultimatum was acceptable."

Having reaffirmed the decision—or assumption—which had guided policy since April, Truman turned to the problem of Soviet entry into the war. Again, he continued to follow the earlier tactics of delay. When on July 18 Stalin had personally brought copies of the latest Japanese messages to the President's attention, Truman had made no attempt to follow up the Japanese overtures. Instead, he had simply agreed with Stalin's suggestion that "it might be desirable to lull the Japanese to sleep . . . [through an] unspecific answer." When the full report of the unexpected power of the test reached the President, however, he went beyond the vagaries and ambivalence of his initial position.

As early as July 18, having heard from the President that "the war might come to a speedy end," Prime Minister Churchill was quite aware of a new confidence in Truman's approach to military problems in the Pacific. When the full report of the test arrived, there could no longer be any question. On July 23, Alanbrooke noted one of the "American exaggerations" Churchill had absorbed and taken as his own: "It was now no longer necessary for the Russians to come into the Japanese war; the new explosive alone was sufficient to settle the matter." Later the same day, reporting to the Cabinet on a conversation with Byrnes, Churchill cabled: "It is quite clear that the United States do not at the present time desire Russian participation in the war against Japan."

Churchill's observation was completely accurate. As Byrnes has written, "The reports made it clear that the bomb had met our highest hopes and that the shock of its use would very likely knock our already wavering enemy out of the war." On July 23, Stimson recorded that even the cautious General Marshall "felt, as I felt sure he would, that now with our new weapon we would not need the assistance of the Russians to conquer Japan." This confiming view was reported to the President the next day, and now there was unanimity; the ambivalent strategy of delay had paid off; it was no longer even necessary to attempt to maintain the insurance of a Soviet declaration of war. Thus, there was a double irony in the Potsdam meeting, for not only was it too early to settle European matters, but the only other reason for coming to the Conference—to insure a Soviet declaration of war—had now also disappeared. . . .

This essay has attempted to describe the influence of the atomic bomb on certain questions of diplomacy. I do not believe that the reverse question—the influence of diplomacy upon the decision to use the atomic bomb—can be answered on the basis of the presently available evidence. However, it is possible to define the nature of the problem which new materials and further research may be able to solve.

A fruitful way to begin is to note General Eisenhower's recollection of the Potsdam discussion at which Stimson told him the weapon would be used against Japan:

> During his recitation of the relevant facts, I had been conscious of a feeling of depression and so I voiced to him my grave misgivings, first on the basis of my belief that Japan was already defeated and that dropping the bomb was completely unnecessary, and secondly because I thought that our country should avoid shocking world opinion by the use of a weapon whose employment was, I thought, no longer mandatory as a measure to save American lives. It was my belief that Japan was, at that very moment, seeking some way to surrender with a minimum loss of "face."

"It wasn't necessary to hit them with that awful thing," Eisenhower concluded.

Perhaps the most remarkable aspect of the decision to use the atomic bomb is that the President and his senior political advisers do not seem ever to have shared Eisenhower's "grave misgivings." As we have seen, they simply assumed that they would use the bomb, never really giving serious consideration to not using it. Hence, to state in a precise way the question "Why was the atomic bomb used?" is to ask why senior political officials did *not* seriously question its use as Eisenhower did.

The first point to note is that the decision to use the weapon did not derive from overriding military considerations. Despite Truman's subsequent statement that the weapon "saved millions of lives," Eisenhower's judgment that it was "completely unnecessary" as a measure to save lives was almost certainly correct. This is not a matter of hindsight; *before the atomic bomb was dropped each of the Joint Chiefs of Staff advised that it was highly likely that Japan could be forced to surrender "unconditionally," without use of the bomb and without an invasion.* Indeed, this characterization of the position taken by the senior military advisers is a conservative one.

General Marshall's June 18 appraisal was the most cautiously phrased advice offered by any of the Joint Chiefs: "The impact of Russian entry on the already hopeless Japanese may well be the decisive action levering them into capitulation. . . ." Admiral Leahy was absolutely certain there was no need for the bombing to obviate the necessity of an invasion. His judgment after the fact was the same as his view before the bombing: "It is my opinion that the use of this barbarous weapon at Hiroshima and Nagasaki was of no material assistance in our war against Japan. The Japanese were already defeated and ready to surrender. . . ." Similarly, through most of 1945 Admiral King believed the bomb unnecessary, and Generals Arnold and LeMay defined the official Air Force position in this way: Whether or not the atomic bomb should be dropped was not for the Air Force to decide, but explosion of the bomb was not necessary to win the war or make an invasion unnecessary.

Similar views prevailed in Britain long before the bombs were used. General Ismay recalls that by the time of Potsdam, "for some time past it had been firmly fixed in my mind that the Japanese were tottering." Ismay's reaction to the suggestion of the bombing was, like Eisenhower's and Leahy's, one of "revulsion." And Churchill, who as early as September 1944, felt that Russian entry was likely to force capitulation, has written: "It would be a mistake to suppose that the fate of Japan was settled by the atomic bomb. Her defeat was certain before the first bomb fell. . . ."

The military appraisals made before the weapons were used have been confirmed by numerous postsurrender studies. The best known is that of the United States Strategic Bombing Survey. The Survey's conclusion is unequivocal: "Japan would have surrendered even if the atomic bombs had not been dropped, even if Russia had not entered the war, and even if no invasion had been planned or contemplated."[2]

That military considerations were not decisive is confirmed—and illuminated —by the fact that the President did not even ask the opinion of the military adviser most directly concerned. General MacArthur, Supreme Commander of Allied Forces in the Pacific, was simply informed of the weapon shortly before it was used at Hiroshima. Before his death he stated on numerous occasions that, like Eisenhower, he believed the atomic bomb was completely unnecessary from a military point of view.

Although military considerations were not primary, as we have seen, unquestionably political considerations related to Russia played a major role in the de-

[2] See also Marshall's postwar statement that the atomic bombs precipitated the surrender only "by months"; Bush's view that "the war would have ended before long in any case, for Japan had been brought nearly to her knees"; Curtis LeMay's opinion that the war would have ended in two weeks ("the atomic bomb had nothing to do with the end of the war"); Claire Chennault's view that the Russian declaration of war was the decisive factor; and the arguments of Morton, Baldwin, Blackett, and Craven and Cate, that the atomic bomb was not needed to force a surrender before an invasion. (J. P. Sutherland, "The Story General Marshall Told Me," *U.S. News & World Report,* Nov. 2, 1959, p. 52; Bush, V., *Modern Arms and Free Men,* p. 101; *New York Herald Tribune,* Sept. 21, 1945; *New York Times,* Aug. 15, 1945; Morton, "The Decision to Use the Atomic Bomb," *Command Decisions,* ed. K. R. Greenfield, p. 408; *Military and Political Consequences of Atomic Energy,* pp. 116–30; Baldwin, *Great Mistakes of the War,* p. 84; Craven and Cate, *Air Forces in World War II,* Vol. V, p. 726).

cision; from at least mid-May American policy makers hoped to end the hostilities before the Red Army entered Manchuria. For this reason they had no wish to test whether Russian entry into the war would force capitulation—as most thought likely—long before the scheduled November invasion. Indeed, they actively attempted to delay Stalin's declaration of war.

Nevertheless, it would be wrong to conclude that the atomic bomb was used simply to keep the Red Army out of Manchuria. Given the desperate efforts of the Japanese to surrender, and Truman's willingness to offer assurances to the Emperor, it is entirely possible that the war could have been ended by negotiation before the Red Army had begun its attack. But, again, as we have seen, after Alamogordo neither the President nor his senior advisers were interested in exploring this possibility.

One reason may have been their fear that if time-consuming negotiations were once initiated, the Red Army might attack in order to seize Manchurian objectives. But, if this explanation is accepted, once more one must conclude that the bomb was used primarily because it was felt to be politically important to prevent Soviet domination of the area.

Such a conclusion is very difficult to accept, for American interests in Manchuria, although historically important to the State Department, were not of great significance. The further question therefore arises: Were there other political reasons for using the atomic bomb? In approaching this question, it is important to note that most of the men involved at the time who since have made their views public always mention *two* considerations which dominated discussions. The first was the desire to end the Japanese war quickly, which, as we have seen, was not primarily a military consideration, but a political one. The second is always referred to indirectly.

In June, for example, a leading member of the Interim Committee's scientific panel, A. H. Compton, advised against the Franck report's suggestion of a technical demonstration of the new weapon: Not only was there a possibility that this might not end the war promptly, but failure to make a combat demonstration would mean the "loss of the opportunity to impress the world with the national sacrifices that enduring security demanded." The general phrasing that the bomb was needed "to impress the world" has been made more specific by J. Robert Oppenheimer. Testifying on this matter some years later he stated that the second of the two "overriding considerations" in discussions regarding the bomb was "the effect of our actions on the stability, on our strength, and the stability of the postwar world." And the problem of postwar stability was inevitably the problem of Russia. Oppenheimer has put it this way: "Much of the discussion revolved around the question raised by Secretary Stimson as to whether there was any hope at all of using this development to get less barbarous relations with the Russians."

Vannevar Bush, Stimson's chief aide for atomic matters, has been quite explicit: "That bomb was developed on time. . . ." Not only did it mean a quick end to the Japanese war, but "it was also delivered on time so that there was no necessity for any concessions to Russia at the end of the war."

In essence, the second of the two overriding considerations seems to have been that a combat demonstration was needed to convince the Russians to accept the American plan for a stable peace. And the crucial point of this effort was the need to force agreement on the main questions in dispute: the American proposals for Central and Eastern Europe. President Truman may well have expressed the key consideration in October 1945; publicly urging the necessity of a more conventional form of military power (his proposal for universal military training), in a personal appearance before Congress the President declared: "It is only by strength that we can impress the fact upon possible future aggressors that we will tolerate no threat to peace. . . ."

If indeed the "second consideration" involved in the bombing of Hiroshima and Nagasaki was the desire to impress the Russians, it might explain the strangely ambiguous statement by Truman that not only did the bomb end the war, but it gave the world "a chance to face the facts." It would also accord with Stimson's private advice to McCloy: "We have got to regain the lead and perhaps do it in a pretty rough and realistic way. . . . We have coming into action a weapon which will be unique. Now the thing [to do is] . . . let our actions speak for themselves." Again, it would accord with Stimson's statement to Truman that the "greatest complication" would occur if the President negotiated with Stalin before the bomb had been "laid on Japan." It would tie in with the fact that from mid-May strategy toward all major diplomatic problems was based upon the assumption the bomb would be demonstrated. Finally, it might explain why none of the highest civilian officials seriously questioned the use of the bomb as Eisenhower did; for, having reversed the basic direction of diplomatic strategy *because* of the atomic bomb, it would have been very difficult indeed for anyone subsequently to challenge an idea which had come to dominate all calculations of high policy.

At present no final conclusion can be reached on this question. But the problem can be defined with some precision: Why did the American government refuse to attempt to exploit Japanese efforts to surrender? Or, alternatively, why did they refuse to test whether a Russian declaration of war would force capitulation? Were Hiroshima and Nagasaki bombed primarily to impress the world with the need to accept America's plan for a stable and lasting peace—that is, primarily, America's plan for Europe? The evidence strongly suggests that the view which the President's personal representative offered to one of the atomic scientists in May 1945 was an accurate statement of policy: "Mr. Byrnes did not argue that it was necessary to use the bomb against the cities of Japan in order to win the war. . . . Mr. Byrnes's . . . view [was] that our possessing and demonstrating the bomb would make Russia more manageable in Europe. . . ."

Chapter 8   "BELIEVING THE UNBELIEVABLE"

MICHAEL AMRINE *(1918–   ), a journalist
and author of* The Great Decision: The Secret History
of the Atomic Bomb *(1959), takes issue with
Alperovitz on diplomatic maneuverings and the
rationale for use of atomic weapons by the United
States. In the following review of Alperovitz' book
Amrine finds his thesis unsupported by the
available evidence and needlessly convoluted.**

In the immediate post-war period, as we saw how atomic policy was developing, influencing and being influenced by the cold war, many indeed wondered if the speed we had used in delivering the newly-tested bomb had been related to some maneuver against the Russians. We did not know as much then as we know now about "the Japanese willingness to surrender," or more persons might have asked still more questions in those days. When Americans set foot in Japan—30 days after Trinity—any sergeant could know more than Truman and Churchill had known for sure about Japan's capabilities to fight indefinitely or surrender.

In 1946 and 1947 the eminent British physicist P. M. S. Blackett repeatedly

*Michael Amrine, Review of *Atomic Diplomacy: Hiroshima and Potsdam*, by Gar Alperovitz, *Book Week*, "The Day the Sun Rose Twice," July 18, 1965, *The New York Herald Tribune*, pp. 8–9. Reprinted through the courtesy of the *World Journal Tribune*.

raised this anti-Russian question and attempted to document it. His line, as of around 1947, is far clearer than most of Alperovitz' intimations, innuendoes and "beliefs." Blackett said: "The dropping of the atomic bombs was not so much the last military act of the Second World War, as the first major operation of the cold diplomatic war." Blackett put forth these sentiments with vigor and clarity, but they were not accepted by those who have since studied these matters. It has been years, to my knowledge, since anyone has brought up the Blackett viewpoint. Alperovitz sidesteps any credit to Blackett for his thesis, giving his name the merest mention in his acknowledgments. Similarly he ignores the many careful men who disagreed with Blackett, and wrote careful analyses of his views in the late Forties. All the facts were fresher then.

Churchill said of the atomic decisions, "The historical fact remains and must be judged in the after time. . . ." It surely is proper that history will "try" Truman and Churchill again and again, but on "the Blackett viewpoint" are we really to assume there was no good evidence brought out by either side in the first trial?

Those interested enough to read the basic documents will find an excellent antidote to Alperovitz in the memoirs of Truman, Stimson, and Churchill, or in the comprehensive special volumes on the atomic decision done by Louis Morton, Herbert Feis, and Hewlett and Anderson. All these men have had full access to secret documents. Yet there is scarcely a hint in any of their pages to support the contention that we dropped the bomb not to save lives but to bolster a threat against Russia.

Here are the basic points on which Alperovitz attempts to prove the Hiroshima and Nagasaki bombs were dropped not to end a hot war but to build up pressure for a cold war.

1. Truman's temperament and outlook on foreign affairs, coupled with possession of the new weapon, changed the American relations to the Soviets in the spring and summer of 1945. Our position changed from one in which we were comrades in arms and Stalin and FDR were very co-operative into one in which we "threatened the Soviets." Alperovitz has rounded up all sorts of bits and pieces, many of them from Stimson's diary. There are some interesting side-by-side notes of news from the atomic tests and of a "new confidence" being shown by Truman at the Potsdam conference table. But all of it is far short of showing that before or at Potsdam the beginnings of the cold war were "atomic diplomacy." Judgment after judgment is on a par with Alperovitz' explanation that Truman's famous angry greetings to Molotov, on the latter's arrival in Washington, could not possibly be construed as off-the-cuff peppery comments. No, they represented a carefully prepared position of HST. Well, HST may even agree, and all his friends may agree, but the facts are that Truman had been in office only 11 days.

You will not find here much substantive information on the Polish question, nor on the number of dead at Hiroshima, on the different intelligence estimates of loss of life through Japanese invasion plans, etc., etc. Nor will you find any human notes that Stimson was 76 and frail, that Byrnes was younger—and fantastically jealous of Truman, who had nosed him out for the Vice-Presidency and hence the Presidency, or that Truman had a thousand other topics on his mind in these 100 days. While the U.S. position—on Poland, say—is seen, for devious reasons, as alternating between plans for early showdown and a delayed showdown, Alperovitz' major conclusion is that "Stalin's approach seems to have been cautiously moderate during the brief few months here described." But you will not find any human understanding that somewhere there were real Polish people with a passion for freedom, many of whom looked to the West for help when the war was over.

2. Another set of "evidence" has to do with Alperovitz' theory that the atomic test in Alamogordo was hurried up and the Potsdam meeting was postponed in order that the Big Three meeting should not be held before the test. Here Alperovitz does indeed make a contribution in showing that the atomic test was an important factor in postponing the Potsdam meeting. But there is nowhere any proof that the first part of his theory is correct.

He quotes Oppenheimer—no date given—as saying: "I don't think there was a time where we worked harder at the speed-up than in the period after the German surrender." That's all he quotes. This statement was made by Oppenheimer many years later—in his famous security hearings, in 1954. The text of the book merely slides it in dateless as a major item of evidence. But in the same breath, the same day, Oppenheimer had said about deadlines at Los Alamos: ". . . The deadline never changed. It was as soon as possible."

Alperovitz has left out of his book any contemporary document from anyone in authority that says either (A) speed up Trinity for diplomatic reasons or (B) hurry to bomb Japan in order to speak loudly to Russia. These documents have also been missing from the memoirs of every man who has spoken out on these processes.

For the record, the bomb was delivered within an eyelash of the date which General Groves had predicted a year before. The Russians entered the war against Japan on a date they had set months before—three months after V-E Day.

Few persons ever knew both projected dates. There is no direct evidence anywhere in this book of any concerted effort to get these events together, to spread them apart and/or to use one to prevent the other. Not here or anywhere known to this writer is there any real evidence that we did not want Russia in the Japanese war, nor that we used A-bombs in a vain effort to keep them out.

3. The capstone of the book is that there was no military reason to drop the bomb on Japan, and that "everyone" knew it. He gives very few pros or cons. He doesn't dwell on the Navy people who think a blockade would have brought

surrender, nor on the psychological warfare people who have thought their broadcasts were turning the critical corner. He doesn't question the Air Force men who think conventional bombs would have done it, and he does not dwell on the fact that we can never really know, because we can't play the game over.

What he does is assert this as a firmly established fact and establish that all in command knew it then. Time and again he hits Truman and Churchill with this hindsight—and he gives short shrift to any of the abundant evidence that our side could not assume Japan would soon quit.

The worst claim in the book is that "before the atomic bomb was dropped each of the Joint Chiefs advised that it was highly likely that Japan could be forced to surrender 'unconditionally' without use of the bomb and without an invasion." Where did this claim come from? I never heard of it before and find it out of key with statements of that summer by the Joint Chiefs, when the facts were fresh. There is no documentation for this staggering claim, which Alperovitz quite rightly puts in italics. Nor is there documentation anywhere in the book to back up the assertion that the top military advisers of the U.S. thought the bomb and the invasion unnecessary. To Alperovitz this is the master card, because if there were no military reason, and the military knew it beforehand, then it becomes obvious that Hiroshima and Nagasaki died for diplomatic reasons. Lest this sound nasty, he concludes by saying the evidence "strongly suggests" we used the bomb to make Russia more manageable in Europe. But a few pages earlier, he said cautiously: "I do not believe that . . . the influence of diplomacy upon the decision to use the atomic bomb . . . can be answered on the basis of the presently available evidence."

He might at that point have mentioned some of the contrary testimony by all hands concerned, but their names are buried in the 1,399 footnotes from 188 books and articles and periodicals which he has either read or used.

Alperovitz never really confronts or condemns the memoirs of the principals. He never does them the courtesy of setting out in detail their explanation of why they did what they did. His book is full of the most insidious hints of Machiavellian plots and counter-plots, and always, of course, he is implying that Truman, Stimson, Byrnes, Churchill—everybody—has been lying, lying, lying when they said the atomic bomb was used to end the war and saved lives. He says: "I have made no attempt, however, to take up the various arguments offered by the great number of writers. . . . who have touched upon the subject." Adding high-toned rhetoric to his air of being above the arena where men like Churchill and Stimson have labored to set out the record, Alperovitz says: "I have eschewed contention. . . . " Others may decide he has evaded confrontation, and that in the matter of contention he has bitten off more than he can eschew.

Gar Alperovitz is a product of an age which has not only by now made thousands of atomic bombs, but has produced computerized war games at research centers based upon real bombs and paper people. We have escalators which go all the way up—to hell. Alperovitz strikes me as a cold-blooded cousin of Herman Kahn and Dr. Strangelove. But to look at the records of Truman and Stimson and believe they were mordant Machiavellis is more than thinking about the unthinkable. It is believing the unbelievable.

Chapter 9 A QUESTION OF POWER

*As an historian taking a radical perspective, Gabriel
Kolko (1932–   ) has published several important books
reassessing significant aspects of American capitalism
and foreign policy. Educated at Kent State, Wisconsin,
and Harvard Universities, he was a member of the faculty
at the University of Pennsylvania, 1964–68, and the
State University of New York at Buffalo, 1968–70;
and since 1970 he has been professor of history at
York University, Toronto, Canada. His books include*
Wealth and Power in America *(1962)*, The Triumph of
Conservatism, 1900–1916 *(1963)*, Railroads and
Regulation, 1877–1916 *(1965)*, The Politics of War,
1943–45 *(1968)*, The Roots of American Foreign Policy
(1969), and, with Joyce Kolko, The Limits of Power:
The World and United States Foreign Policy, 1945–1954
*(1972). What perspective does the author present here
on the great decision?**

From the moment work began on the construction of the atomic bomb in
1941 until the Americans dropped it on Hiroshima on August 6, 1945, none of
the American leaders involved ever had any doubt that they were building the
bomb to be used. This assumption was axiomatic at the time, and it was only
later revulsion that led to the artificial investigation of the relatively unimportant
spring 1945 debate on the moral problems of using the bomb. The war and the
mass destruction of civilians posed all the moral questions well before August
1945, by which time years of sustained murder and brutality had grotesquely
distorted men's sensibilities.

The nuclear scientists of all the major warring powers were aware of the

*Gabriel Kolko, *The Politics of War: The World and United States Foreign Policy, 1943–1945*
(New York: Random House, 1968), pp. 538–43, 566–67. By permission of Random House,
Inc. and George Wiedenfeld & Nocolson Ltd.

military potentialities of nuclear physics, and we now know the Germans conducted their own lethargic research program into the bomb throughout the war. At the end of 1944 and during 1945 both the Russians and special American units picked up German scientists as quickly as they could find them. We now also know that the Russians created their first laboratory to build a bomb in the summer of 1942, by which time they were familiar with the existence of programs in the United States and Germany, and that they accelerated their activity in February 1943. By September 1943 Stimson was certain the Russians were spying on the American program, and by the end of 1944 most of the executives connected with the project assumed this to be the case. Late in 1943 Peter Kapitza, the leading Soviet nuclear physicist, formally invited Niels Bohr, the great Danish physicist, to settle in Russia, where he would receive all the facilities he required. In July 1944 one of the French scientists working on the bomb project in Canada told De Gaulle of its development, and in late 1944 even Soong informed Ambassador Gauss of a vast American project devoted to producing a decisive secret weapon that would end the war. At the beginning of 1945 Jean F. Joliot, the Communist head of the French Government's research center, discussed possible French involvement in the atomic bomb project with British authorities. In brief, the only secret connected with the bomb was whether the United States had produced it, and how, and not in its anticipated construction.

When Stimson, who was the primary head of the atomic-bomb development, thought about the problem of the bomb in relation to the Russians it was always with the knowledge that the Russians knew the Americans were building such a weapon. To tell them officially merely created problems involving sharing technical knowledge, and from this viewpoint such discussion was unacceptable. At no time did the Americans believe they could surprise the Russians with a weapon that would cause them to cower, and at every stage in their diplomacy the Russians acted with full knowledge that the United States was likely to be the first to have an atomic bomb. At the end of 1944 Stimson thought the Russians were a long way from obtaining the secret of how to build a bomb, and he felt it unwise to tell them anything about the method until America obtained "a real quid pro quo" on diplomatic questions.[1] Roosevelt agreed.

As Major General Leslie R. Groves, the head of the Manhattan Project under Stimson, summarized the prospect for the bomb in December 1944, the first

---

[1]Stimson Diary, December 31, 1944. See also Henry L. Stimson, "The Decision to Use the Atomic Bomb," *Harper's Magazine,* 194 (February, 1947), 98; *New York Times*, August 19, 1966; Stimson Diary, September 8, 1943, HLS Mss; Leslie R. Groves, *Now It Can Be Told: The Story of the Manhattan Project* (New York, 1962), chaps. XIII, XVI, XVII; Hewlett and Anderson, *The New World*, 334–35; Herbert Feis, *The Atomic Bomb and the End of World War II* (Princeton, 1966), 31–32; FR (1945), II, 2–3; Alice K. Smith, *A Peril and a Hope: The Scientists' Movement in America: 1945–47* (Chicago, 1965), 316–17.

one would be ready about August 1 of the following year, with another before the end of the year. He expected it to be 10 kilotons, the equivalent of 10,000 tons of TNT. The implosion bomb also being developed would not be ready before late July and would be about .5 kiloton, and probably not exceed 2.5 kilotons for some time. Although the maximum prediction was for 18 kilotons, most of the scientists connected with the project thought until as late as May that the first bomb would be a relatively modest .7 to 1.5 kilotons. Given this timetable and this expected range of power, the military based their planning for the war on known, controllable, conventional weapons, weapons that were quite sufficient in the march toward victory in early 1945. Moreover, to both the Navy and Army the theory of strategic bombing inherent in the weapons was not very persuasive, and they consistently denied the premise that air power might win the war.

During November 1944 American B-29's began their first incendiary bomb raids on Tokyo, and on March 9, 1945, wave upon wave dropped masses of small incendiaries containing an early version of napalm on the city's population —for they directed this assault against civilians. Soon small fires spread, connected, and grew into a vast firestorm that sucked the oxygen out of the lower atmosphere. The bomb raid was a "success" for the Americans; they killed 125,000 Japanese in one attack. The Allies bombed Hamburg and Dresden in the same manner, and Nagoya, Osaka, and Kobe, and Tokyo again on May 24. The basic moral decision that the Americans had to make during the war was whether or not they would violate international law by indiscriminately attacking and destroying civilians, and they resolved that dilemma within the context of conventional weapons. Neither fanfare nor hesitation accompanied their choice, and in fact the atomic bomb used against Hiroshima was less lethal than massive fire bombing. The war had so brutalized the American leaders that burning vast numbers of civilians no longer posed a real predicament by the spring of 1945. Given the anticipated power of the atomic bomb, which was far less than that of fire bombing, no one expected small quantities of it to end the war. Only its technique was novel—nothing more.

By June 1945 the mass destruction of civilians via strategic bombing did impress Stimson as something of a moral problem, but the thought no sooner arose than he forgot it, and in no appreciable manner did it shape American use of conventional or atomic bombs. "I did not want to have the United States get the reputation of outdoing Hitler in atrocities," he noted telling the President on June 6. There was another difficulty posed by mass conventional bombing, and that was its very success, a success that made the two modes of human destruction qualitatively identical in fact and in minds of the American military. "I was a little fearful," Stimson told Truman, "that before we could get ready the Air Force might have Japan so thoroughly bombed out that the new weapon would not have a fair background to show its strength." To this the President "laughed and said he understood."[2]

Early in 1945 Groves had asked Marshall for authorization to draw up detailed plans for use of the bomb, and the head of the Joint Chiefs merely passed the responsibility back to Groves. After Yalta, Stimson for his part still preferred "to tread softly" on discussing the existence of the bomb with the Russians and to wait "until we have some much more tangible 'fruits of repentance' from the Russians as a quid pro quo. . . . "[3] This attitude defined the very general plans for postwar atomic energy control that various officials raised during the spring of 1945, plans that dealt essentially with American development of atomic energy. The actual thought that went into the matter of the new genie was on how best to employ it against Japan. A group of scientists defined the principles of targeting, and in April, Stimson urged the new President to create a committee to advise him on the use and future of the atomic bomb. Truman appointed such an "Interim Committee" consisting of Stimson, Byrnes, Clayton, Ralph A. Bard of the Navy, and George L. Harrison, Stimson's deputy, and the scientists Vannevar Bush, Karl T. Compton, and James B. Conant, although it did not meet until the last day of May. He added a scientific panel of four to advise the committee, but all of the scientists were well known for their cooperative attitude toward Washington officials, and in fact were administrative scientists with declining personal interests in research. The committee excluded the younger and more liberal scientists connected with the Manhattan Project, who were now much alarmed at an American policy that might encourage a postwar arms race.

By the time the committee began to function the Allies had effectively defeated Japan and reduced its industrial capacity and manpower to nearly a last-stand posture. The Navy knew this and so argued, but from its strategic position and not convincingly. At the end of May, although Stimson had thought continuously about the problem during the prior weeks, the Americans now tried to weigh the atomic bomb both from the viewpoint of its use against Japan and its implications to future relations with the Soviet Union. Stimson knew the bomb would influence many phases of postwar relations with the U.S.S.R., and he also reviewed the problem of Soviet entry into the war against Japan in this light. But one should not make too much of these thoughts or link them too closely, for once the Americans built and used the bomb they had to reconsider its relationship to the Russians and everything else, but such new reassessments are not the same as basic alterations in policy. In reality the issues are whether the United States would have dropped the bomb even if it had per-

[2]Memo of Conference with the President, June 6, 1945; HLS Mss. See also *Yalta Papers*, 383–84.
[3]Stimson Diary, February 13, 1945, HLS Mss.

fect relations with the Russians, and also what did its refusal to share the information imply about the American vision of its future power. The actual policy Washington adopted toward the Russians in the end, as events showed, reflected the same mechanistic attitudes that left unchallenged its decision to drop the bomb. One must remember that at no time did the Americans see the bomb as a weapon for defeating the formidable Japanese army in China, and at no time did they consider it desirable that the Soviets invade the Japanese mainland. The bomb did not reduce the importance of Soviet entry into Manchuria and north China, for the Chinese were surely not going to be able to eliminate the Japanese army there even after the United States had devastated all of Japan itself, and not for a moment did anyone in Washington think of using the atomic bomb in Manchuria. Since they knew the Russians based their diplomacy on premises which assumed the existence of the Manhattan Project, any American revelation—in whatever form—designed to effect Soviet diplomacy was superfluous.

Truman and Grew at the end of May finally suggested that other officials consider the issue of dropping the bomb in the context of a prior warning to Japan to surrender. On May 29 Marshall, McCloy, Elmer Davis, the head of the Office of War Information, and a group of leaders who were not all aware of the Manhattan Project, but only of the American prospect of doing "something worse" to Japan, rejected the idea.[4] In the context of a warning to Japan, or the mechanics of its use, and not whether the bomb should be used, the planning proceeded from the end of May onward. On May 31 and June 1 the Interim Committee met for the first time, and the scientists held forth first, estimating that a bomb would kill perhaps 20,000 people, or, to interpolate, less than many conventional attacks. Some pleaded for a continuation of the vast government appropriations for their labs, estimating the length of time it would take to construct a thermonuclear or hydrogen bomb. They considered the possibility of "a competitor" overtaking America in the field, to use the exact term in the official history, and all resolved that the United States should keep its atomic plant intact and develop it. The problem of telling the Russians of the project was really one of sharing knowledge, and on this the scientists disagreed; Bush and Conant, who had prepared a memo on the matter earlier, urged international control with inspection. Both Byrnes and Marshall discouraged such talk, Marshall citing Russia's lack of cooperation, and Byrnes the need to stay ahead—even of the British—and to deal with future relations with the U.S.S.R. on a political level. They always discussed the question of using the bomb itself in the context of choosing a target—Bard wished an advance warning, but this

---

[4]Stimson Diary, May 29, 1945, HLS Mss. See also Hewlett and Anderson, *The New World*, 338–40; Robert Jungk, *Brighter Than a Thousand Suns: A Personal History of the Atomic Scientists* (New York, 1958), 181.

they hardly considered—and after some debate they concluded that the United States would use the bomb as soon as it was ready, against a military target surrounded by workers' homes, and without warning.[5]

The committee immediately informed Truman of its decisions, and on June 6 Stimson visited him for a more systematic discussion of the problems involved. One must remember that at this time Stimson opposed diplomatic conferences with the U.S.S.R., including the one at Potsdam, and Truman was well aware of his position. For reasons . . . having nothing to do with the atomic bomb, and over the objection of Churchill and Harriman, the President delayed the Potsdam meeting, and implied to Stimson additional time to develop the bomb *and use it* against Japan was a reason. In reality, by July 15 and for several weeks thereafter no one, including Stimson, expected the bomb to be ready for use, and obviously the statement was a sop to Stimson but inconsistent with all the facts, for a delay of the conference for this reason should have been until late July at the earliest. The two men decided that until they dropped the bomb on Japan they would not tell the Russians of its existence, and later they would deflect any questions about sharing information. Stimson agreed to such cooperation only after the Allies established full means of preventing its misuse, and also in return for quid pro quos in Poland, Yugoslavia, Rumania, and Manchuria—at that point the United States could release its secrets. At no time did Stimson imply that the Russians should not enter the war, and in fact no one thought that they were unnecessary by virtue of the existence of a bomb which they expected to be less destructive than the average fire raid. On June 18 Truman had authorized preparations for the landing on the Japanese mainland on November 1, employing a million and a half men. By that time the United States would have dropped several bombs.

During these same days a committee of seven scientists chaired by James Franck, but also representative of a much larger group, heard of the Interim Committee's decisions and decided to issue a modest, contrite protest. They confessed ignorance of military and foreign affairs, but they urged that a demonstration of the bomb on a barren area or island serve as a substitute for an attack on Japan, and that the United States make a sincere attempt at international control. They gave their recommendation to Stimson, who in turn passed it along to the scientific panel, which promptly decided to leave the subject to the domain of those who knew more about politics than they. In reality the proposal was rather too modest to regard seriously, and no one ever did save those who favored it, for it failed to question any of the basic assumptions of United States policy. The top-flight scientists connected with the entire

[5]Jungk, *Brighter Than A Thousand Suns*, 182; Hewlett and Anderson, *The New World*, 338, 356–57; Herbert Feis, *Japan Subdued: The Atomic Bomb and the End of the War in the Pacific* (Princeton, 1961), 38.

program were for the most part busy arguing for future funds to retain the new empires of big research in the postwar era.[6] In the last analysis, what the scientists said would worry the politicians less than what they refused to do, and none showed readiness to boycott a policy they opposed. The relationship established an important precedent, one that became mutually profitable in the future.

The question of the bomb was not so much an issue of diplomacy and the Russians as it was of power—American power. For that power involved not merely excluding the Russians from access to the secret of the bomb, but retaining a monopoly of power where possible, which meant barring the English as well. The British early in the war gave heavily of their scientific knowledge and resources to help build the bomb, and at Quebec the prior September the two nations agreed to share the knowledge in the postwar era and to use the bomb only after joint agreement. By June the United States had given the British nothing, and Truman decided to confirm his Interim Committee's decisions without reference to Churchill, to whom he finally presented the matter on July 4 after American plans were well advanced. In fact, every concerned American leader agreed by May 31 that they would keep not only the Russians out of the atomic club, but they would do nothing more to aid the English, whom Stimson even wished to see deprived of information of the first test. Later the British complained and protested, and developed their own bomb themselves.[7]

Throughout the period before Potsdam the decision to use a bomb to destroy 20,000 people posed no personal moral dilemmas to men who had already ordered far more destructive attacks on civilian populations. They continued to base their planning on the premises of a long war and a need for Russian aid. No one ever doubted that they would drop the bomb when ready. When Truman came to the White House he took the ultimate responsibility for the decision, but as Groves later assessed it, "As far as I was concerned, his decision was one of noninterference—basically, a decision not to upset the existing plans."[8]

Mechanism prevailed. No one seriously explored any of the options—neither Japanese surrender, nor delay, nor withholding the bomb. The leaders of the United States considered, and for a moment rethought, but in the end they did not alter their course, not merely because there was no effective way of preventing the Russians from doing what they had been asked to undertake for several years, but because the United States still felt the Russians had something left to offer that might save time and American blood. In fact the leaders of the United

[6]Hewlett and Anderson, *The New World*, 358–60; Stimson Diary, June 6, 1945, HLS Mss; Memo for Talk With the President, June 6, 1945, HLS Mss; FR (1945), II, 13; Groves, *Now It Can Be Told*, 264; Jungk, *Brighter Than a Thousand Suns*, 183–86.

[7]Feis, *Japan Subdued*, 46–47; Groves, *Now It Can Be Told*, 265; Hewlett and Anderson, *The New World*, 357; *Potsdam Papers*, II, 1371; Memo of Conference with the President, June 6, 1945, IILS Mss.

[8]Groves, *Now It Can Be Told*, 265.

States decided to continue the war on the basis of known and predictable factors: they took a conservative position and would not risk the alternatives of possibly fighting the war in China. Any realistic assessment of the objective conditions of the Japanese during those weeks might have convinced a reasonable group of men that significant alternatives to prolonged war existed, but the Japanese leaders themselves were incapable of confronting their defeat and acting accordingly. The United States would take no chances. For precisely the same reasons of mechanism and conservatism, which the Japanese in their own desperate way shared, the Americans decided to use the bomb as a known and now predictable factor of war, an economical means of destroying vast numbers of men, women, and children, soldiers and civilians. Well before August 1945 they had reduced this to a routine.

The United States could have won the war without the Russians and without the atomic bomb.

Chapter 10 THE BOMB AND THE ORIGINS OF THE COLD WAR

MARTIN J. SHERWIN *(1937–   ) was educated at Dartmouth College and the University of California at Los Angeles. He has been a member of the faculties of the History Department at the University of California at Berkeley, of the Program of Science, Technology and Society and the Peace Studies Program of Cornell University, and of the Princeton University History Department. He has written* A World Destroyed: The Atomic Bomb and the Grand Alliance *(1975) and published articles on different aspects of the politics of atomic science. In what ways does Sherwin's analysis enlarge historical understanding of atomic diplomacy and the origins of the Cold War?**

During the Second World War the atomic bomb was seen and valued as a potential rather than an actual instrument of policy. Responsible officials believed that its impact on diplomacy had to await its development and, perhaps, even a demonstration of its power. As Henry L. Stimson, the secretary of war, observed in his memoirs: "The bomb as a merely probable weapon had seemed a weak reed on which to rely, but the bomb as a colossal reality was very different." That policy makers considered this difference before Hiroshima has been well documented, but whether they based wartime diplomatic policies upon an anticipated successful demonstration of the bomb's power remains a source of controversy. Two questions delineate the issues in this debate. First, did the

*Martin J. Sherwin, "The Atomic Bomb and the Origins of the Cold War: U.S. Atomic-Energy Policy and Diplomacy, 1941–45," *American Historical Reivew*, Vol. 78, no. 4 (October 1973), pp. 945–968. Footnotes omitted. By permission of the author.

development of the atomic bomb affect the way American policy makers conducted diplomacy with the Soviet Union? Second, did diplomatic considerations related to the Soviet Union influence the decision to use the atomic bomb against Japan?

These important questions relating the atomic bomb to American diplomacy, and ultimately to the origins of the cold war, have been addressed almost exclusively to the formulation of policy during the early months of the Truman administration. As a result, two anterior questions of equal importance, questions with implications for those already posed, have been overlooked. Did diplomatic considerations related to Soviet postwar behavior influence the formulation of Roosevelt's atomic-energy policies? What effect did the atomic legacy Truman inherited have on the diplomatic and atomic-energy policies of his administration?

To comprehend the nature of the relationship between atomic-energy and diplomatic policies that developed during the war, the bomb must be seen as policy makers saw it before Hiroshima, as a weapon that might be used to control postwar diplomacy. For this task our present view is conceptually inadequate. After more than a quarter century of experience we understand, as wartime policy makers did not, the bomb's limitations as a diplomatic instrument. To appreciate the profound influence of the unchallenged wartime assumption about the bomb's impact on diplomacy we must recognize the postwar purposes for which policy makers and their advisers believed the bomb could be used. In this effort Churchill's expectations must be scrutinized as carefully as Roosevelt's, and scientists' ideas must be considered along with those of politicians. Truman's decision to use the atomic bomb against Japan must be evaluated in the light of Roosevelt's atomic legacy, and the problems of impending peace must be considered along with the exigencies of war. To isolate the basic atomic-energy policy alternatives that emerged during the war requires that we first ask whether alternatives were, in fact, recognized.

What emerges most clearly from a close examination of wartime formulation of atomic-energy policy is the conclusion that policy makers never seriously questioned the assumption that the atomic bomb should be used against Germany or Japan. From October 9, 1941, the time of the first meeting to organize the atomic-energy project, Stimson, Roosevelt, and other members of the "top policy group" conceived of the development of the atomic bomb as an essential part of the total war effort. Though the suggestion to build the bomb was initially made by scientists who feared that Germany might develop the weapon first, those with political responsibility for prosecuting the war accepted the circumstances of the bomb's creation as sufficient justification for its use against any enemy.

Having nurtured this point of view during the war, Stimson charged those who later criticized the use of the bomb with two errors. First, these critics asked the wrong question: it was not whether surrender could have been obtained without using the bomb but whether a different diplomatic and military course from that followed by the Truman administration would have achieved an earlier surrender. Second, the basic assumption of these critics was false: the idea that American policy should have been based primarily on a desire not to employ the bomb seemed as "irresponsible" as a policy controlled by a positive desire to use it. The war, not the bomb, Stimson argued, had been the primary focus of his attention; as secretary of war his responsibilities permitted no alternative.

Stimson's own wartime diary nevertheless indicates that from 1941 on, the problems associated with the atomic bomb moved steadily closer to the center of his own and Roosevelt's concerns. As the war progressed, the implications of the weapon's development became diplomatic as well as military, postwar as well as wartime. Recognizing that a monopoly of the atomic bomb gave the United States a powerful new military advantage, Roosevelt and Stimson became increasingly anxious to convert it to diplomatic advantage. In December 1944 they spoke of using the "secret" of the atomic bomb as a means of obtaining a *quid pro quo* from the Soviet Union. But viewing the bomb as a potential instrument of diplomacy, they were not moved to formulate a concrete plan for carrying out this exchange before the bomb was used. The bomb had "this unique peculiarity," Stimson noted several months later in his diary; "Success is 99% assured, yet only by the first actual war trial of the weapon can the actual certainty be fixed." Whether or not the specter of postwar Soviet ambitions created "a positive desire" to ascertain the bomb's power, until that decision was executed "atomic diplomacy" remained an idea that never crystallized into policy.

Although Roosevelt left no definitive statement assigning a postwar role to the atomic bomb, his expectations for its potential diplomatic value can be recalled from the existing record. An analysis of the policies he chose from among the alternatives he faced suggests that the potential diplomatic value of the bomb began to shape his atomic-energy policies as early as 1943. He may have been cautious about counting on the bomb as a reality during the war, but he nevertheless consistently chose policy alternatives that would promote the postwar diplomatic potential of the bomb if the predictions of scientists proved true. These policies were based on the assumption that the bomb could be used effectively to secure postwar diplomatic aims; and this assumption was carried over from the Roosevelt to the Truman administration.

Despite general agreement that the bomb would be an extraordinarily important diplomatic factor after the war, those closely associated with its development did not agree on how to use it most effectively as an instrument of diplomacy. Convinced that wartime atomic-energy policies would have postwar diplomatic consequences, several scientists advised Roosevelt to adopt policies aimed at achieving a postwar international control system. Churchill, on the other hand, urged the president to maintain the Anglo-American atomic monopoly as a diplomatic counter against the postwar ambitions of other nations—particularly against the Soviet Union. Roosevelt fashioned his atomic-energy policies from the choices he made between these conflicting recommendations. In 1943 he rejected the counsel of his science advisers and began to consider the diplomatic component of atomic-energy policy in consultation with Churchill alone. This decision-making procedure and Roosevelt's untimely death have left his motives ambiguous. Nevertheless it is clear that he pursued policies consistent with Churchill's monopolistic, anti-Soviet views.

The findings of this study thus raise serious questions concerning generalizations historians have commonly made about Roosevelt's diplomacy: that it was consistent with his public reputation for cooperation and conciliation; that he was naive with respect to postwar Soviet behavior; that, like Wilson, he believed in collective security as an effective guarantor of national safety; and that he made every possible effort to assure that the Soviet Union and its allies would continue to function as postwar partners. Although this article does not dispute the view that Roosevelt desired amicable postwar relations with the Soviet Union, or even that he worked hard to achieve them, it does suggest that historians have exaggerated his confidence in (and perhaps his commitment to) such an outcome. His most secret and among his most important long-range decisions —those responsible for prescribing a diplomatic role for the atomic bomb—reflected his lack of confidence. Finally, in light of this study's conclusions, the widely held assumption that Truman's attitude toward the atomic bomb was substantially different from Roosevelt's must also be revised.

Like the Grand Alliance itself, the Anglo-American atomic-energy partnership was forged by the war and its exigencies. The threat of a German atomic bomb precipitated a hasty marriage of convenience between British research and American resources. When scientists in Britain proposed a theory that explained how an atomic bomb might quickly be built, policy makers had to assume that German scientists were building one. "If such an explosive were made," Vannevar Bush, the director of the Office of Scientific Research and Development, told Roosevelt in July 1941, "it would be thousands of times more powerful than existing explosives, and its use might be determining." Roosevelt assumed nothing less. Even before the atomic-energy project was fully organized he assigned it the highest priority. He wanted the program "pushed not only in regard to development, but also with due regard to time. This is very much of the essence," he told Bush in March 1942. "We both felt painfully the dangers of doing nothing," Churchill recalled, referring to an early wartime discussion with Roosevelt about the bomb.

The high stakes at issue during the war did not prevent officials in Great Britain or the United States from considering the postwar implications of their atomic-energy decisions. As early as 1941, during the debate over whether to join the United States in an atomic-energy partnership, members of the British government's atomic-energy committee argued that the matter "was so important for the future that work should proceed in Britain." Weighing the obvious difficulties of proceeding alone against the possible advantages of working with the United States, Sir John Anderson, then lord president of the council and the minister responsible for atomic-energy research, advocated the partnership. As he explained to Churchill, by working closely with the Americans British scientists would be able "to take up the work again [after the war], not where we left off, but where the combined effort had by then brought it."

As early as October 1942 Roosevelt's science advisers exhibited a similar concern with the potential postwar value of atomic energy. After conducting a full-scale review of the atomic-energy project, James B. Conant, the president of Harvard University and Bush's deputy, recommended discontinuing the Anglo-American partnership "as far as development and manufacture is concerned." Conant had in mind three considerations when he suggested a more limited arrangement with the British: first, the project had been transferred from scientific to military control; second, the United States was doing almost all the developmental work; and third, security dictated "moving in a direction of holding much more closely the information about the development of this program." Under these conditions it was difficult, Conant observed, "to see how a joint British-American project could be sponsored in this country." What prompted Conant's recommendations, however, was his suspicion—soon to be shared by other senior atomic-energy administrators—that the British were rather more concerned with information for postwar industrial purposes than for wartime use. What right did the British have to the fruits of American labor? "We were doing nine-tenths of the work," Stimson told Roosevelt in October. By December 1942 there was general agreement among the president's atomic-energy advisers that the British no longer had a valid claim to all atomic-energy information.

Conant's arguments and suggestions for a more limited partnership were incorporated into a "Report to the President by the Military Policy Committee." Roosevelt approved the recommendations on December 28. Early in January the British were officially informed that the rules governing the Anglo-American atomic-energy partnership had been altered on "orders from the top."

By approving the policy of "restricted interchange" Roosevelt undermined a major incentive for British cooperation. It is not surprising, therefore, that Churchill took up the matter directly with the president and with Harry Hopkins, "Roosevelt's own, personal Foreign Office." The prime minister's initial response to the new policy reflected his determination to have it reversed: "That we should each work separately," he threatened, "would be a sombre decision."

Conant and Bush understood the implications of Churchill's intervention and sought to counter its effect. "It is our duty," Conant wrote Bush, "to see to it that the President of the United States, in writing, is informed of what is involved in these decisions." Their memorandums no longer concentrated on tortuous discussions differentiating between the scientific research and the manufacturing stages of the bomb's development but focused on what to Conant was "the major consideration . . . that of *national security and postwar strategic signifi- cance.*" Information on manufacturing an atomic bomb, Conant noted, was a "military secret which is in a totally different class from anything the world has ever seen if the potentialities of this project are realized." To provide the British with detailed knowledge about the construction of a bomb "might be the equi- valent to joint occupation of a fortress of strategic harbor in perpetuity." Though British and American atomic-energy policies might coincide during the war, Conant and Bush expected them to conflict afterward.

The controversy over the policy of "restricted interchange" of atomic- energy information shifted attention to postwar diplomatic considerations. As Bush wrote to Hopkins. "We can hardly give away the fruits of our develop- ments as a part of postwar planning except on the basis of some overall agree- ment on that subject, which agreement does not now exist." The central issue was clearly drawn. The atomic-energy policy of the United States was related to the very fabric of Anglo-American postwar relations and, as Churchill would insist, to postwar relations between each of them and the Soviet Union. Just as the possibility of British postwar commercial competition had played a major role in shaping the U.S. policy of restricted interchange, the specter of Soviet postwar military power played a major role in shaping the prime min- ister's attitude toward atomic-energy policies in 1943.

"We cannot," Sir John Anderson wrote Churchill, "afford after the war to face the future without this weapon and rely entirely on America should Russia or some other power develop it." The prime minister agreed. The atomic bomb was an instrument of postwar diplomacy that Britain had to have. He could cite numerous reasons for his determination to acquire an independent atomic arsenal after the war, but Great Britain's postwar military-diplomatic position with respect to the Soviet Union invariably led the list. When Bush and Stimson visited London in July, Churchill told them quite frankly that he was "vitally interested in the possession of all [atomic-energy] information because this will be necessary for Britain's independence in the future as well as for success during the war." Nor was Churchill evasive about his reasoning: "It would never do to have Germany or Russia win the race for something which might be used for international blackmail," he stated bluntly and then pointed out that "Russia might be in a position to accomplish this result unless we worked together." In Washington, two months earlier, Churchill's science adviser Lord Cherwell had told Bush and Hopkins virtually the same thing. The British government, Cherwell stated, was considering "the whole [atomic-energy] affair on an after-the-war military basis." It intended, he said, "to manufacture and produce the weapon." Prior to the convening of the Quebec Conference, Anderson explained his own and Churchill's view of the bomb to the Canadian prime minister, Mackenzie King. The British knew, Anderson said, "that both Germany and Russia were working on the same thing," which, he noted, "would be a terrific factor in the postwar world as giving an absolute control to whatever country possessed the secret." Convinced that the British attitude toward the bomb would undermine any possibility of postwar cooperation with the Soviet Union, Bush and Conant vigorously continued to oppose any revival of the Anglo-American atomic-energy partnership.

On July 20, however, Roosevelt chose to accept a recommendation from Hopkins to restore full partnership, and he ordered Bush to "renew, in an inclusive manner, the full exchange of information with the British." A garbled trans-Atlantic cable to Bush reading "review" rather than "renew" gave him the opportunity to continue his negotiations in London with Churchill and thereby to modify the president's order. But Bush could not alter Roosevelt's intentions. On August 19, at the Quebec Conference, the president and the prime minister agreed that the British would share the atomic bomb. Despite Bush's negotiations with Churchill, the Quebec Agreement revived the principle of an Anglo-American atomic-energy partnership, albeit the British were reinstated as junior rather than equal partners.

The president's decision was not a casual one taken in ignorance. As the official history of the Atomic Energy Commission notes: "Both Roosevelt and Churchill knew that the stake of their diplomacy was a technological breakthrough so revolutionary that it transcended in importance even the bloody work of carrying the war to the heartland of the Nazi foe." The president had been informed of Churchill's position as well as of Bush's and Conant's. But how much closer Roosevelt was to Churchill than to his own advisers at this time is suggested by a report written after the war by General Leslie R. Groves, military director of the atomic-energy project. "It is not known what if any Americans President Roosevelt consulted at Quebec," Groves wrote. "It is doubtful if there were any. All that is known is that the Quebec Agreement was signed by President Roosevelt and that, as finally signed, it agreed practically in toto with the version presented by Sir John Anderson to Dr. Bush in Washington a few weeks earlier."

The debate that preceded the Quebec Agreement is noteworthy for yet another reason: it led to a new relationship between Roosevelt and his atomic-energy advisers. After August 1943 the president did not consult with them about the diplomatic aspects of atomic-energy policy. Though he responded politely when they offered their views, he acted decisively only in consultation with Churchill. Bush and Conant appear to have lost a large measure of their influence because they had used it to oppose Churchill's position. What they did not suspect was the extent to which the president had come to share the prime minister's view.

It can be argued that Roosevelt, the political pragmatist, renewed the wartime atomic-energy partnership to keep relations with the British harmonious rather than disrupt them on the basis of a postwar issue. Indeed it seems logical that the president took this consideration into account. But it must also be recognized that he was perfectly comfortable with the concept Churchill advocated—that military power was a prerequisite to successful postwar diplomacy. As early as August 1941, during the Atlantic Conference, Roosevelt had rejected the idea that an "effective international organization" could be relied upon to keep the peace; an Anglo-American international police force would be far more effective, he told Churchill. By the spring of 1942 the concept had broadened; the two "policemen" became four, and the idea was added that every other nation would be totally disarmed. "The Four Policemen" would have "to build up a reservoir of force so powerful that no aggressor would dare to challenge it," Roosevelt told Arthur Sweetser, an ardent internationalist. Violators first would be quarantined, and, if they persisted in their disruptive activities, bombed at the rate of a city a day until they agreed to behave. The president told Molotov about this idea in May, and in November he repeated it to Clark Eichelberger, who was coordinating the activities of the American internationalists. A year later, at the Teheran Conference, Roosevelt again discussed his idea, this time with Stalin. As Robert A. Divine has noted: "Roosevelt's concept of big power domination remained the central idea in his approach to international organization throughout World War II."

Precisely how Roosevelt expected to integrate the atomic bomb into his plans for keeping the peace in the postwar world is not clear. However, against the background of his atomic-energy policy decisions of 1943 and his peace-keeping concepts, his actions in 1944 suggest that he intended to take full advantage of the bomb's potential as a postwar instrument of Anglo-American diplomacy. If Roosevelt thought the bomb could be used to create a more peaceful world order, he seems to have considered the threat of its power more effective than any opportunities it offered for international cooperation. If Roosevelt was less worried than Churchill about Soviet postwar ambitions, he was no less determined than the prime minister to avoid any commitments to the Soviets for the international control of atomic energy. There could still be four policemen, but only two of them would have the bomb.

The atomic-engery policies Roosevelt pursued during the remainder of his life reinforce this interpretation of his ideas for the postwar period. The following three questions offer a useful framework for analyzing his intentions. Did Roosevelt make any additional agreements with Churchill that would further support the view that he intended to maintain an Anglo-American monopoly after the war? Did Roosevelt demonstrate any interest in the international control of atomic energy? Was Roosevelt aware that an effort to maintain an

Anglo-American monopoly of the atomic bomb might lead to a postwar atomic arms race with the Soviet Union?

An examination of the wartime activities of the eminent Danish physicist, Niels Bohr, who arrived in America early in 1944 as a consultant to the atomic-bomb project, will help answer these questions. "Officially and secretly he came to help the technical enterprise," noted J. Robert Oppenheimer, the director of the Los Alamos atomic-bomb laboratory, but "most secretly of all . . . he came to advance his case and his cause." Bohr was convinced that a postwar atomic armaments race with the Soviet Union was inevitable unless Roosevelt and Churchill initiated efforts during the war to establish the international control of atomic energy. Bohr's attempts to promote this idea in the United States were aided by Justice Felix Frankfurter.

Bohr and Frankfurter were old acquaintances. They had first met in 1933 at Oxford and then in 1939 on several occasions in London and the United States. At these meetings Bohr had been impressed by the breadth of Frankfurter's interests and, perhaps, overimpressed with his influence on Roosevelt. In 1944 the Danish minister to the United States brought them together, once again, at his home in Washington. Frankfurter, who appears to have suspected why Bohr had come to America and why this meeting had been arranged, had learned about the atomic-bomb project earlier in the war when, as he told the story, several troubled scientists had sought his advice on a matter of "greatest importance." He therefore invited Bohr to lunch in his chambers and, by dropping hints about his knowledge, encouraged Bohr to discuss the issue.

After listening to Bohr's analysis of the postwar alternatives—an atomic armaments race or some form of international control—Frankfurter saw Roosevelt. Bohr had persuaded him, Frankfurter reported, that disastrous consequences would result if Russia learned on her own about the atomic-bomb project. Frankfurter suggested that it was a matter of great importance that the president explore the possibility of seeking an effective arrangement with the Soviets for controlling the bomb. He also noted that Bohr, whose knowledge of Soviet science was extensive, believed that the Russians had the capability to build their own atomic weapons. If the international control of atomic energy was not discussed among the Allies during the war, an atomic arms race between the Allies would almost certainly develop after the war. It seemed imperative, therefore, that Roosevelt consider approaching Stalin with a proposal as soon as possible.

Frankfurter discussed these points with the president for an hour and a half, and he left feeling that Roosevelt was "plainly impressed by my account of the matter." When Frankfurter had suggested that the solution to this problem might be more important than all the plans for a world organization, Roosevelt had agreed. Moreover he had authorized Frankfurter to tell Bohr, who was scheduled to return to England, that he might inform "our friends in London that the President was most eager to explore the proper safeguards in relation to X [the atomic bomb]." Roosevelt also told Frankfurter that the problem of the atomic bomb "worried him to death" and that he was very eager for all the help he could have in dealing with it.

The alternatives placed before Roosevelt posed a difficult dilemma. On the one hand, he could continue to exclude the Soviet government from any official information about the development of the bomb, a policy that would probably strengthen America's postwar military-diplomatic position. But such a policy would also encourage Soviet mistrust of Anglo-American intentions and was bound to make postwar cooperation more difficult. On the other hand, Roosevelt could use the atomic-bomb project as an instrument of cooperation by informing Stalin of the American government's intention of cooperating in the development of a plan for the international control of atomic weapons, an objective that might never be achieved.

Either choice involved serious risks. Roosevelt had to balance the diplomatic advantages of being well ahead of the Soviet Union in atomic-energy production after the war against the advantages of initiating wartime negotiations for postwar cooperation. The issue here, it must be emphasized, is not whether the initiative Bohr suggested would have led to successful international control, but rather whether Roosevelt demonstrated any serious interest in laying the groundwork for such a policy.

Several considerations indicate that Roosevelt was already committed to a course of action that precluded Bohr's internationalist approach. First, Frankfurter appears to have been misled. Though Roosevelt's response had been characteristically agreeable, he did not mention Bohr's ideas to his atomic-energy advisers until September 1944, when he told Bush that he was very disturbed that Frankfurter had learned about the project. Roosevelt knew at this time, moreover, that the Soviets were finding out on their own about the development of the atomic bomb. Security personnel had reported an active Communist cell in the Radiation Laboratory at the University of California. Their reports indicated that at least one scientist at Berkeley was selling information to Russian agents. "They [Soviet agents] are already getting information about vital secrets and sending them to Russia," Stimson told the president on September 9, 1943. If Roosevelt was indeed worried to death about the effect the atomic bomb could have on Soviet-American postwar relations, he took no action to remove the potential danger, nor did he make any effort to explore the possibility of encouraging Soviet postwar cooperation on this problem. The available evidence indicates that he never discussed the merits of the international control of atomic energy with his advisers after this first or any subsequent meeting with Frankfurter.

How is the president's policy of neither discussing international control nor promoting the idea to be explained if not by an intention to use the bomb as an instrument of Anglo-American postwar diplomacy? Perhaps his concern for maintaining the tightest possible secrecy against German espionage led him to oppose any discussion about the project. Or he may have concluded, after considering Bohr's analysis, that Soviet suspicion and mistrust would be further aroused if Stalin were informed of the existence of the project without receiving detailed information about the bomb's construction. The possibility also exists that Roosevelt believed that neither Congress nor the American public would approve of a policy giving the Soviet Union any measure of control over the new weapon. Finally Roosevelt might have thought that the spring of 1944 was not the proper moment for such an initiative.

Though it would be unreasonable to state categorically that these considerations did not contribute to his decision, they appear to have been secondary. Roosevelt was clearly, and properly, concerned about secrecy, but the most important secret with respect to Soviet-American relations was that the United States was developing an atomic bomb. And that secret, he was aware, already had been passed on to Moscow. Soviet mistrust of Anglo-American postwar intentions could only be exacerbated by continuing the existing policy. Moreover an attempt to initiate planning for international control of atomic energy would not have required the revelation of technical secrets. Nor is it sufficient to cite Roosevelt's well-known sensitivity to domestic politics as an explanation for his atomic-energy policies. He was willing to take enormous political risks, as he did at Yalta, to support his diplomatic objectives.

Had Roosevelt avoided all postwar atomic-energy commitments, his lack of support for international control could have been interpreted as an attempt to reserve his opinion on the best course to follow. But he had made commitments in 1943 supporting Churchill's monopolistic, anti-Soviet position, and he continued to make others in 1944. On June 13, for example, Roosevelt and Churchill signed an Agreement and Declaration of Trust, specifying that the United States and Great Britain would cooperate in seeking to control available supplies of uranium and thorium ore both during and after the war. This commitment, taken against the background of Roosevelt's peace-keeping ideas and his other commitments, suggests that the president's attitude toward the international control of atomic energy was similar to the prime minister's.

Churchill had dismissed out of hand the concept of international control when Bohr talked with him about it in May 1944. Their meeting was not long under way before Churchill lost interest and became involved in an argument with Lord Cherwell, who was also present. Bohr, left out of the discussion, was frustrated and depressed; he was unable to return the conversation to what he considered the most important diplomatic problem of the war. When the allotted half hour elapsed, Bohr asked if he might send the prime minister a memorandum on the subject. A letter from Niels Bohr, Churchill bitingly replied, was always welcome, but he hoped it would deal with a subject other than politics. As Bohr described their meeting: "We did not even speak the same language."

Churchill rejected the assumption upon which Bohr's views were founded—that international control of atomic energy could be used as a cornerstone for constructing a peaceful world order. An atomic monopoly would be a significant diplomatic advantage in postwar diplomacy, and Churchill did not believe that anything useful could be gained by surrendering this advantage. The argument that a new weapon created a unique opportunity to refashion international affairs ignored every lesson Churchill read into history. "You can be quite sure," he would write in a memorandum less than a year later, "that any power that gets hold of the secret will try to make the article and this touches the existence of human society. This matter is out of all relation to anything else that exists in the world, and I could not think of participating in any disclosure to third or fourth parties at the present time."

Several months after Bohr met Churchill, Frankfurter arranged a meeting between Bohr and Roosevelt. Their discussion lasted an hour and a half. Roosevelt told Bohr that contact with the Soviet Union along the lines he suggested had to be tried. The president also said he was optimistic that such an initiative would have a "good result." In his opinion Stalin was enough of a realist to understand the revolutionary importance of this development and its consequences. The president also expressed confidence that the prime minister would eventually share these views. They had disagreed in the past, he told Bohr, but they had always succeeded in resolving their differences.

Roosevelt's enthusiasm for Bohr's ideas was more apparent than real. The president did not mention them to anyone until he met with Churchill at Hyde Park on September 18, following the second wartime conference at Quebec. The decisions reached on atomic energy at Hyde Park were summarized and documented in an *aide-mémoire* signed by Roosevelt and Churchill on September 19, 1944. The agreement bears the markings of Churchill's attitude toward the atomic bomb and his poor opinion of Bohr. "Enquiries should be made," the last paragraph reads, "regarding the activities of Professor Bohr and steps taken to ensure that he is responsible for no leakage of information particularly to the Russians." If Bohr's activities prompted Roosevelt to suspect his loyalty, there can be no doubt that Churchill encouraged the president's suspicions. Atomic energy and Britain's future position as a world power had become part of a single equation for the prime minister. Bohr's ideas, like the earlier idea of restricted interchange, threatened the continuation of the Anglo-American atomic-energy partnership. With such great stakes at issue Churchill did not hesitate to discredit Bohr along with his ideas. "It seems to me," Churchill wrote to Cherwell soon after Hyde Park, "Bohr ought to be confined or at any rate made to see that he is very near the edge of mortal crimes."

The *aide-mémoire* also contained an explicit rejection of any wartime efforts toward international control: "The suggestion that the world should be informed regarding tube alloys [the atomic bomb], with a view to an international agreement regarding its control and use, is not accepted. The matter should continue to be regarded as of the utmost secrecy." But Bohr had never suggested that the world be informed about the atomic bomb. He had argued in memorandums and in person that peace was not possible unless the Soviet government—not the world—was officially notified only about the project's existence before the time when any discussion would appear coercive rather than friendly.

It was the second paragraph, however, that revealed the full extent of Roosevelt's agreement with Churchill's point of view. "Full collaboration between the United States and the British Government in developing tube alloys for military and commercial purposes," it noted, "should continue after the defeat of Japan unless and until terminated by joint agreement." Finally the *aide-mémoire* offers some insight into Roosevelt's intentions for the military use of the weapon in the war: "When a bomb is finally available, it might perhaps, after mature consideration, be used against the Japanese, who should be warned that this bombardment will be repeated until they surrender."

Within the context of the complex problem of the origins of the cold war the Hyde Park meeting is far more important than historians of the war generally have recognized. Overshadowed by the Second Quebec Conference on one side and by the drama of Yalta on the other, its significance often has been overlooked. But the agreements reached in September 1944 reflect a set of attitudes, aims, and assumptions that guided the relationship between the atomic bomb and American diplomacy during the Roosevelt administration and, through the transfer of its atomic legacy, during the Truman administration as well. Two alternatives had been recognized long before Roosevelt and Churchill met in 1944 at Hyde Park: the bomb could have been used to initiate a diplomatic effort to work out a system for its international control, or it could remain isolated during the war from any cooperative initiatives and held in reserve should cooperation fail. Roosevelt consistently favored the latter alternative. An insight into his reasoning is found in a memorandum Bush wrote following a conversation with Roosevelt several days after the Hyde Park meeting: "The President evidently thought he could join with Churchill in bringing about a US-UK postwar agreement on this subject [the atomic bomb] by which it would be held closely and presumably to control the peace of the world." By 1944 Roosevelt's earlier musings about the four policemen had faded into the background. But the idea behind it, the concept of controlling the peace of the world by amassing overwhelming military power, appears to have remained a prominent feature of his postwar plans.

In the seven months between his meeting with Churchill in September and his death the following April Roosevelt did not alter his atomic-energy policies. Nor did he reverse his earlier decision not to take his advisers into his confidence about diplomatic issues related to the new weapon. They were never told about the Hyde Park agreements, nor were they able to discuss with him their ideas for the postwar handling of atomic-energy affairs. Though officially uninformed, Bush suspected that Roosevelt had made a commitment to continue the atomic-energy partnership exclusively with the British after the war, and he, as well as Conant, opposed the idea. They believed such a policy "might well lead to extraordinary efforts on the part of Russia to establish its own position in the field secretly, and might lead to a clash, say 20 years from now." Unable to reach the president directly, they sought to influence his policies through Stimson, whose access to Roosevelt's office (though not to his thoughts on atomic energy) was better than their own.

Summarizing their views on September 30 for the secretary of war, Bush and Conant predicted that an atomic bomb equivalent to from one to ten thousand tons of high explosive could be "demonstrated" before August 1, 1945. They doubted that the present American and British monopoly could be maintained for more than three or four years, and they pointed out that any nation with good technical and scientific resources could catch up: accidents of research, moreover, might even put some other nation ahead. In addition atomic bombs were only the first step along the road of nuclear weapons technology. In the not-too-distant future loomed the awesome prospect of a weapon perhaps a thousand times more destructive—the hydrogen bomb. Every major center of population in the world would then lie at the mercy of a nation that struck first in war. Security therefore could be found neither in secrecy nor even in the control of raw materials, for the supply of heavy hydrogen was practically unlimited.

These predictions by Bush and Conant were more specific than Bohr's, but not dissimilar. They, too, believed that a nuclear arms race could be prevented only through international control. Their efforts were directed, however, toward abrogating existing agreements with the British rather than toward initiating new agreements with the Soviets. Like Bohr they based their hope for Stalin's eventual cooperation on his desire to avoid the circumstances that could lead to a nuclear war. But while Bohr urged Roosevelt to approach Stalin with the carrot of international control before the bomb became a reality, Bush and Conant were inclined to delay such an approach until the bomb was demonstrated, until it was clear that without international control the new weapon could be used as a terribly effective stick.

In their attempt to persuade Roosevelt to their point of view Bush and Conant failed. But their efforts were not in vain. By March 1945 Stimson shared their concerns, and he agreed that peace without international control was a forlorn hope. Postwar problems relating to the atomic bomb "went right down to the bottom facts of human nature, morals and government, and it is by far the most searching and important thing that I have had to do since I have been here in the office of Secretary of War," Stimson wrote on March 5. Ten days later he presented his views on postwar atomic-energy policy to Roosevelt. This was their last meeting. In less than a month a new president took the oath of office.

Harry S. Truman inherited a set of military and diplomatic atomic-energy policies that included partially formulated intentions, several commitments to Churchill, and the assumption that the bomb would be a legitimate weapon to be used against Japan. But no policy was definitely settled. According to the Quebec Agreement the president had the option of deciding the future of the commercial aspects of the atomic-energy partnership according to his own estimate of what was fair. Although the policy of "utmost secrecy" had been confirmed at Hyde Park the previous September, Roosevelt had not informed his atomic-energy advisers about the *aide-mémoire* he and Churchill signed. Although the assumption that the bomb would be used in the war was shared by those privy to its development, assumptions formulated early in the war were not necessarily valid at its conclusion. Yet Truman was bound to the past by his own uncertain position and by the prestige of his predecessor. Since Roosevelt had refused to open negotiations with the Soviet government for the international control of atomic energy, and since he had never expressed any objection to the wartime use of the bomb, it would have required considerable political courage and confidence for Truman to alter those policies. Moreover it would have required the encouragement of his advisers, for under the circumstances the most serious constraint on the new president's choices was his dependence upon advice. So Truman's atomic legacy, while it included several options, did not necessarily entail complete freedom to choose from among all the possible alternatives.

"I think it is very important that I should have a talk with you as soon as possible on a highly secret matter," Stimson wrote to Truman on April 24. It has "such a bearing on our present foreign relations and has such an important effect upon all my thinking in this field that I think you ought to know about it without further delay." Stimson had been preparing to brief Truman on the atomic bomb for almost ten days, but in the preceding twenty-four hours he had been seized by a sense of urgency. Relations with the Soviet Union had declined precipitously during the past week, the result, he thought, of the failure of the State Department to settle the major problems between the Allies before going ahead with the San Francisco Conference on the United Nations Organization. The secretary of state, Edward R. Stettinius, Jr., along with the department's Soviet specialists, now felt "compelled to bull the thing through." To get out of the "mess" they had created, Stimson wrote in his diary, they were urging Truman to get tough with the Russians. He had. Twenty-four hours earlier the president met with the Soviet foreign minister, V. M. Molotov, and "with rather brutal frankness" accused his government of breaking the Yalta Agreement. Molotov was furious. "I have never been talked to like that in my life," he told the president before leaving.

With a memorandum on the "political aspects of the S-1 [atomic bomb's] performance" in hand and General Groves in reserve, Stimson went to the White House on April 25. The document he carried was the distillation of numerous decisions already taken, each one the product of attitudes that developed along with the new weapon. The secretary himself was not entirely aware of how various forces had shaped these decisions: the recommendations of Bush and Conant, the policies Roosevelt had followed, the uncertainties inherent in the wartime alliance, the oppressive concern for secrecy, and his own inclination to consider long-range implications. It was a curious document. Though its language revealed Stimson's sensitivity to the historic significance of the atomic bomb, he did not question the wisdom of using it against Japan. Nor did he suggest any concrete steps for developing a postwar policy. His objective was to inform Truman of the salient problems: the possibility of an atomic arms race, the danger of atomic war, and the necessity for international control if the United Nations Organization was to work. "If the problem of the proper use of this weapon can be solved," he wrote, "we would have the opportunity to bring the world into a pattern in which the peace of the world and our civilizations can be saved." To cope with this difficult challenge Stimson suggested the "establishment of a select committee" to consider the postwar problems inherent in the development of the bomb. If his presentation was the "forceful statement" of the problem that historians of the Atomic Energy Commission have described it as being, its force inhered in the problem itself, not in any bold formulations or initiatives he offered toward a solution. If, as another historian has claimed, this meeting led to a "strategy of delayed showdown," requiring "the delay of all disputes with Russia until the atomic bomb had been demonstrated," there is no evidence in the extant records of the meeting that Stimson had such a strategy in mind or that Truman misunderstood the secretary's views.

What emerges from a careful reading of Stimson's diary, his memorandum of April 25 to Truman, a summary by Groves of the meeting, and Truman's recollections is an argument for overall caution in American diplomatic relations with the Soviet Union: it was an argument against any showdown. Since the atomic bomb was potentially the most dangerous issue facing the postwar world and since the most desirable resolution of the problem was some form of international control, Soviet cooperation had to be secured. It was imprudent, Stimson suggested, to pursue a policy that would preclude the possibility of international cooperation on atomic-energy matters after the war ended. Truman's overall impression of Stimson's argument was that the secretary of war was "at least as much concerned with the role of the atomic bomb in the shaping of history as in its capacity to shorten the war." These were indeed Stimson's dual concerns on April 25, and he could see no conflict between them.

Despite the profound consequences Stimson attributed to the development of the new weapon, he had not suggested that Truman reconsider its use against Japan. Nor had he thought to mention the possibility that chances of securing

Soviet postwar cooperation might be diminished if Stalin did not receive a commitment to international control prior to an attack. The question of why these alternatives were overlooked naturally arises. Perhaps what Frankfurter once referred to as Stimson's habit of setting "his mind at one thing like the needle of an old victrola caught in a single groove" may help to explain his not mentioning these possibilities. Yet Bush and Conant never raised them either. Even Niels Bohr had made a clear distinction between the bomb's wartime use and its postwar impact on diplomacy. "What role it [the atomic bomb] may play in the present war," Bohr had written to Roosevelt in July 1944, was a question "quite apart" from the overriding concern: the need to avoid an atomic arms race.

The preoccupation with winning the war obviously helped to create this seeming dichotomy between the wartime use of the bomb and the potential postwar diplomatic problems with the Soviet Union raised by its development. But a closer look at how Bohr and Stimson each defined the nature of the diplomatic problem created by the bomb suggests that for the secretary of war and his advisers (and ultimately for the president they advised) there was no dichotomy at all. Bohr apprehended the meaning of the new weapon even before it was developed, and he had no doubt that scientists in the Soviet Union would also understand its profound implications for the postwar world. He was also certain that they would interpret the meaning of the development to Stalin just as scientists in the United States and Great Britain had explained it to Roosevelt and Churchill. Thus the diplomatic problem, as Bohr analyzed it, was not the need to convince Stalin that the atomic bomb was an unprecedented weapon that threatened the life of the world but the need to assure the Soviet leader that he had nothing to fear from the circumstances of its development. By informing Stalin during the war that the United States intended to cooperate with him in neutralizing the bomb through international control, Bohr reasoned that its wartime use could be considered apart from postwar problems.

Stimson approached the problem rather differently. Although he believed that the bomb "might even mean the doom of civilization or it might mean the perfection of civilization" he was less confident than Bohr that the weapon in an undeveloped state could be used as an effective instrument of diplomacy. Until its "actual certainty [was] fixed," Stimson considered any prior approach to Stalin as premature. But as the uncertainties of impending peace became more apparent and worrisome, Stimson, Truman, and the secretary of state–designate, James F. Byrnes, began to think of the bomb as something of a diplomatic panacea for their postwar problems. Byrnes had told Truman in April that the bomb "might well put us in a position to dictate our own terms at the end of the war." By June, Truman and Stimson were discussing "further *quid pro quos* which should be established in consideration for our taking them [the Soviet Union] into [atomic-energy] partnership." Assuming that the bomb's impact on diplomacy would be immediate and extraordinary, they agreed on no less than "the settlement of the Polish, Rumanian, Yugoslavian, and Manchurian problems." But they also concluded that no revelation would be made "to Russia or anyone else until the first bomb had been successfully laid on Japan." Truman and Stimson based their expectations on how they saw and valued the bomb; its use against Japan, they reasoned, would transfer this view to the Soviet Union.

Was an implicit warning to Moscow, then, the principal reason for deciding to use the atomic bomb against Japan? In light of the ambiguity of the available evidence the question defies an unequivocal answer. What can be said with certainty is that Truman, Stimson, Byrnes, and several others involved in the decision consciously considered two effects of a combat demonstration of the bomb's power: first, the impact of the atomic attack on Japan's leaders, who might be persuaded thereby to end the war; and second, the impact of that attack on the Soviet Union's leaders, who might then prove to be more cooperative. But if the assumption that the bomb might bring the war to a rapid conclusion was the principal motive for using the atomic bomb, the expectation that its use would also inhibit Soviet diplomatic ambitions clearly discouraged any inclination to question that assumption.

Policy makers were not alone in expecting a military demonstration of the bomb to have a salubrious effect on international affairs. James Conant, for example, believed that such a demonstration would further the prospects for international control. "President Conant has written me," Stimson informed the news commentator Raymond Swing in February 1947, "that one of the principal reasons he had for advising me that the bomb must be used was that that was the only way to awaken the world to the necessity of abolishing war altogether." And the director of the atomic-energy laboratory at the University of Chicago made the same point to Stimson in June 1945: "If the bomb were not used in the present war," Arthur Compton noted, "the world would have no adequate warning as to what was to be expected if war should break out again." Even Edward Teller, who has publicly decried the attack on Hiroshima and declared his early opposition to it, adopted a similar position in July 1945. "Our only hope is in getting the facts of our results before the people," he wrote to his colleague, Leo Szilard, who was circulating a petition among scientists opposing the bomb's use. "This might help to convince everybody that the next war would be fatal," Teller noted. "For this purpose actual combat use might even be the best thing."

Thus by the end of the war the most influential and widely accepted attitude toward the bomb was a logical extension of how the weapon was seen and valued earlier—as a potential instrument of diplomacy. Caught between the remnants of war and the uncertainties of peace, scientists as well as policy makers were trapped by the logic of their own unquestioned assumptions. By the summer of 1945 not only the conclusion of the war but the organization of an acceptable peace seemed to depend upon the success of the atomic attacks against Japan. When news of the successful atomic test of July 16 reached the president at the Potsdam Conference, he was visibly elated. Stimson noted that Truman "was tremendously pepped up by it and spoke to me of it again and again when I saw him. He said it gave him an entirely new feeling of confidence." The day after receiving the complete report of the test Truman altered his negotiating style. According to Churchill the president "got to the meeting after having read this report [and] he was a changed man. He told the Russians just where they got on and off and generally bossed the whole meeting." After the plenary session on July 24 Truman "casually mentioned to Stalin" that the United States had "a new weapon of unusual destructive force." Truman took this step in response to a recommendation by the Interim Committee, a group of political and scientific advisers organized by Stimson in May 1945 to advise the president on atomic-energy policy. But it is an unavoidable conclusion that what the President told the premier followed the letter of the recommendation rather than its spirit, which embodied the hope that an overture to Stalin would initiate the process toward international control. In less than three weeks the new weapon's destructive potential would be demonstrated to the world. Stalin would then be forced to reconsider his diplomatic goals. It is no wonder that upon learning of the raid against Hiroshima Truman exclaimed: "This is the greatest thing in history."

As Stimson had expected, as a colossal reality the bomb was very different. But had American diplomacy been altered by it? Those who conducted diplomacy became more confident, more certain that through the accomplishments of American science, technology, and industry the "new world" could be made into one better than the old. But just how the atomic bomb would be used to help accomplish this ideal remained unclear. Three months and one day after Hiroshima was bombed Bush wrote that the whole matter of international relations on atomic energy "is in a thoroughly chaotic condition." The wartime relationship between atomic-energy policy and diplomacy had been based upon the simple assumption that the Soviet government would surrender important geographical, political, and ideological objectives in exchange for the neutralization of the new weapon. As a result of policies based on this assumption American diplomacy and prestige suffered grievously: an opportunity to gauge the Soviet Union's response during the war to the international control of atomic energy was missed, and an atomic-energy policy for dealing with the Soviet government after the war was ignored. Instead of promoting American postwar aims, wartime atomic-energy policies made them more difficult to achieve. As a group of scientists at the University of Chicago's atomic-energy laboratory presciently warned the government in June 1945: "It may be difficult to persuade the world that a nation which was capable of secretly preparing and suddenly releasing a weapon as indiscriminate as the [German] rocket bomb and a million times more destructive, is to be trusted in its proclaimed desire of having such weapons abolished by international agreement." This reasoning, however, flowed from alternative assumptions formulated during the closing months of the war by scientists far removed from the wartime policy-making process. Hiroshima and Nagasaki, the culmination of that process, became the symbols of a new American barbarism, reinforcing charges, with dramatic circumstantial evidence, that the policies of the United States contributed to the origins of the cold war.

Part Three

THE ADMINISTRATIVE CONTEXT

Chapter 11 ADMINISTRATIVE AND PROCEDURAL CONSIDERATIONS

*The death of Franklin D. Roosevelt on April 12, 1945,
suddenly thrust Vice President Harry S. Truman into
an office for which he had scarcely been prepared at all.
In the following selection, KENNETH M. GLAZIER
(1948–   ) views the great decision in its
administrative-bureaucratic context. A graduate of
Harvard College and the Yale University School of Law,
Glazier is presently a practicing attorney. What elements
of this administrative context were especially significant
in formulating the 1945 decision?**

Late in the afternoon of April 12, 1945, Vice President Harry S. Truman
received a call asking him to report immediately to the White House. On his
arrival, he was quickly ushered into Mrs. Roosevelt's study and there told that
President Roosevelt was dead. The stunned Truman finally found his voice and
asked Mrs. Roosevelt if there was anything he could do. " 'Is there anything *we*
can do for *you*?' she asked. 'For you are the one in trouble now.' " Shortly thereafter Harry Truman took the oath of office and became the thirty-third President
of the United States.

At the time of Truman's accession to the presidency, the Manhattan Project
was nearing its goal of producing the world's first atomic bomb. But the bril-

*Kenneth M. Glazier, Jr., "The Decision to Use Atomic Weapons Against Hiroshima and
Nagasaki," *Public Policy*, XVIII, no. 4 (summer 1970), pp. 465–475, 512–516. Footnotes
omitted. By permission of *Public Policy*.

liant technical achievements of the Manhattan Project at this stage were not accompanied by any comparably impressive systematic consideration of the way in which the new weapon would be used. The one major policy decision up to this time—the shift of the target for the bombs from Germany to Japan—was made without any comprehensive discussion of the political implications of that shift. And no other policy guidelines were worked out for bomb use despite the fact that atomic weapons development by the American government was entering its fifth and climactic year.

The decision to use atomic weapons, made as it was during a period of presidential transition, reflected the influence of that transition. The over-all concern of this section, then, is the context in which Truman made his decision. The argument is not that Roosevelt would necessarily have made a different decision, but only that he would have made it under a completely different set of circumstances.

The most obvious effect of the change in presidents was that Harry Truman instead of Franklin Roosevelt made the final decision on the use of the atomic bomb. The obvious nature of the observation should not detract from its importance. Had Roosevelt lived long enough to make a decision about bomb use, he would have had behind him more than a decade of presidential experience and five years of thinking about atomic weapons. Truman, on the other hand, had been Vice President only eighty-two days and had seen Roosevelt only twice during this period. Furthermore, Truman did not learn of the purpose of the Manhattan Project until he became President. In short, the new President was utterly unable to bring to bear on the atomic decision the sort of executive experience and long-range thinking that his predecessor would have been able to muster.

No one was more conscious of his lack of experience than Truman himself: "Now the lightning had struck, and events beyond anyone's control had taken command. America had lost a great leader, and I was faced with a terrible responsibility." A decade of service in the U.S. Senate and a few months as a largely ignored vice president meant that while Truman knew a good deal about the federal government, he knew virtually nothing about being President. Stimson's diary indicates the Secretary of War's reaction to the new President:

> He made the impression on me of a man who is willing and anxious to learn and to do his best but who was necessarily laboring with the terrific handicap of coming into such an office where the threads of information were so multitudinous that only long previous familiarity could allow him to control them.

In other words, Truman had a great deal to learn about the mechanics of being President—staff organization, intragovernmental relations, information-sifting, and so forth—and so had less time than an experienced President to devote to long-range thinking about problems like atomic weapons.

Because of Truman's inexperience he relied on advisers and advisory committees to a much greater extent than had Roosevelt. Realizing that he still had much to learn about being President, Truman also showed a willingness to delegate authority which would have been out of place for his more experienced predecessor. Admiral Leahy, top military adviser to both Truman and Roosevelt, writes:

> His [Truman's] method of administration differed from that of Mr. Roosevelt in that after reaching a decision he delegated full responsibility for its execution to the department of the government charged by custom or law with that duty. . . .
>
> Mr. Roosevelt . . . differed from Mr. Truman in that he had little confidence in some of his executive departments, and therefore took detailed action with his own hands, assisted when necessary by some of his personal secretaries.

A second major consequence of the change in Presidents was the policy confusion which resulted from such an unexpected transition. Truman had no indication of Roosevelt's plans for the use of the atomic bomb. Furthermore, Roosevelt's failure to discuss his intentions with Stimson or any other top advisers meant that Truman lacked even informal information about Roosevelt's plans. Roosevelt had undoubtedly thought about the matter, but whatever conclusions he reached were buried with him.

Thus Truman came into office with no guidelines from his predecessor about what he should do with the bomb. In one sense, Truman was therefore fortunate in that he was free to make any decision without being constrained by policies he had not made. But in another sense he was trapped by the very lack of established policy. Roosevelt, as the initiator and prime mover behind the atomic bomb project, would have been in a much better position to decide for no use or limited use of the bomb than Truman, who arrived on the atomic scene at the last moment. Stimson describes the crucial difference in the political "strength" of the two Presidents: "Roosevelt had such immense prestige politically arising from his four successful campaigns for President that he carried a weight with the Congress and with general politicians of the country which Truman of course could not possibly have." Truman, therefore, would have had a much more difficult time than Roosevelt in justifying the atomic bomb effort had he decided not to use the bomb at all. In short, Truman was not as free to make *any* decision on use of the bomb as the lack of inherited policy might suggest.

A third consequence of the confusion that to some extent always surrounds a transfer of presidential power was the shifting degree of influence upon the President wielded by various members of the government. Roosevelt's top advisers would not necessarily remain as Truman's top advisers, and the early months of the Truman administration saw government leaders trying to maintain or establish influence with the new President. This period of jockeying for presidential approval took place at precisely the time that the decision was being made on what to do with the atomic bomb.

A good illustration of the shifts in the influence of presidential advisers which occurred during this period concerns Secretary of War Henry L. Stimson. Stimson's governmental career had spanned forty years and included service as Taft's Secretary of War and Hoover's Secretary of State. Although he was a prominent Republican he agreed to join Roosevelt's cabinet in 1940 as Secretary of War. Roosevelt soon gave Stimson full authority and responsibility for the Manhattan Project and made Stimson his chief adviser on atomic matters. Truman originally maintained that relationship, but after a few months the influence of the seventy-eight-year-old Stimson had declined precipitously. By July, 1945, Truman's chief adviser on the bomb was his new Secretary of State, James F. Byrnes; Stimson was so far from being influential that he had to ask for an invitation to attend the important Potsdam Conference of late July. The effect of Stimson's declining influence will be dealt with later; the important point here is that the decision on the use of the bomb was made at a time when various officials were involved in a struggle for presidential favor. The lines of influence were not clearly drawn, and the shifting influence of presidential advisers added a chaotic note to the already confused decision-making process.

The decision to drop the atomic bomb, therefore, must be understood in terms of a new President trying to run a nation at the same time that he was learning *how* to run it; of an almost total lack of established policy regarding possible uses of atomic weapons; and of the constant shifting of influence among old and new presidential advisers.

Truman's first act as President was to call a brief cabinet meeting at which, according to Stimson, "The new President on the whole made a pleasant impression but it was very clear that he knew very little of the task into which he was stepping. . . ." Truman recalls that after the meeting Stimson told him

> . . . that he wanted me to know about an immense project that was under way—a project looking to the development of a new explosive of almost unbelievable destructive power. That was all he felt free to say at the time, and his statement left me puzzled. It was the first bit of information that had come to me about the atomic bomb, but he gave me no details.

It seems incredible that the Vice President had not been informed of the purpose of the Manhattan Project. Vice President Wallace had been told, but apparently no one had got around to telling Truman.

The best indication of the degree to which the Manhattan Project was shrouded in secrecy even at the highest levels of government is the fact that Stimson felt reluctant to tell Truman the full story of the atomic bomb even after Truman had been sworn in as President. A certain amount of secrecy about the project was necessary to prevent important technical secrets from falling into the hands of the Germans or the Russians, but the secrecy in question involved refraining from even mentioning the existence of the atomic effort. As James F. Byrnes, who learned of the bomb in 1943, put it, "No one ever talked about it [the bomb] unless it was absolutely necessary." Stimson notes the same phenomenon, saying, "On grounds of secrecy the bomb was never mentioned except when absolutely necessary."

A meeting on the first full day of Truman's presidency indicates how narrowly "absolute necessity" was defined as a cause for discussion of the atomic bomb. On April 13, Truman called together his top military advisers to discuss the military situation with regard to Germany and Japan. Although everyone in the room knew of the Manhattan Project, it was never mentioned in the course of the discussion. Thus the military gave Truman its estimates of the state of the war without ever discussing the effect that atomic weapons might have on that war. What Admiral Leahy called "the best kept secret of the entire war" was so well kept that Truman as Vice President was not informed of the project, that the new President was not immediately given all the details he wanted, and that full discussion of the use of the new weapon did not take place even among those who knew about it.

The secrecy which surrounded the Manhattan Project severely limited President Truman's possible sources of advice from outside the regular governmental framework. One group which might have provided original policy suggestions and reviewed official thinking on bomb use was the *ad hoc* committee appointed by Truman to advise him on atomic matters. Known as the Interim Committee, it was composed of five government officials (including Stimson and James Byrnes, soon to be Secretary of State) and three scientists then administering government projects. Their discussions focused on the question of *how* rather than *whether* to use the bomb, since some use of atomic weapons was apparently a foregone conclusion. The presence of Byrnes and Stimson on the Committee ensured that its efforts would produce more of a reaffirmation than a review of official thinking, and therefore the Committee's recommendation that the bomb be used without warning against a populated target in Japan simply confirmed official attitudes on bomb use. Stimson recalls, "The conclusions of the committee were similar to my own, although I reached mine independently." A better illustration of the influence of the Committee concerns its recommendation that the Soviets be told of the atomic bomb before its use against Japan. This recommendation ran counter to official thinking and was consequently ignored. Thus the Interim Committee had little impact beyond the reinforcement of existing governmental attitudes.

The second "outside" group—or rather collection of individuals—to offer

Truman advice about the use of the bomb was composed of those scientists working on the Manhattan Project who were aware of the purpose of their labors. But the scientists had little information on what policy decisions were being made and were systematically discouraged from considering the political implications of their work. Hence the few efforts by scientists at influencing policy had little impact. For example, when one Chicago atomic scientist drew up a petition calling for full disclosure of American surrender terms for Japan before the use of atomic weapons, General Groves (head of the Manhattan Project) halted its circulation by the simple expedient of having it declared classified and then refusing to provide the military guard required for circulation of all classified material. Another group of scientists led by James Franck drew up a report calling for a demonstration of the bomb's power before combat use. Although the Franck Report was considered by a subgroup of the Interim Committee, the actual text was never dealt with, and the subgroup had little chance of influencing policy anyway. In short, the Interim Committee and the atomic scientists were largely overlooked as potential sources of valid criticism and new ideas, thereby limiting consideration of what to do with the bomb to a tiny circle of top governmental officials.

Although Truman was interested in the Manhattan Project, he made little effort to get a detailed understanding of the Project or to exert his influence over it. At the beginning of May, Stimson and Groves brought Truman a twenty-four-page report on the bomb. "I don't like to read long reports," the President told them. "Your present course is sound. Carry on as you are doing now." Either Truman was too busy to consider the report or, as his answer suggests, he had the sort of absolute faith in his subordinates that subordinates so much admire.

Truman's lack of concern over the administration of the Manhattan Project did not mean that he failed to appreciate the significance of atomic weapons. On hearing of the success of the atomic bomb at Hiroshima, Truman said, "This is the greatest thing in history." He saw the project to build the bomb as "the greatest achievement of organized science in history."

Truman recognized the importance of atomic weapons but was strangely untroubled by the implications of their military use. For Truman, the decision to use atomic energy for destructive purposes "was not any decision you had to worry about. It was just the same as getting a bigger gun than the other fellow had to win a war and that's what it was used for. Nothing else but an artillery weapon." It seems incongruous that the "artillery weapon" Truman speaks of was also "the greatest thing in history."

Truman has stated clearly his view of the nature of the questions raised by the "bigger gun" developed by the Manhattan Project: "Let there be no mistake about it. I regarded the bomb as a military weapon and *never had any doubt that it should be used*" (italics added). For Truman, then, the question was not *whether* but *how* the bomb should be used.

Truman's perception of the bomb as a military weapon makes it reasonable to suppose that the military would play a major role in deciding on its use. But such does not seem to have been the case. Although the Joint Chiefs of Staff worked closely with both Roosevelt and Truman on problems of war strategy, and the four individual Chiefs all had been informed of the bomb project, the Joint Chiefs never discussed the atomic bomb at any of their meetings prior to its use. Not only were the Joint Chiefs left out of the discussion of what to do with the new military weapon, but key military commanders were informed of the existence of the bomb only at the last possible moment. For example, General Douglas MacArthur, Supreme Commander of the Allied Forces in the Pacific, was told about the atomic bomb only five days before it was dropped on Hiroshima. Had bad weather not delayed the first bombing, MacArthur might have learned of the bomb only on the day that it was dropped. Stimson notes one consequence of Truman's failure to consult the military on the use of atomic weapons: "The strategic plans of our armed forces for the defeat of Japan, as they stood in July [1945], had been prepared without reliance upon the atomic bomb, which had not yet been tested in New Mexico."

Truman's explanation for the use of the new military weapon was, not surprisingly, a military one: "It was a question of saving hundreds of thousands of American lives." Secretary of State Byrnes felt that "by bringing the war to an end, the atomic bomb saved the lives of thousands of American boys." Secretary of War Stimson used the same justification: "The destruction of Hiroshima and Nagasaki put an end to the Japanese war. . . . It ended the ghastly specter of a clash of great land armies."

At the time the bomb was used, the next major Allied operation planned against Japan was an invasion of Kyushu scheduled for November 1, 1945. When Truman, Byrnes, and Stimson argued that the bombs were used to save thousands of American lives they apparently meant that using the bombs made an invasion of the Japanese home islands unnecessary. Since MacArthur's forces had suffered an average of fewer than 1,000 deaths per month since March 1944, elimination of the need for the Kyushu invasion was the only way such a large number of lives could have been saved. The official explanation for use of atomic weapons may therefore be rephrased to say that the bomb was used to make an invasion of Japan unnecessary and thereby save thousands of American lives.

But would an invasion have been necessary to defeat Japan without the use of atomic weapons? Many military leaders *at that time*, including three of the four Joint Chiefs of Staff, felt that an invasion would *not be necessary*. Admiral King stated: "It was the belief of the Navy that Japan could and should be defeated without an invasion of the home islands"; Admiral Leahy and other naval officers agreed. Major General LeMay said: "Most of us in the Army Air Forces had been convinced for a long time that it would be possible to defeat the Japanese without invading their home islands"; Air Force Generals Arnold and Twining expressed similar views. Army Chief of Staff George C. Marshall did not say that the invasion would be unnecessary, but did oppose use of the atomic bomb without prior warning to the Japanese. Although no one could predict with absolute certainty whether an invasion was necessary, many or most military leaders at the time felt that an invasion would not be needed. The Truman-Byrnes-Stimson explanation that use of the bomb obviated the need for an invasion therefore rests on a questionable assumption about the necessity for that invasion.

Two general conclusions may be reached about the context in which President Truman made the decision on use of atomic weapons. First, the decision was made in a time of presidential transition and was significantly affected by that situation. Truman lacked both presidential experience and familiarity with the Manhattan Project, and delegated much more authority than had his more experienced predecessor. The new President inherited no guidelines for use of the bomb, but Truman's political weakness limited the range of options open to him on bomb use. Finally, the shifting influence of presidential advisers caused a lack of continuity in the advice the President received, and further complicated the already complex decision-making process.

A second conclusion concerns, in a more general way, the manner in which the President was exposed to advice from other members of the government, both civilian and military. The tremendous secrecy of the project meant that very few officials knew of it, and hence the number of officials who could give Truman advice on bomb use was severely limited. Furthermore, the few officials who did know of the bomb subscribed to the informal rule that discussion of the bomb would take place only when "absolutely necessary." Therefore Truman's advisers reached their conclusions after individual deliberation rather than after discussion among the various officials concerned. On atomic matters, then, civilian advice was limited in scope and value, while military advice was either not solicited or was ignored.

The decision to use atomic bombs against Hiroshima and Nagasaki presents, at best, an unsettling picture of routine consideration of "the greatest thing in history." Roosevelt's failure to consider systematically the implications of atomic weapons left his successor with little time and less background to decide on their use. Truman relied heavily on the advice of Byrnes and to a lesser extent Stimson, but never sought the advice of military leaders on bomb use and ignored the suggestions made by the only knowledgeable "outside" group—the atomic scientists. The Interim Committee, lacking both detachment from official views and adequate information, could only reinforce current government thinking or be ignored. The two policy alternatives to the bomb—Russian entry and clarification of surrender terms—were never fully explored. Finally, the politically important operational decisions were delegated to military commanders who lacked perspective on the proper role of the bomb as well as any qualifications for dealing with the political issues involved. The decision to use atomic weapons was made, therefore, without any systematic consideration of either the political implications or the alternatives to that decision.

However, the question of *why* the bombs were dropped remains. Neither the conventional wisdom of Truman and his colleagues nor the revisionist interpretation adequately explains the reasons behind the decision.

Truman, Byrnes, and Stimson explained the use of the bomb in terms of military necessity: The atomic attacks would obviate the need for a bloody invasion of Japan. But their explanation is not convincing on several counts. First, by this explanation, the necessity for bomb use hinged on the necessity for an invasion and, as all three leaders were undoubtedly aware, the need for an invasion was being seriously questioned by the military commanders concerned. Secondly, justification for bomb use on military grounds is invariably explained in terms of saving "thousands" or "hundreds of thousands" of American lives by the elimination of any need for an invasion. But if desire to avoid an invasion necessitated use of atomic weapons, what necessitated use of those weapons at the earliest possible moment? The invasion was not due until November, yet the bombs were dropped in early August. The atomic bomb could not have saved "thousands" of lives, since in August thousands of lives were not in jeopardy. Finally, if Truman and his advisers were primarily motivated by desire to save American lives, why were the alternative methods of bringing an early Japanese surrender—Russian entry or clarification of surrender terms—not given more thorough consideration? Military necessity, then, is an unconvincing explanation because the invasion was not due for several months, and because such an explanation fails to account for either the haste of the bombings or the lack of consideration of the policy alternatives.

The revisionist interpretation of bomb use is equally unconvincing. [William Appleman] Williams writes: "The United States dropped the bomb to end the war against Japan and thereby stop the Russians in Asia, and to give them sober pause in eastern Europe." P.M.S. Blackett concludes that "the dropping of the atomic bombs were not so much the last military act of the second World War, as the first major operation in the cold diplomatic war with Russia. . . ." Gar Alperovitz suggests that besides an American desire for a quick end to the war, the overriding consideration prompting bomb use was that "A combat demonstration was needed to convince the Russians to accept the American plan for a stable peace." By the revisionist interpretation, then, Truman's "purely military decision" was a cynical exercise in *Realpolitik*: 100,000 Japanese were incinerated to impress the Russians with the power of the new weapon. But such an explanation accounts for the bombing of Hiroshima and Nagasaki only if a *combat* demonstration was the only way to impress the Russians. Truman saw atomic weapons as "the greatest thing in history" before he received any details of the Hiroshima attack, and perhaps Stalin could have been expected to be equally perceptive; Soviet scientists were not so backward that they could not inform their leaders of the awesome destructive power of nuclear fission. But the major flaw in the revisionist argument lies in the fact that the chaotic early months of the Truman presidency show no evidence at all of long-range thinking about the political effects of atomic weapons. Rather, the one thread which runs throughout the entire history of the Manhattan Project is the extent to which political considerations were consistently separated from "atomic" issues and then ignored.

A third and somewhat more plausible explanation for bomb use is suggested by Truman himself: "Let there be no mistake about it. I regarded the bomb as a military weapon and never had any doubt that it should be used." In a sense, the decision was not "military" because military advice was never solicited and many military factors were ignored. But Truman's perception of the bomb as "a military weapon" was crucial since it meant that bomb use "was not any decision you had to worry about." Extensive civilian intervention in routine military procedures was simply not appropriate if in fact the bomb was just "an artillery weapon."

Truman was not alone in his belief that combat use of atomic weapons was an obvious consequence of their development. Churchill recalls, "The historic fact remains, and must be judged in the after time, that the decision whether or not to use the atomic bomb to compel the surrender of Japan was never even an issue." Stimson agrees, saying, "At no time, from 1941 to 1945, did I ever hear it suggested by the President, or by any other responsible member of the government, that atomic energy should not be used in the war." Therefore, as Oppenheimer suggests, "The decision was implicit in the project."

Use of the atomic bombs, then, was assumed rather than decided. Such an interpretation accounts for many of the otherwise inexplicable aspects of the decision. Roosevelt and Truman did not *need* to consider the political implications of a weapon that was going to be used anyway, and low-level operational decisions were logical once the political implications had been disregarded. Advice from military leaders or the Interim Committee on *how* the bomb should be used lost its significance if the decision on full military use had already been made. The suggestions of the atomic scientists on bomb use were based on humanitarian and political considerations and so were seen as irrelevant to the "purely military decision." The haste with which the weapon was dropped was natural if use of the bomb had never been questioned since the Army Air Force and Manhattan Project officials had an interest in seeing that the bombs were dropped before the end of the war. Alternative methods of ending the war were predictably overlooked if bomb use was assumed in the first place. Finally, the lack of systematic decision-making procedure and Truman's failure to make any recorded formal decision is explained if, in fact, there was no decision to make.

Secretary of War Stimson has written:

In this last great action of the Second World War we were given final proof that war is death. War in the twentieth century has grown steadily more barbarous, more destructive, more debased in all its aspects. Now, with the release of atomic energy, man's ability to destroy himself is very nearly complete.

America's use of atomic weapons clearly demonstrated the cataclysmic potential of nuclear war. Somewhat less clear is the question of the effect of bomb use in 1945 on the ultimate likelihood of man's self-destruction. Perhaps the carnage at Hiroshima and Nagasaki has served as a vivid example of the destructive capacity of atomic bombs and hence has made their further use less likely. But the routine manner in which the leaders of a peace-loving democracy "assumed" the decision to use atomic weapons against an already defeated enemy raises the possibility that some future leader may feel, as Truman did, that use of nuclear weapons is "not any decision you had to worry about."

Part Four

THE MORAL DIMENSIONS

Chapter 12 CHANGING ETHICS IN THE CRUCIBLE OF WAR

*The moral aspects of the dropping of the atomic
bomb have been a major concern since 1945.*
ROBERT C. BATCHELDER *(1926–   ), a
clergyman trained at Yale University, has written a
book-length study of the ethical implications of the
use of the bomb. In* The Irreversible Decision,
1939–1950 *(1962) he investigates the background of the
development of atomic energy and focuses
particularly on the questions of shortening the war
and the moral implications of different possible
courses of action. A good part of the discussion uses
as a frame of reference the well-developed positions
of Roman Catholic theology. What long-term
significance should be attached to ethical changes that
occurred in "the crucible of war"?**

The decision to use the atomic bomb took place within a historical situation with a peculiar political-military configuration. This context shaped the way in which policymakers thought about the bomb and its relation to the war, and heavily influenced the outcome of the decision itself. In particular, the gradual acceptance of obliteration bombing as a military necessity, until the mass-bombing of Japanese cities was regarded as standard procedure, largely determined that the atomic bomb—once it was decided to use it—would be dropped on the center of a large city, despite the professed concern of our leaders to avoid the killing of undefended civilians.

This particular decision took place within a larger context, a significant characteristic of which was the tendency on the part of American leaders (both

*Robert C. Batchelder, *The Irreversible Decision, 1939–1950* (Boston: Houghton Mifflin Company, 1962), pp. 211–222. Reprinted by permission. Footnotes omitted (except for footnote 1).

military and civilian) to think of the war in purely military rather than in political terms. As a result, the goal of the war was military victory; the way to victory was the military defeat of the enemy armed forces; since the major decisions to be made were of a military character, policy formation was delegated to military men. The result was a whole series of decisions: to treat the atomic bomb as a bigger and better military weapon, to exclude civilian leaders from the highest war councils of the nation, to accept the judgment of generals that obliteration bombing was necessary for victory, to try a political method to end the war only as an afterthought, to ignore vital intelligence because it did not indicate that the enemy was ready to accept total surrender, to let a military commander decide on purely tactical grounds how much time the Japanese government should have to decide to surrender after the first atomic bomb—a series of decisions which tended to mold events in such a way that the atomic bomb would finally be used in a total and unrestrained military manner. Any one of these decisions, had the emphasis lain on the political rather than on the military way of thinking, *might* have precluded or tempered our use of the atomic bomb; the cumulative effect of making all these decisions on political rather than on military grounds could well have resulted in termination of the war by diplomatic means, and prevented the destruction of Hiroshima and Nagasaki.

Focusing more narrowly upon the specific decision to drop the atomic bomb— and taking as given the political failure and the war situation as it stood in mid-1945—one cannot escape the conclusion that the atomic bombing of Hiroshima and Nagasaki caused less loss of life (and general human suffering and chaos) than would have come about had the new weapon been withheld and the war been allowed to continue by conventional means, with or without invasion of the Japanese home islands. Within this narrow context Truman and Stimson were right: the atomic bomb did cut short the war and save thousands of lives. Nevertheless, even within the situation as it had developed by August 1945, alternatives were still open—such as a demonstration of the atomic bomb against a large military installation in Japan, followed by a stern warning— which probably would have brought about Japan's surrender without the great toll of civilian lives resulting from atomic attacks upon two large cities.

. . . Certain of the cherished ethical principles held by scientists were transformed under the impact of the threat posed to the civilized world by Hitler's emerging power. Something of the same transformation was wrought in the ethical principles of United States leaders, both military and political, during World War II. Our Air Force had entered the war proud of its Norden bomb-sight, and was committed to the superior morality and military effectiveness of daylight precision bombing of purely military objectives. Our government was on record as opposed, on humane grounds, to the bombing of civilian areas. The transformation both of practice and of official justification [developed] under the demands of "military necessity. . . ." Churchmen proved only slightly more resistant than political leaders to this erosion of moral principles during war-time. . . .

Two fundamental ways of judging the morality of the use of the atomic bomb appeared during 1945 and 1946. The first was (in the broadest sense) utilitarian; the primary concern of those using this approach was the consequences of the act in question. Will the war be shortened? How many lives will be lost? Will long-term consequences be good or evil? The method is calculative: good and evil consequences are balanced one against the other, and the right act is that which produces the most good—or, at any rate, the least evil. America's leaders used this method in determining to drop the atomic bomb on Japan. It was the choice, made with awareness of its inherent horror, of the lesser evil. Yet the results produced by this method appalled many who were disposed to follow it. Once the result was faced for what it was—the deliberate bombing of two cities, resulting in death to more than a hundred thousand, and agonizing injury to as many more—many felt that the intrinsic character of the act in itself, completely apart from any consequences stemming from it, was so clearly immoral that any ethical system justifying such an act must be bankrupt. It is impossible to predict accurately the consequences of any major decision, or to calculate good and evil results numerically. This impossibility, together with the lack of any objective moral standard by which to judge the quality of an act, means in the end that a purely calculative ethical theory will permit the plausible justification of almost any atrocity, no matter how repugnant to man's innate sense of decency.

The second basic ethical approach to the question of the atomic bombing of Japan was formalistic: it was concerned with the rightness or wrongness of the act in itself. What determines the rightness or wrongness of an act is not its consequences but its inherent quality. If the act conforms to an objective moral standard, it is permissible; if not, it is forbidden or condemned. The standard to be applied in the case of Hiroshima may be summed up in the commandment "Thou shalt not attack noncombatants directly." If an act has the form of a direct and deliberate attack upon noncombatants—no matter how many or how few, no matter what the consequences—it is a violation of the commandment and therefore wrong.[1]

For example, had the atomic bomb been withheld from use, Hiroshima might have been attacked the same week by 500 B-29's dropping incendiaries;

[1]As derived from Christian ethical theory, the proscription of direct military attack upon noncombatants is not an external limitation imposed upon a supposed right of self-defense. Rather, it roots in Christian love for neighbor which (1) imposes *as a duty* the physical restraint of an aggressor *for the sake of preventing him from harming the innocent*, and (2) at the same time prohibits direct attack upon noncombatants and the fabric of civilian life—because protection of these is the very reason for restraint of the aggressor in the first place.

the center of the city could have been burned to the ground, with the loss of 10,000 or 20,000 civilian lives. For Roman Catholic moral theory, such an incendiary raid and the atomic bombing of Hiroshima would be on the same level of immorality. Both would equally be condemned as direct and indiscriminate attacks upon the innocent.

It may be noted, however, that despite its clarity of moral theory the Roman Catholic Church probably would not have specifically condemned such an incendiary raid upon Hiroshima in the actual situation existing in August 1945. In spite of a few lonely voices like that of Father Ford, and the often expressed concern of the Pope that aerial warfare respect the immunity of noncombatants, the fire raids had been going on regularly since March. During this time the American Catholic hierarchy had taken no forthright and united stand in opposition to mass-bombing (nor had the Protestant churches). The leading American Jesuit theologian, John Courtney Murray, later commented on the silence of the Roman Catholic Church regarding the incendiary mass-bombing attacks of World War II:

> Nor was any substantial effort made [by Catholic publicists or even bishops] to clarify by moral judgment the thickening mood of savage violence that made possible the atrocities of Hiroshima and Nagasaki. I think it is true to say that the traditional doctrine was irrelevant during World War II. This is no argument against the traditional doctrine. . . . But there is place for an indictment of all of us who failed to make the traditional doctrine relevant.

Despite the immediate clarity of moral judgment provided by the formalistic approach to ethics, it is not devoid of dilemmas. In the example just cited it is too simple, in that it would leave out of consideration the consequences flowing from the two raids. An incendiary raid on Hiroshima, like those on dozens of other Japanese cities during the summer of 1945, would have advanced the end of the war somewhat, but only imperceptibly. In contrast, the atomic raid, as we have seen, was the decisive factor that brought the war to a halt within eight days. Although in one dimension (that of form) the two raids are morally equivalent, in another dimension (that of consequences) one is morally much better than the other. To be concerned only for form and to ignore consequences is to miss much of ethical significance; for certainly it was better on moral grounds that the killing and the disruption of Japanese civil life should stop than that it should continue.

Again, let it be assumed, for the sake of argument, that Truman's estimate of the alternatives before him was accurate: it was a choice between dropping the atomic bomb on Hiroshima and proceeding with the invasion of Japan. A formalist would be compelled to judge the atomic bombing of Hiroshima as impermissible, and therefore to recommend the invasion, which would be justifiable since it would proceed by conventional and discriminate attack on the military forces of the enemy. Having accepted as justifiable the killing of 317,000 Japanese soldiers in the Philippines campaign, and the killing of 107,000 of the total garrison of 120,000 on Okinawa, the Roman Catholic position would now forbid the killing of 110,000 civilians with the atomic bomb but condone a conventional invasion even though the preliminaries and the invasion itself took the lives of ten times that number of Japanese and Allied soldiers in Manchuria, China, and the Japanese home islands. In addition, it would reluctantly "permit" the death of many civilians and the destruction of many cities from battle causes, the freezing and starvation of refugee children during the approaching winter, and the complete breakdown and disruption of the fabric of Japanese civil life—provided only that all these evils were unintended and unavoidable effects of the direct attack of the invaders upon the defenders.

It must parenthetically be stated that Roman Catholic moral theology does specify that an act right in itself (such as an attack upon enemy armed forces in a just war) is not permissible if its unintended and indirect evil consequences are of such great magnitude as to be disproportionate to the good produced by the act. Yet the principle of disproportionate evil was not applied to the invasion of Germany, which resulted in just such death, suffering, and disruption of civil life; and there is no reaon to believe that it would have been the basis of Catholic condemnation of the invasion of Japan (provided that generals considered invasion a military necessity).

In contrast to a moral theory that would condone the greater evil consequences, provided only that they be produced by "legitimate" means, one cannot help feeling a certain respect for the elemental morality of Truman and Stimson in their determination to avoid the massive evil of invasion if humanly possible. They realistically surveyed the situation confronting them, estimated (probably correctly) that had they refrained from using the atomic bomb the war would have continued without much change in basic character—and then resolutely chose what appeared to them to be the lesser evil, regardless of the fine points of ethical theory.

It would appear, then, that just as a purely calculative approach to ethics has no inner principle to prevent the final bankrupty of justifying an atrocity as "the lesser evil," so an ethical approach concerned exclusively with conformity to laws or norms, to the neglect of consequences, has its own peculiar form of bankruptcy. To forbid an atomic attack upon a city because of its indiscriminateness but complacently to recommend an invasion which, by "legitimate" means, would produce massive evil, death, and suffering borders on hypocrisy, or at least callousness.

The conflict between the calculative and formalistic approaches to the bombing of Hiroshima can be focused in a single question: is it right to perform an inherently immoral act in order to achieve a good end and avoid a massive evil?

For the formalists the answer is easy—no, it is never permissible to do evil as a means to a good end. Considered in the abstract the problem is simple. But in a particular historical context the answer is not so simple.

The bare act of dropping an atomic bomb upon a city—considered in itself alone—is clearly immoral because it constitutes a direct attack upon noncombatants. Yet it is inconsistent to single out for condemnation the act of dropping an atomic bomb and at the same time implicitly to recommend continuation of a war that one knows will include direct attack upon noncombatants with incendiary bombs. In the midst of a historical context already compromised by past and present mass bombing of civilians, which would undoubtedly have continued in the future, can Truman justly be condemned for authorizing an atomic attack (no more and no less immoral than the fire raids) which promised to put an end to the whole badly compromised situation?

The formal nature of the act in itself apart from its consequences, and the calculation of greater good and lesser evil—concern with either one of these to the exclusion of the other leads only to corruption. Ethical theory that will stand the stress of the massive evils inherent in war must include *both* a calculation of consequences *and* a concern for the intrinsic morality of the act. Paul Ramsey, a Protestant moralist, has recently suggested that Roman Catholic moral theory (or, rather, the traditional *Christian* moral theory) at its best combines both. Calculation of probable consequences and the choosing of the greater good and the lesser evil are essential, but properly come only *after* determination of the intrinsic morality of the act itself.

Thus in the case of bringing about the surrender of Japan in 1945: dropping the atomic bomb on a city would be ruled out at the start because of its violation of the immunity of civilians from direct attack. Among the remaining legitimate alternatives, a calculation of probable consequences would show that a diplomatic offensive, or even a military demonstration with the A-bomb, was morally better than invasion which, because of the enormous evil it would produce, could be considered only as a last resort,

The elimination at the outset of certain possible alternatives as inherently immoral does not remove the need for calculation of consequences among the remaining legitimate alternatives. It may stimulate more creative calculation and imaginative searching for a course of action which is both effective and morally acceptable. A firm policy decision not to indulge in mass fire-bombing of Japanese cities would probably have resulted in an early and systematic attack upon the extremely vulnerable Japanese railroad network—a course that the United States Strategic Bombing Survey suggests would have crippled Japan's entire war industry sooner and more effectively than did the incendiary raids. It might also have led to an earlier re-examination of our policies regarding unconditional surrender and the status of the Emperor, and a careful use of diplomatic and political tools which, in the actual event, were never tried. Closing the door to immoral means may provide the opportunity for more creative use of legitimate means.

The failure of moral theory in those who made the decision to drop the atomic bomb was not that they failed to replace their dominant concern for "calculating the lesser evil" with a one-sided concern for the ethical principle of "noncombatant immunity, regardless of consequences." The failure lay in their inability to maintain simultaneously *both* a commitment to ethical principle *and* a realistic calculation of consequences in some such fashion as that suggested here. The tension between the two having been lost in the acceptance of obliteration bombing in March of 1945, it proved to be impossible to reestablish the tension in August.

While it is important to recognize the ethical failures in the making of a particular crucial decision, it is even more important to be aware of the ethical failures implicit in the unquestioned assumptions about the nature of war that were shared in 1945 by American leaders and people alike. The assumptions that war is primarily a military matter, that war is now total, that the purpose of fighting a war is to achieve military victory, and that war can end in victory only if the enemy is forced to surrender unconditionally—these came to be accepted as self-evident and unquestionable truths by the vast majority of the American people, despite the fact that such axioms stand in direct contradiction to the main stream of Christian ethical thought about war. Such general assumptions about modern war were at least as important—if not more so—in the shaping of the decision to drop the atomic bomb as were the ethical considerations consciously brought to bear upon that particular choice. What is required for the future is not only that proper ethical thinking be applied to the making of each particular policy decision affecting nuclear weapons. It is even more important that our whole style of thinking about war be such that these particular decisions are not—as in 1945—morally compromised before they are reached.

Chapter 13 THE "DECLINE TO BARBARISM"

The next essay by DWIGHT MACDONALD *(1906–   ), written in the fall of 1945, immediately after the dropping of the bombs, expresses vividly the moral revulsion to this act that some Americans felt—the response of the critical observer who sees how far short of traditional ideals his country has fallen. A social critic and essayist, Macdonald writes regularly for* The New Yorker *and is author of* Fascism and the American Scene *(1938);* Memoirs of a Revolutionist *(1957);* Against the American Grain *(1962), a look at American mass culture;* Dwight Macdonald on Movies *(1969); and* Politics Past *(1970).* *

At 9:15 on the morning of August 6, 1945, an American plane dropped a single bomb on the Japanese city of Hiroshima. Exploding with the force of 20,000 tons of TNT, The Bomb destroyed in a twinkling two-thirds of the city, including, presumably, most of the 343,000 human beings who lived there.[1] No warning was given. This atrocious action places "us," the defenders of civilization, on a moral level with "them," the beasts of Maidanek. And "we," the American people, are just as much and as little responsible for this horror as "they," the German people.

*This essay first appeared in *Politics*, II (August-September, 1945), 225, 257–260, reprinted, in *Memoirs of a Revolutionist* (New York, 1957). Copyright © 1957 by Dwight Macdonald. Reprinted by permission of the author.

[1]The death toll at Hiroshima was first estimated by the Japanese govenment at 71,379; the figure, including subsequent deaths arising from the bombing, was later reduced to 60,175. – *Ed.*

So much is obvious. But more must be said. For the atomic bomb renders anticlimactical even the ending of the greatest war in history. *(1) The concepts, "war" and "progress," are now obsolete.* Both suggest human aspirations, emotions, aims, consciousness. "The greatest achievement of organized science in history," said President Truman after the Hiroshima catastrophe—which it probably was, and so much the worse for organized science. *(2) The futility of modern warfare should now be clear.* Must we not now conclude, with Simone Weil, that the technical aspect of war today is the evil, regardless of political factors? Can one imagine that The Bomb could ever be used "in a good cause"? Do not such means instantly, of themselves, corrupt *any* cause? *(3) The Bomb is the natural product of the kind of society we have created.* It is as easy, normal and unforced an expression of the American Way of Life as electric iceboxes, banana splits, and hydromatic-drive automobiles. We do not dream of a world in which atomic fission will be "harnessed to constructive ends." The new energy will be at the service of the rulers; it will change their strength but not their aims. The underlying populations should regard this new source of energy with lively interest—the interest of victims. *(4) Those who wield such destructive power are outcasts from humanity.* They may be gods, they may be brutes, but they are not men. *(5) We must "get" the national State before it "gets" us.* Every individual who wants to save his humanity—and indeed his skin—had better begin thinking "dangerous thoughts" about sabotage, resistance, rebellion, and the fraternity of all men everywhere. The mental attitude known as "negativism" is a good start.

What first appalled us was its blast. "TNT is barely twice as strong as black powder was six centuries ago. World War II developed explosives up to 60% more powerful than TNT. The atomic bomb is more than 12,000 times as strong as the best improvement on TNT. One hundred and twenty-three planes, each bearing a single atomic bomb, would carry as much destructive power as all the bombs (2,453,595 tons) dropped by the Allies on Europe during the war" (*Time*, August 20, 1945).

It has slowly become evident, however, that the real horror of The Bomb is not blast but radioactivity. Splitting the atom sets free all kinds of radioactive substances, whose power is suggested by the fact that at the Hanford bomb plant, the water used for cooling the "pile" (the structure of uranium and other substances whose atomic interaction produces the explosive) carried off enough radiation to "heat the Columbia River appreciably." *Time* added: "Even the wind blowing over the chemical plant picked up another load of peril, for the stacks gave off a radioactive gas." And Smyth notes: "The fission products produced in one day's run of a 100,000-kilowatt chain-reacting pile of uranium might be sufficient to make a large area uninhabitable."

There is thus no question as to the potential horror of The Bomb's radio-activity. The two bombs actually used were apparently designed as explosive and not gas bombs, perhaps from humanitarian considerations, perhaps to protect the American troops who will later have to occupy Japan. But intentions are one thing, results another. So feared was radioactivity at Hanford that the most elaborate precautions were taken in the way of shields, clothes, etc. No such precautions were taken, obviously, on behalf of the inhabitants of Hiroshima; the plane dropped its cargo of half-understood poisons and sped away. What happened? The very sensitivity of the army and the scientists on the subject is ominous. When one of the lesser experts who had worked on the bomb, a Dr. Harold Jacobson of New York, stated publicly that Hiroshima would be "uninhabitable" for seventy years, he was at once questioned by FBI agents, after which, "ill and upset," he issued another statement emphasizing that this was merely his own personal opinion, and that his colleagues disagreed with him.

The point is that none of those who produced and employed this monstrosity really knew just how deadly or prolonged these radioactive poisons would be. Which did not prevent them from completing their assignment, nor the army from dropping the bombs. Perhaps only among men like soldiers and scientists, trained to think "objectively"—i.e., in terms of means, not ends—could such irresponsibility and moral callousness be found. In any case, it was undoubtedly the most magnificent scientific experiment in history, with cities as the laboratories and people as the guinea pigs.

The official platitude about Atomic Fission is that it can be a Force for Good (production) or a Force for Evil (war), and that the problem is simply how to use its Good rather than its Bad potentialities. This is "just common sense." But, as Engels once remarked, Common Sense has some very strange adventures when it leaves its cozy bourgeois fireside and ventures out into the real world. For, given our present institutions—and the official apologists, from Max Lerner to President Conant of Harvard, envisage at most only a little face-lifting on these—how can The Bomb be "controlled," how can it be "internationalized"? Already the great imperialisms are jockeying for position in World War III. How can we expect them to give up the enormous advantage offered by The Bomb? May we hope that the destructive possibilities are so staggering that, for simple self-preservation, they will agree to "outlaw" The Bomb? Or that they will foreswear war itself because an "atomic" war would probably mean the mutual ruin of all contestants? The same reasons were advanced before World War I to demonstrate its "impossibility"; also before World War II. The devastation of these wars was as terrible as had been predicted—yet they took place. Like all the great advances in technology of the past century, Atomic Fission is something in which Good and Evil are so closely intertwined that it is hard to see how the Good can be extracted and the Evil thrown away. A century of effort has failed to separate the Good of capitalism (more production) from the Evil (exploitation, wars, cultural barbarism). *This* atom has never been split, and perhaps never will be.

The Marxian socialists, both revolutionary and reformist, also accept the potentialities-for-Good-or-for-Evil platitude, since this platitude is based on a faith in Science and Progress which is shared by Marxists as well as conservatives, and is indeed still the basic assumption of Western thought. (In this respect, Marxism appears to be simply the most profound and consistent intellectual expression of this faith.) Since the Marxists make as a precondition of the beneficial use of Atomic Fission a basic change in present institutions, their position is not open to the objections noted just above. But if one looks deeper than the political level, the Marxist version of the platitude seems at the very least inadequate. It blunts our reaction to the present horror by reducing it to an episode in an historical schema which will "come out all right" in the end, and thus makes us morally callous (with resulting ineffectuality in our actions against the *present* horror) and too optimistic about the problem of evil; and it ignores the fact that such atrocities as The Bomb and the Nazi death camps are *right now* brutalizing, warping, deadening the human beings who are expected to change the world for the better; that modern technology has its own anti-human dynamics which has proved so far much more powerful than the liberating effects the Marxist schema expects from it.

The bomb produced two widespread and, from the standpoint of The Authorities, undesirable emotional reactions in this country: a feeling of guilt at "our" having done this to "them," and anxiety lest some future "they" do this to "us." Both feelings were heightened by the superhuman *scale* of The Bomb. The Authorities have therefore made valiant attempts to reduce the thing to a human context, where such concepts as Justice, Reason, Progress could be employed. Such moral defenses are offered as: the war was shortened and many lives, Japanese as well as American, saved; "we" had to invent and use The Bomb against "them" lest "they" invent and use it against "us"; the Japanese deserved it because they started the war, treated prisoners barbarously, etc., or because they refused to surrender. The flimsiness of these justifications is apparent; *any* atrocious action, absolutely *any* one, could be excused on such grounds. For there is really only one possible answer to the problem posed by Dostoievski's Grand Inquisitor: if all mankind could realize eternal and complete happiness by torturing to death a single child, would this act be morally justified?

Somewhat subtler is the strategy by which The Authorities—by which term I mean not only the political leaders but also the scientists, intellectuals, trade-unionists and businessmen who function on the top levels of our society—tried to ease the deep fears aroused in everyone by The Bomb. From President Truman down, they emphasized that The Bomb has been produced in the normal, orderly course of scientific experiment, that it is thus simply the latest step in man's long struggle to control the forces of nature, in a word that it is Progress. But this is a knife that cuts both ways: the effect on me, at least, was to intensify some growing doubts about the "Scientific Progress" which had whelped this monstrosity. Last April, I noted that in our movies "the white coat of the scientist is as blood-chilling a sight as Dracula's black cape. . . . If the scientist's laboratory has acquired in Popular Culture a ghastly atmosphere, is this not perhaps one of those deep intuitions of the masses? From Frankenstein's laboratory to Maidanek [or, now, to Hanford and Oak Ridge] is not a long journey. Was there a popular suspicion, perhaps only half conscious, that the 19th century trust in science was mistaken . . . ?"

These questions seem more and more relevant. I doubt if we shall get satisfactory answers from the scientists (who, indeed, seem professionally incapable even of asking, let alone answering, them). The greatest of them all, who in 1905 constructed the equation which provided the theoretical basis for Atomic Fission, could think of nothing better to tell us after the bombings than: "No one in the world should have any fear or apprehension about atomic energy being a supernatural product. In developing atomic energy, science merely imitated the reaction of the sun's rays. ["Merely" is good!—DM] Atomic power is no more unnatural than when I sail my boat on Saranac Lake." Thus, Albert Einstein. As though it were not precisely the natural, the perfectly rational and scientifically demonstrable that is now chilling our blood! How human, intimate, friendly by comparison are ghosts, witches, spells, werewolves and poltergeists! Indeed, all of us except a few specialists know as much about witches as we do about atom-splitting; and all of us with no exceptions are even less able to defend ourselves against The Bomb than against witchcraft. No silver bullet, no crossed sticks will help us there. As though to demonstrate this, Einstein himself, when asked about the unknown radioactive poisons which were beginning to alarm even editorial writers, replied "emphatically": "I will not discuss that." Such emphasis is not reassuring.

Nor was President Truman reassuring when he pointed out: "This development, which was carried forward by the many thousand participants with the utmost energy and the very highest sense of national duty . . . probably represents the greatest achievement of the combined efforts of science, industry, labor and the military in all history." Nor Professor Smyth: "The weapon has been created not by the devilish inspiration of some warped genius but by the arduous labor of thousands of normal men and women working for the safety of their country." Again, the effort to "humanize" The Bomb by showing how it fits into our normal, everyday life also cuts the other way: it reveals how inhuman our normal life has become.

The pulp writers could imagine things like the atom bomb; in fact, life is becoming more and more like a Science Fiction story, and the arrival on earth of a few six-legged Martians with Death Rays would hardly make the front page. But the pulp writers' imaginations were limited; *their* atom bombs were created by "devilish" and "warped" geniuses, not by "thousands of normal men and women"—including some of the most eminent scientists of our time, the labor movement (the army "warmly" thanked the AFL and the CIO for achieving "what at times seemed impossible provision of adequate manpower"), various great corporations (DuPont, Eastman, Union Carbon & Carbide), and the president of Harvard University.

Only a handful, of course, knew what they were creating. None of the 125,000 construction and factory workers knew. Only three of the plane crew that dropped the first bomb knew what they were letting loose. It hardly needs to be stressed that there is something askew with a society in which vast numbers of citizens can be organized to create a horror like The Bomb without even knowing they are doing it. What real content, in such a case, can be assigned to notions like "democracy" and "government of, by and for the people"? The good Professor Smyth expresses the opinion that "the people of this country" should decide for themselves about the future development of The Bomb. To be sure, no vote was taken on the creation and employment of the weapon. However, says the Professor reassuringly, these questions "have been seriously considered by all concerned [i.e., by the handful of citizens who were permitted to know what was going on] and vigorously debated among the scientists, and the conclusions reached have been passed along to the highest authorities.

"These questions are not technical questions; they are political and social questions, and the answers given to them may affect all mankind for generations. In thinking about them, the men on the project have been thinking as citizens of the United States vitally interested in the welfare of the human race. It has been their duty and that of the responsible high Government officials who were informed to look beyond the limits of the present war and its weapons to the ultimate implications of these discoveries. This was a heavy responsibility.

"In a free country like ours, such questions should be debated by the people and decisions must be made by the people through their representatives."

It would be unkind to subject the above to critical analysis beyond noting that every statement of what-is contradicts every statement of what-should-be.

Atomic fission makes me sympathize, for the first time, with the old Greek notion of *Hubris*, that lack of restraint in success which invited the punishment of the gods. Some scientist remarked the other day that it was fortunate that the only atom we as yet know how to split is that of uranium, a rare substance; for if we should learn how to split the atom of iron or some other common ore, the chain reaction might flash through vast areas and the molten interior of the globe come flooding out to put an end to us and our Progress. It is *Hubris* when President Truman declares: "The force from which the sun draws its powers has been loosed against those who brought war to the Far East." Or when the *Times* editorialist echoes: "The American answer to Japan's contemptuous rejection of the Allied surrender ultimatum of July 26 has now been delivered upon Japanese soil in the shape of a new weapon which unleashes against it the forces of the universe." Invoking the Forces of the Universe to back up the ultimatum of July 26 is rather like getting in God to tidy up the living room.

It seems fitting that the Bomb was not developed by any of the totalitarian powers, where the political atmosphere might at first glance seem to be more suited to it, but by the two "democracies," the last major powers to continue to pay at least ideological respect to the humanitarian-democratic tradition. It also seems fitting that the heads of these governments, by the time The Bomb exploded, were not Roosevelt and Churchill, figures of a certain historical and personal stature, but Attlee and Truman, both colorless mediocrities, Average Men elevated to their positions by the mechanics of the system. All this emphasizes that perfect automatism, that absolute lack of human consciousness or aims which our society is rapidly achieving. As a uranium "pile," once the elements have been brought together, inexorably runs through a series of "chain reactions" until the final explosion takes place, so the elements of our society act and react, regardless of ideologies or personalities, until The Bomb explodes over Hiroshima. The more commonplace the personalities and senseless the institutions, the more grandiose the destruction. It is *Götter-dämmerung* without the gods.

The scientists themselves whose brainwork produced The Bomb appear not as creators but as raw material, to be hauled about and exploited like uranium ore. Thus, Dr. Otto Hahn, the German scientist who in 1939 first split the uranium atom and who did his best to present Hitler with an atom bomb, has been brought over to this country to pool his knowledge with our own atomic "team" (which includes several Jewish refugees who were kicked out of Germany by Hitler). Thus Professor Kapitza, Russia's leading experimenter with uranium, was decoyed from Cambridge University in the thirties back to his native land, and, once there, refused permission to return. Thus a recent report from Yugo-slavia tells of some eminent native atom-splitter being high-jacked by the Red Army (just like a valuable machine tool) and rushed by plane to Moscow.

Insofar as there is any moral responsibility assignable for The Bomb, it rests with those scientists who developed it and those political and military leaders who employed it. Since the rest of us Americans did not even know what was being done in our name—let alone have the slightest possibility of stopping it—The Bomb becomes the most dramatic illustration to date of the fallacy of "The Responsibility of Peoples."

Yet how can even those immediately concerned be held responsible? A general's function is to win wars, a president's or prime minister's to defend the interests of the ruling class he represents, a scientist's to extend the frontiers of knowledge; how can any of them, then, draw the line at the atom bomb, or indeed anywhere, regardless of their "personal feelings"? The dilemma is absolute, when posed in these terms. The social order is an impersonal mechanism, the war is an impersonal process, and they grind along automatically; if some of the human parts rebel at their function, they will be replaced by more amenable ones; and their rebellion will mean that they are simply thrust aside, without changing anything. The Marxists say this must be so until there is a revolutionary change; but such a change never seemed farther away. What, then, can a man do *now*? How can he escape playing his part in the ghastly process?

Quite simply by not playing it. Many eminent scientists, for example, worked on The Bomb: Fermi of Italy, Bohr of Denmark, Chadwick of England, Oppenheimer, Urey and Compton of USA. It is fair to expect such men, of great knowledge and intelligence, to be aware of the consequences of their actions. And they seem to have been so. Dr. Smyth observes: "Initially, many scientists could and did hope that some principle would emerge which would prove that atomic bombs were inherently impossible. The hope has faded gradually. . . . " Yet they all accepted the "assignment," and produced The Bomb. Why? Because they thought of themselves as specialists, technicians, and not as complete men. Specialists in the sense that the process of scientific discovery is considered to be morally neutral, so that the scientist may deplore the uses to which his discoveries are put by the generals and politicians but may not refuse to make them for that reason; and specialists also in that they reacted to the war as partisans of one side, whose function was the narrow one of defeating the Axis governments even if it meant sacrificing their broader responsibilities as human beings.

But, fortunately for the honor of science, a number of scientists refused to take part in the project. I have heard of several individual cases over here, and Sir James Chadwick has revealed "that some of his colleagues refused to work on the atomic bomb for fear they might be creating a planet-destroying monster." These scientists reacted as whole men, not as special-ists or part-isans. Today the tendency is to think of peoples as responsible and individuals as irresponsible. The reversal of both these conceptions is the first condition of escaping the present decline to barbarism. The more each individual thinks and behaves as a whole Man (hence responsibly) rather than as a specialized part of some nation or profession (hence irresponsibly), the better hope for the future. To insist on acting as a responsible individual in a society which reduces the individual to impotence may be foolish, reckless, and ineffectual; or it may be wise, prudent and effective. But whichever it is, only thus is there a chance of changing our present tragic destiny. All honor then to the as yet anonymous British and American scientists—Men I would rather say—who were so wisely foolish as to refuse their cooperation on The Bomb! This is "resistance," this is "negativism," and in it lies our best hope.

Part Five

THE BOMB AND THE WORLD TODAY

Chapter 14 THE BOMB: A DETERRENT OF WAR

RICHARD H. ROVERE *(1915–   ), an analyst of domestic and international affairs, has long been a contributer to* The New Yorker, *and he has written widely for other journals. His books include* The General and the President *(1951; with A. M. Schlesinger, Jr.),* Senator Joe McCarthy *(1959),* The American Establishment *(1962),* The Goldwater Caper *(1945), and* Waist Deep in the Big Muddy *(1968). In this selection from* Hiroshima Plus 20 *(1965), he looks at some of the implications of the bombing of Hiroshima and Nagasaki for postwar diplomacy. In evaluating the 1945 decision to use the new weapon, what weight should be given to the main arguments he presents?**

Before it was dropped or even tested, the bomb had an immense impact on American diplomacy. On May 16, 1945, Henry L. Stimson, the Secretary of War, told President Truman that "We shall probably hold more cards in our hands later than now." He meant that nuclear weapons were on the way and that, when the Russians saw what they could do, they would behave themselves in Eastern Europe. Stimson was trying to dissuade the President from seeking an early showdown with the Soviets and a face-to-face meeting with Stalin. Stimson believed, as Truman and just about everyone else did at the time, that a showdown was inevitable. He wanted, however, to delay it until the scientists of the Manhattan Project dealt the President what he needed for a Grand Slam. The President accepted Stimson's view. Almost immediately, he abandoned the "hard line" he had been pursuing and became—to the astonishment of most of his associates—almost conciliatory. He would wait for the bomb, which his Secretary of State, James F. Byrnes, had told him "could put us in a position to dictate our own terms at the end of the war."

Until very recently, this view of American strategy in mid-1945 would have been a difficult one to support. But now a young and brilliant historian, Gar Alperovitz, has produced a book—*Atomic Diplomacy: Hiroshima and Potsdam*—which pretty well cinches the case. According to Alperovitz, who was eight years old when the events he describes occurred, it was only in the last few months of the war that anyone thought of the diplomatic consequences of nuclear weapons. In the early and middle phases of its development the bomb was thought of as a bomb—one more instrument of destruction. There was never any debate over whether or not it would be put to the use for which it was intended. "At no time between 1941 and 1945," Stimson later said, "did I ever hear it suggested by the President or any other responsible member of the government that atomic energy should not be used in the war." As Alperovitz writes, "It was *assumed*—not decided—that the bomb would be used." But as things turned out, the war was really over by the time the bomb was ready. Germany had fallen and Japan was suing for peace. Though it no doubt hastened the Japanese surrender, military strategy did not require its use. Nevertheless it was used, and although Alperovitz cannot prove it—crucial documents are still classified—and does not try to, the implication of all that he has learned by piecing together the political and diplomatic events of the preceding months is that given our diplomatic reliance on it, the *bomb had to be used in order to show the Kremlin that it existed and could be used.*

Not only was the bomb central in pre-Hiroshima diplomatic thinking and planning; it was detonated over Hiroshima on August 6, 1945, as a *diplomatic instrument.* It did not produce the expected results—or at least the ones that seemed the most important at the time to Stimson, Byrnes, and Truman. They were thinking primarily of Eastern and Central Europe; they wished to compel the Russians to honor the Yalta agreements as the Truman administration interpreted them. This seems to have been what Stimson and Truman meant when they talked about the role of the bomb, as Truman put it, "in shaping history." Their scheme in its fulness—and also in its Europe-centered narrowness—was overtaken by events. Germany fell before the burst at Alamogordo. The confrontation they had wanted months earlier and then decided to postpone simply had to be arranged—and it was, at Potsdam, in the latter half of July. Informed that the Alamogordo tests had exceeded all expectations, Truman confided to Stimson, who recorded it in the diary he deposited at Yale, that the bomb "gave him an entirely new feeling of confidence." But Truman's "confidence" was not enough to move the Red Army east, and Herbert Feis, another historian of the period, was essentially right in saying that "the light of the explosion 'brighter than a thousand suns' filtered into the conference rooms at Potsdam only as a distant gleam." Two years later, Byrnes resigned as Secretary of State feeling that he had been a failure and believing that there could be no resolution of our differences with the Russians except through preventive war. In 1965, it is startling to revisit those years and discover how many wise and well-informed men shared that view. In his journal for November 1, 1949, David E. Lilienthal, then chairman of the Atomic Energy Commission, records an evening spent with Senator Brien McMahon, of Connecticut, who was, next to Lilienthal himself, the most knowledgeable man in Washington on matters of atomic energy and was certainly the most circumspect of senators: "What he is talking about," Lilienthal wrote, "is the inevitability of war with the Russians, and what he says adds up to one thing: blow them off the face of the earth, quick, before they do the same to us."

In the late forties, then, the bomb as a diplomatic weapon—as a force for "shaping history"—seemed a dud. It was once again being thought of as a purely military weapon. But of course it was shaping history all the time and in many ways, and even in 1949 it was possible, as Alperovitz points out, to argue that without it, the Red Army might not have left Iran and Manchuria, Czechoslovakia and Hungary. In retrospect, it is clear that every new atomic development, every technological "advance," was an event in diplomatic history as well as in military and scientific history. Some of these events, such as the acquisition of the bomb by France and China, were events in diplomatic history alone. And, putting aside for the moment the notion of the bomb as a diplomatic "instrument," one can say with certainty that it has been a great and constant "presence" in diplomacy since 1945. It is almost as if it were itself a great sovereignty—an awesome independent power. We can talk about the bomb nowadays without drawing any important distinction between "theirs" and "ours." The thing itself is a problem for diplomacy.

In a sense, the bomb is what most postwar diplomacy has been all about. In a relatively short time, diplomats almost everywhere came to see that the fact that the United States and the U.S.S.R. were atomic powers was vastly more important than the fact that they were ideologically hostile powers. The diplomacy of Gaullist France is an almost perfect example of this. In its relations with the Soviet Union, China, and the United States, France is dealing not with Communist powers and capitalist or democratic powers but with *nuclear* powers. It is impossible to explain its diplomacy in any other way. And while there are diplomatic issues that do not appear to involve the great nuclear powers or any of the disputes between them, hardly any affairs of nations anywhere can be seriously and profitably considered without keeping the bomb at the forefront of consciousness.

The bomb has given the whole enterprise of diplomacy a new objective, a new imperative. It has radically changed the old concept of "national interest."

By adding a new factor—human extinction as an unarguable possibility—to every calculation, it has created a "supranational interest" which is openly acknowledged by most of the great powers. It is true, to be sure, that there have always been nations which insisted that "peace" was the highest and noblest of their aims—not to be sacrificed for any merely national aspiration—and the insistence has not always been hypocritical. Neville Chamberlain's England was certainly earnest in its desire for peace. But peace has never before had the meaning or value it has had since 1945. Certainly as far as the great European powers were concerned, it was never for any length of time the *sine qua non* of foreign policy. To put it another way, there was never, in our part of the world, a pacifist nation. It can, I think, be maintained that with the advent of the bomb, or at least with the advent of the Soviet bomb, all the great Western powers became pacifist in the sense that they identified the avoidance of war as the fundamental objective of their diplomacy. "Better Red than Dead" may be a despised slogan in most of the great Western capitals, but it nevertheless states a proposition—a proposition that underlies most of their foreign policies. Washington may say that it plays no part in our diplomacy and cite as proof our response in the Cuban missile crisis. But French diplomacy isn't so sure about this. General de Gaulle thinks we might sooner see Europe red than ourselves dead, and there are Americans who think he may be right—if not about this generation of diplomats, then about some of their successors. And there have been occasions in the past when some of our most dedicated Cold War commanders have behaved in such a way as to encourage this view, e.g., the late John Foster Dulles at the time of Suez and Hungary.

In the cant of pre-bomb diplomacy, peace was rarely a value of which diplomats spoke without mentioning certain other values, such as "honor" or "justice." And these were generally considered the superior values—the conditions that made peace defensible. Better, on the whole, righteous strife than ignoble peace. Better to die on one's feet than to live forever on one's knees. Things have changed. Diplomats don't talk much of honor nowadays, though there is no evidence that they think less well of it than once they did. It is simply that they know that too dogged an insistence on "peace with honor" could lead to a dreadful peace everlasting. Today, what may be in and of itself a just and honorable course of action must be set down as morally indefensible if one of its consequences might be nuclear or thermonuclear war. For the sake of peace alone, we have candidly accepted arrangements that we could not bring ourselves to regard or describe as honorable or just. One need only cite the Berlin Wall.

Besides altering concepts of national interest, the bomb has blunted the force of ideology. It must be conceded that ideology has rarely been a great force in diplomacy. Notable illustrations of how quickly it yields to other considerations are to be found in any history of our own Latin-American policies. And no doubt the Sino-Soviet split would have come sooner or later even if there had been no bomb. It appears to have many causes, some of them, such as chauvinism, going back into pre-history. When it came, it demonstrated what we should have known long before it came—that, where great powers deal with one another, ideology can never be a match for national interest. But the bomb also has the power to override ideology, and it could probably have produced the Sino-Soviet split in the absence of all other causes. If "Better Red than Dead" is what many Westerners really believe, there are Communist diplomats who adhere to a happily complementary slogan—"Worse Dead than Imperialist." The Soviet leaders have publicly declared that ideology must be put aside so long as there exists what Churchill called "the universality of potential destruction." The Chinese may not at present feel that way, but there is reason to suspect that they are acting as they are because they have, now, the opportunity to wring from ideology certain advantages that are in the national interest. As for ourselves, our ardor for democracy and our zealous anti-Communism—for a time, the toughest ideology that ever motivated American diplomacy—are more important in rhetoric than in policy. It is true that we took some heavy risks in the Cuban missile crisis, but this only nails down the proposition. Our response at that time had nothing to do with advancing democracy or combatting Communist ideology. It had to do—as the ultimate Soviet response did —with the bomb and its threat to existence.

History and its precedents have always been as central in diplomatic thinking and procedure as in legal thinking and procedure. The bomb has rendered precedent and historical analogy largely absurd. Some statesmen may go telling us, with pointed examples from the past, that "appeasement never works." This may be no less than the truth, but it is a truth of severely limited utility these days. For appeasement's opposite—"firmness," as it is generally called—may not "work" either. Moreover, Khrushchev "appeased" us in October, 1962, and showed a notable lack of "firmness," and from his point of view, as from ours, it "worked." It may be contended that we are not tyrants and that the old rule applies only to them. Perhaps, but we have never been presented with an ultimatum. What we can be sure of is that if we were, our councils would be divided, and who cannot say that we would not in the end "appease." In any event, the appeal to pre-atomic experience can be taken only when it can be maintained that the experience has not been invalidated by the bomb.

Twenty years after the bomb, however, we have considerable post-atomic experience—far more, really, than 20 years' worth, for the pace of change and of challenge in the last two decades has been so accelerated that we have, as it were, lived through centuries. It is not only, or even primarily, the bomb and related technological developments that account for this acceleration. Many other things—the shattering of empires, the population explosion, advances in communications and other technologies—have quickened history's pace. In certain ways, the changing world might have been easier for diplomacy to deal with if there had been no bomb or if it had been brought quickly under some kind of international control that would have effectively eliminated it as a factor in the relations between powers. On the other hand, a world that did not have to contend with the bomb but did have to contend with all those tensions that would have developed in any case sounds like a world vastly more dangerous than the world between the wars. For my own part, I incline to the view that the bomb and its diplomatic consequences have had, by and large, a stabilizing effect on our time.

For two decades, diplomacy has contrived to avert general war. In the nineteenth century, this might have seemed no great achievement. But the last 20 years have been years of unbroken tensions—as the inter-war years were not —and of provocations that would have snapped the patience of great powers in any earlier period of modern history. The first and perhaps the largest of these was the Soviet occupation of Eastern Europe and the lowering of the Iron Curtain—an insolent exercise of force similar to that which led to World War II. The partition of Germany has been a continuing provocation, and partitioned Berlin has been the scene of a dozen explosive "incidents." And there have been Korea, Hungary, Cuba, Vietnam—and the U-2 and the missile crisis and the flareups in the Middle East and the Straits of Formosa. In any other historical setting, any of these might have led to general war. Surely World War I had no causes comparable in magnitude to that of the Soviet occupation of Eastern Europe, and surely few great and provoked powers have refrained from pressing an advantage comparable to the one the United States had as the sole possessor of an atomic [arsenal] in the first five years after the war.

It was the bomb more than anything else that enabled—or compelled— diplomacy to do its proper work. It was the bomb that made war, as President Eisenhower put it, "unthinkable." And for most reasonable men in this country atomic war was unthinkable even before the Soviet Union developed its own bomb. In 1949, Senator McMahon despairingly talked of putting an end to our troubles by smashing the Soviet Union, but this was never what he advocated in the way of public policy, and a couple of years later he was firmly on the side of President Truman in the President's dispute with General MacArthur, in which MacArthur opposed, and Truman advocated, "limited" war in Korea. Among those who thought preventive war inevitable and even desirable, there were actually very few who put their opinions in the form of specific recommendations.

For the terror of the bomb, even before there was any "balance of terror" or "universality of potential destruction," imposed its own restraint on men of conscience. There may have been no agonizing in the government over whether or not to use the bomb at Hiroshima, but there was a national agony after Hiroshima, and one must toy with the awful thought that a defense for Hiroshima may be found in the very revulsion it produced here in the United States. The use of the bomb was militarily unnecessary and diplomatically ineffective— at least by the prevalent criteria of effectiveness. It seems possible, though, that if we had spared Hiroshima and Nagasaki, we would have been all the more strongly tempted to use it on Moscow and Leningrad a couple of years later. It is unlikely that a dozen tests or public demonstrations at Alamogordo or in the Pacific atolls would have affected us as Hiroshima did.

During the period of monopoly, the peace was not kept solely through the workings of American conscience. Hiroshima had produced revulsion elsewhere in the world, and we were in those early post-war years becoming acutely aware of the desirability of alliances, of winning, so far as we possibly could, the good opinion of mankind. We were trying to build a system of European security, and we saw a promising future for the United Nations. There was probably more external than internal pressure for restraint. And it cannot be overlooked that some of this external pressure came from the Soviet Union—partly through its massive and ready conventional power in Eastern Europe and on its own frontiers, and partly through its own diplomatic restraint. This may have been purely out of fear, but that is beside the point. It knew when to stop crowding us and pressing its own advantages, and in Iran and elsewhere it did pull back.

In any case, restraint prevailed through the early years and into the period of "mutual deterrence," when general war became "unthinkable." To say that war is unthinkable is not, as Herman Kahn has instructed us, to say that it is impossible. At this moment, it seems a good deal more possible, or less unthinkable, than it has at any time in more than a decade, save for that terrible week in October, 1962. In Vietnam, we may shortly find ourselves confronting a power which, thanks largely to what may be the one great failure of our diplomacy, has shared little in the diplomatic history of the past 20 years and which professes to scorn the notion that the bomb has altered anything fundamental in the relations between powers. China may in the next few months put our diplomacy to the severest test it has ever known. But it has known some severe ones since 1945, and one can only hope that it will find a way of applying what it has known.

Chapter 15 PERVASIVE CONSEQUENCES OF NUCLEAR STALEMATE

According to CARROLL QUIGLEY *(1910–   )*
the ramifications of the decision by the United States
to use the bomb against Japan have been extensive
in many aspects of twentieth-century life.
A faculty member at Georgetown University, and the
author of The World Since 1939 *(1968), he is*
especially interested in the large patterns of change
in world civilization. Does Quigley in this selection
from Tragedy and Hope: The World in Our Time
(1966) find too much significance arising
directly *from use of the bomb, to the neglect*
of other important sociological and historical
developments?*

The decision to use the bomb against Japan marks one of the critical turning points in the history of our times. We cannot now say that the world would have been better, but we can surely say that it would have been different. We can also say, with complete assurance, that no one involved in the decision had a complete or adequate picture of the situation. The scientists who were consulted had no information on the status of the war itself, had no idea how close to the end Japan already was, and had no experience to make judgments on this matter. The politicians and military men had no real conception of the nature of the new weapon or of the drastic revolution it offered to human life. To them it was simply a "bigger bomb," even a "much bigger bomb," and, by that fact alone, they welcomed it.

*Reprinted with permission of The Macmillan Company from *Tragedy and Hope: The World In Our Time* by Carroll Quigley. Copyright © Carroll Quigley 1966. Pp. 862–869.

Some people, like General Groves, wanted it to be used to justify the $2 billion they had spent. A large group sided with him because the Democratic leaders in the Congress had authorized these expenditures outside proper congressional procedures and had cooperated in keeping them from almost all members of both houses by concealing them under misleading appropriation headings. Majority Leader John W. McCormack (later Speaker) once told me, half joking, that if the bomb had not worked he expected to face penal charges. Some Republicans, notably Congressman Albert J. Engel of Michigan, had already shown signs of a desire to use congressional investigations and newspaper publicity to raise questions about misuse of public funds. During one War Department discussion of this problem, a skilled engineer, Jack Madigan, said: "If the project succeeds, there won't be any investigation. If it doesn't, they won't investigate anything else." Moreover, some air-force officers were eager to protect the relative position of their service in the postwar demobilization and drastic reduction of financial appropriations by using a successful Abomb drop as an argument that Japan had been defeated by air power rather than by naval or ground forces.

After it was all over, Director of Military Intelligence for the Pacific Theater of War Alfred McCormack, who was probably in as good position as anyone for judging the situation, felt that the Japanese surrender could have been obtained in a few weeks by blockade alone: "The Japanese had no longer enough food in stock, and their fuel reserves were practically exhausted. We had begun a secret process of mining all their harbors, which was steadily isolating them from the rest of the world. If we had brought this operation to its logical conclusion, the destruction of Japan's cities with incendiary and other bombs would have been quite unnecessary. But General Norstad declared at Washington that this blockading action was a cowardly proceeding unworthy of the Air Force. It was therefore discontinued."

Even now it is impossible to make any final and impartial judgment of the merits of this decision. The degree to which it has since been distorted for partisan purposes may be seen from the contradictory charges that the efforts to get a bomb slowed down after the defeat of Germany and the opposite charge that they speeded up in that period. The former charge, aimed at the scientists, especially the refugees at Chicago who had given America the bomb by providing the original impetus toward it, was that these scientists, led by Szilard, were anti-Nazi, pro-Soviet, and un-American, and worked desperately for the bomb so long as Hitler was a threat, but on his demise opposed all further work for fear it would make the United States too strong against the Soviet Union. The opposite charge was that the Manhattan District worked with increasing frenzy after Germany's defeat, because General Groves was anti-Soviet. A variant of this last charge is that Groves was a racist and was willing to use the bomb on nonwhites like the Japanese but unwilling to use it against the Germans. It is true that Groves in his report of April 23, 1945, which was presented to President Truman by Secretary Stimson two days later, said that Japan had always been the target. The word "always" here probably goes back only to the date on which it was realized that the bomb would be so heavy that it could not be handled by any American plane in the European theater and, if used there, would have to be dropped from a British Lancaster, while in the Pacific the B-29 could handle it.

It seems clear that no one involved in making the decision in 1945 had any adequate picture of the situation. The original decision to make the bomb had been a correct one based on fear that Germany would get it first. On this basis the project might have been stopped as soon as it was clear that Germany was defeated without it. By that time other forces had come into the situation, forces too powerful to stop the project. It is equally clear that the defeat of Japan did not require the A-bomb, just as it did not require Russian entry into the war or an American invasion of the Japanese home islands. But, again, other factors involving interests and nonrational considerations were too powerful. However, if the United States had not finished the bomb project or had not used it, it seems most unlikely that the Soviet Union would have made its postwar efforts to get the bomb.

There are several reasons for this: (1) the bomb's true significance was even more remote from Soviet political and military leaders than from our own, and would have been too remote to make the effort to get it worthwhile if the bomb had never been demonstrated; (2) Soviet strategy had no interest in strategic bombing, and their final decision to make the bomb, based on our possession of it, involved changes in strategic ideas, and the effort, almost from scratch, to obtain a strategic bombing plane (the Tu-4) able to carry it; and (3) the strain on Soviet economic resources from making the bomb was very large, in view of the Russian war damage. Without the knowledge of the actual bomb which the Russian leaders obtained from our demonstration of its power, they would almost certainly not have made the effort to get the bomb if we had not used it on Japan.

On the other hand, if we had not used the bomb on Japan, we would have been quite incapable of preventing the Soviet ground forces from expanding wherever they were ordered in Eurasia in 1946 and later. We do not know where they might have been ordered because we do not know if the Kremlin is insatiable for conquest, as some "experts" claim, or is only seeking buffer security zones, as other "experts" believe, but it is clear that Soviet orders to advance were prevented by American possession of the A-bomb after 1945. It does seem clear that ultimately Soviet forces would have taken all of Germany, much of the Balkans, probably Manchuria, and possibly other fringe areas across central Asia, including Iran. Such an advance of Soviet power to the Rhine, the Adriatic, and the Aegean would have been totally unacceptable to the United States, but, without the atom bomb, we could hardly have stopped it. Moreover, such an advance would have led to Communist or Communist-dominated coalition governments in Italy and France. If the Soviet forces had advanced to the Persian Gulf across Iran, this might have led to such Communist-elected governments in India and much of Africa.

From these considerations it seems likely that American suspension of the atomic project after the defeat of Germany or failure to use the bomb against Japan would have led eventually to American possession of the bomb in an otherwise intolerable position of inferiority to Russia or even to war in order to avoid such a position (but with little hope, from war, to avoid such inferiority). This would have occurred even if we assume the more optimistic of two assumptions about Russia: (1) that they would not themselves proceed to make the bomb and (2) that they are not themselves insatiably expansionist. On the whole, then, it seems that the stalemate of mutual nuclear terror without war in which the world now exists is preferable to what might have occurred if the United States had made the decision either to suspend the atomic project after the defeat of Germany or to refuse to use it on Japan. Any other possible decisions (such as an open demonstration of its power before an international audience in order to obtain an international organization able to control the new power) would probably have led to one of the two outcomes already described. But it must be clearly recognized that the particular stalemate of nuclear terror in which the world now lives derives directly from the two decisions made in 1945 to continue the project after the defeat of Germany and to use the bomb on Japan.

This nuclear stalemate, in turn, leads to pervasive consequences in all aspects of the world in the twentieth century. It gives rise to a frenzied race between the two super-Powers to outstrip each other in the application of science and rationality to life, beginning with weapons. This effort provides such expensive equipment and requires such skill from the operators of this equipment that it makes obsolete the army of temporarily drafted citizen-soldiers of the nineteenth century and of "the armed hordes" of World War I and even of World War II, and requires the use of highly trained, professional, mercenary fighting men.

The growth of the army of specialists, foretold by General de Gaulle in 1934 and foreseen by others, destroys one of the three basic foundations of political democracy. These three bases are (1) that men are relatively equal in factual power; (2) that men have relatively equal access to the information needed to make a government's decisions; and (3) that men have a psychological readiness to accept majority rule in return for those civil rights which will allow any minority to work to build itself up to become a majority.

Just as weapons development has destroyed the first of these bases, so secrecy, security considerations, and the growing complexity of the issues have served to undermine the second of these. The third, which was always the weakest of the three, is still in the stage of relative vitality and relative acceptability that it had in the nineteenth century, but is in much greater danger from the threat of outside forces, notably the changes in the other two bases, plus the greater danger today from external war or from domestic economic breakdown.

One great danger in regard to the second of these basic foundations (availability of information necessary for decision-making) is the impact upon it of the expansion of rationalization. While this has led to automatic and mechanical storage and retrieval of information, it has also led to efforts to establish automatic electronic decision-making on the basis of the growing volume and complexity of such information. This renunciation of the basic feature of being human—judgment and decision-making—is very dangerous and is a renunciation of the very faculty which gave man his success in the evolutionary struggle with other living creatures. If this whole process of human evolution is now to be abandoned in favor of some other, unconscious and mechanical, method of decision-making, in which the individual's flexibility and awareness are to be subordinated to a rigid group process, then man must yield to those forms of life such as the social insects, which have already carried this method to a high degree of perfection.

This whole process has been made the central focus of a recent novel, *Fail-Safe*, by Eugene Burdick and Harvey Wheeler. The reduction of men to automatons in a complicated nexus of expensive machines is well shown in that book. To its picture must be added two points: (1) It does not require a blown condenser, as in the book, to unleash the full dangers of the situation; it is a situation which is dangerous in itself even if it functions perfectly; and (2) the avoidance of the ultimate total catastrophe in the book, because a few men, at and near the top, were able to resume the human functions of decision, self-sacrifice, love of their fellowmen, and hope for the future, should not conceal the fact that the whole world in that story came within minutes of handing its resources over to the insects.

Regardless of the outcome of the situation, it is increasingly clear that, in the twentieth century, the expert will replace the industrial tycoon in control of the economic system even as he will replace the democratic voter in control of the political system. This is because planning will inevitably replace laissez faire in the relationships between the two systems. This planning may not be single or unified, but it will be *planning*, in which the main framework and operational forces of the system will be established and limited by the experts on the governmental side; then the experts within the big units on the economic side will do their planning within these established limitations. Hopefully, the elements of choice and freedom may survive for the ordinary individual in that he may be free to make a choice between two opposing political groups (even if these groups have little policy choice within the parameters of policy established by the experts) and he may have the choice to switch his economic support from one large unit to another. But, in general, his freedom and choice will be controlled within very narrow alternatives by the fact that he will be numbered from birth and followed, as a number, through his educational training, his required military or other public service, his tax contributions, his health and medical requirements, and his final retirement and death benefits.

Eventually, in two or three generations, as the ordinary individual who is not an expert or a skilled professional soldier or a prominent industrial executive becomes of less personal concern to the government, his contacts with the government will become less direct and will take place increasingly through intermediaries. Some movement in this direction may be seen already in those cases where taxpayers whose incomes are entirely from wages or salaries find that their whole tax is already paid by their employer or in the decreasing need for the military draftee to be called to serve by a letter from the President. The development of such a situation, a kind of neofeudalism, in which the relationships of ordinary people to government cease to be direct and are increasingly through intermediaries (who are private rather than public authorities), is a long way in the future.

One consequence of the nuclear rivalry has been the almost total destruction of international law and the international community as they existed from the middle of the seventeenth century to the end of the nineteenth. That old international law was based on a number of sharp rational distinctions which no longer exist; these include the distinction between war and peace, the rights of neutrals, the distinction between combatants and noncombatants, the nature of the state, and the distinction between public and private authority. These are now either destroyed or in great confusion. We have already seen the obliteration of the distinctions between combatants and noncombatants and between neutrals and belligerents brought on by British actions in World War I. These began with the blockade of neutrals, like the Netherlands, and the use of floating mines in navigational waters. The Germans retaliated with acts against Belgian civilians and with indiscriminate submarine warfare. These kinds of actions continued in World War II with the British night-bombing effort aimed at destroying civilian morale by the destruction of workers' housing (Lord Cherwell's favorite tactic) and the American fire raids against Tokyo. It is generally stated in American accounts of the use of the first atom bomb that target planning was based on selection of military targets, and it is not generally known even today that the official orders from Cabinet level on this matter specifically said "military objectives surrounded by workers' housing." The postwar balance of terror reached its peak of total disregard both of noncombatants and of neutrals in the policies of John Foster Dulles, who combined sanctimonious religion with "massive retaliation wherever and whenever we judge fit" to the complete destruction of any noncombatant or neutral status.

Most other aspects of traditional international law have also been destroyed.

The Cold War has left little to the old distinction between war and peace in which wars had to be formally declared and formally concluded. Hitler's attacks without warning; the Korean War, which was not a "war" in international law or in American constitutional law (since it was not "declared" by Congress); and the fact that no peace treaty has been signed with Germany to end World War II, while we are already engaged in all kinds of undeclared warlike activities against the Soviet Union, have combined to wipe out many of the distinctions between war and peace which were so painfully established in the five hundred years before Grotius died (in 1645).

Most of these losses are obvious but there are others, equally significant but not yet widely recognized. The growth of international law in the late medieval and Renaissance periods not only sought to make the distinctions we have indicated, as a reaction against "feudal disorder"; it also sought to make a sharp distinction between public and private authority (in order to get rid of the feudal doctrine of *dominia*) and to set up sharp criteria of public authority involving the new doctrine of sovereignty. One of the chief criteria of such sovereignty was ability to maintain the peace and to enforce both law and order over a definite territory; one of its greatest achievements was the elimination of arbitrary nonsovereign private powers such as robber barons on land or piracy on the sea. Under this conception, ability to maintain law and order became the chief evidence of sovereignty, and the possession of sovereignty became the sole mark of public authority and the existence of a state. All this has now been destroyed. The Stimson Doctrine of 1931, now carried to its extreme conclusion in the American refusal to recognize Red China, shifted recognition from the objective criterion of ability to maintain order to the subjective criterion of approval of the form of government or liking of a government's domestic behavior.

The destruction of international law, like the destruction of international order, has gone much further than this. As long as the chief criterion for a state's sovereignty, and hence of recognition, was ability to maintain order, states in international law were regarded as equal. This concept is still recognized in theory in such organizations as the Assembly of the United Nations. But the achievement of nuclear weapons, by creating two super-Powers in a Cold War, destroyed the fact of the equality of states. This had the obvious result of creating Powers on two levels: ordinary and super; but it had the less obvious, and more significant, consequence of permitting the existence of states of lower levels of power, far below the level of ordinary Powers. This arose because the nuclear stalemate of the two super-Powers created an umbrella of fear of precipitating nuclear war which falsified their abilities to act at all.

As a result, all kinds of groups and individuals could do all kinds of actions to destroy law and order without suffering the consequences of forcible retaliation by ordinary powers or by the super-Powers, and could become recognized as states when they were still totally lacking in the traditional attributes of statehood. For example, the Léopoldsville group were recognized as the real government of the whole Congo in spite of the fact that they were incapable of maintaining law and order over the area (or even in Léopoldsville itself). In a similar way a gang of rebels in Yemen in 1962 were instantly recognized before they gave any evidence whatever of ability to maintain control or of readiness to assume the existing international obligations of the Yemen state, and before it was established that their claims to have killed the king were true. In Togo in the following year a band of disgruntled soldiers killed the president, Sylvanus Olympio, and replaced him with a recalled political exile.

Under the umbrella of nuclear stalemate, the boundaries of old states are shattered by guerrillas in conflict, supported by outsiders; outside governments subsidize murders or revolts, as the Russians did in Iraq in July 1958, or as Nasser of Egypt did in Jordan, Syria, Yemen, and elsewhere in the whole period after 1953, and as the American CIA did in several places, successfully in Iran in August 1953, and in Guatemala in May 1954, or very unsuccessfully, as in the Cuban invasion of April 1961. Under the Cold War umbrella, small groups or areas can obtain recognition as states without any need to demonstrate the traditional characteristics of statehood, namely, the ability to maintain their frontiers against their neighbors by force and the ability to maintain order within these frontiers. They can do this either by securing the intervention (usually secret) of some outside Power or even by preventing the intervention of a recognized Power fearful of precipitating nuclear or lesser conflict. In this way areas with a few states (such as southeast Asia) were shattered into many; states went out of existence or appeared (as Syria did in 1958 and 1961); and so-called new states came into existence by scores without reference to any traditional realities of political power or to the established procedures of international law.

The number of separate states registered as members in the United Nations rose steadily from 51 in 1945 to 82 in 1958 to 104 in 1961, and continued to rise. The difference in power between the strongest and the weakest became astronomical, and the whole mechanism of international relations, outside the UN organization as well as within it, became more and more remote from power considerations or even from reality, and became enmeshed in subjective considerations of symbols, prestige, personal pride, and petty spites. By 1963 single tribes in Africa were looking toward recognition of statehood through membership in the UN even when they lacked the financial resources to support a delegation at UN headquarters in New York City or in the capitals of any major country and were, indeed, incapable of controlling police forces to maintain order in their own tribal areas.

In this way the existence of nuclear stalemate within the Cold War carried on the total destruction of traditional international law and the gradual loss of meaning of the established concepts of state and public authority, and opened the door to a feudalization of authority somewhat similar to that which the founders of the modern state system and of international law had sought to overcome in the period from the twelfth century to the seventeenth.

Chapter 16   MORAL AND SOCIAL ASPECTS OF SCIENCE AND TECHNOLOGY

*Among those who were concerned with the
long-term effects of the 1945 decision was* NORBERT
WIENER *(1894–1964), one of the great mathe-
maticians of the twentieth century. He is best known
for his work in the field of cybernetics, the theory of
communication and control in the animal and the
machine, basic to automation and computor
technology. For many years a faculty member of the
Massachusetts Institute of Technology, he became
increasingly disturbed by the potentially destructive
uses of military devices based on his work and decided
in 1947 not to contribute to further military research.
His autobiography was published as* Ex-Prodigy
(1953) and I Am a Mathematician *(1956), and this
selection has been taken from the latter. Wiener's
viewpoint was that of the scientist who was sharply
aware of the moral and social meanings of science
and technology. What additional insights are provided
by the perspective he brought to this problem?**

All these emotional experiences were nothing to those through which I went
at the time of the bombing of Hiroshima. At first I was of course startled, but
not surprised, as I had been aware of the possibility of the use of the new
Manhattan Project weapons against an enemy. Frankly, however, I had been
clinging to the hope that at the last minute something in the atomic bomb would
fail to work, for I had already reflected considerably on the significance of the
bomb and on the meaning to society of being compelled to live from that time
on under the shadow of the threat of limitless destruction.

Of course I was gratified when the Japanese war ended without the heavy
casualties on our part that a frontal attack on the mainland would have involved.

*From *I Am a Mathematician* by Norbert Wiener. Copyright © 1956 by Norbert Wiener.
Reprinted by permission of Doubleday & Company, Inc., and Victor Gollancz, Ltd., British
publishers, pp. 299–308.

Yet even this gratifying news left me in a state of profound disquiet. I knew very well the tendency (which is not confined to America, though it is extremely strong here) to regard a war in the light of a glorified football game, at which at some period the final score is in, and which we have to count as either a definite victory or a definite defeat. I knew that this attitude of dividing history into separate blocks, each contained within itself, is by no means weakest in the Army and Navy.

But to me this episodic view of history seemed completely superficial. The most important thing about the atomic bomb was, in my opinion, not the termination of a specific war without undue casualties on our part, but the fact that we were now confronted with a new world and new possibilities with which we should have to live ever after. To me the most important fact about the wars of the past was that, serious as they had been, and completely destructive for those involved in them, they had been more or less local affairs. One country and one civilization might go under, but the malignant process of destruction had so far been localized, and new races and peoples might take up the torch which the others had put down.

I did not in the least underrate the will to destructiveness, which was as much a part of war with a flint ax and of war with a bow and arrow as it is of war with a musket and of war with a machine gun. What came most strongly to my attention was that in previous wars the power of destruction was not commensurate with the will for destruction. Thus, while I realized that as far as the people killed or wounded are concerned, there is very little difference between a cannonade or an aerial bombardment with explosive bombs of the type already familiar and the use of the atomic bomb, there seemed to me to be most important practical differences in the consequences to humanity at large.

Up to now no great war, and this includes World War II, had been possible except by the concerted and prolonged will of the people fighting, and consequently no such war could be undertaken without a profoundly real share in it by millions of people. Now the new modes of mass destruction, expensive as they must be in the bulk, have become so inexpensive per person killed that they no longer take up an overwhelming share of a national budget.

For the first time in history, it has become possible for a limited group of a few thousand people to threaten the absolute destruction of millions, and this without any highly specific immediate risk to themselves.

War had made the transition between an overwhelming assertion of national effort and the push-button declaration of the will of a small minority of people. Fundamentally this is true, even if one includes in the military effort all the absolutely vast but relatively small sums which have been put into the whole body of nuclear research. It is even more devastatingly true if one considers the relatively minimal effort required on the part of a few generals and a few aviators to place on a target an atomic bomb already made.

Thus, war has been transported, at least as a possibility, from the field of national effort to the field of private conspiracy. In view of the fact that the great struggle to come threatens to be one between the United States and the Soviet government, and in view of the additional fact that the whole atmosphere and administration of the Soviet government shares with that of the Nazis an extremely strong conspiratorial nature, we have taken a step which is intrinsically most dangerous for us.

I did not regard with much seriousness the assertions which some of the great administrators of science were making, to the effect that the know-how needed for the construction of the atomic bomb was a purely American thing and could not be duplicated by a possible enemy for many years at least, during which we could be counted upon to develop a new and even more devastating know-how. In the first place, I was acquainted with more than one of these popes and cardinals of applied science, and I knew very well how they underrated aliens of all sorts, in particular those not of the European race. With my wide acquaintance among scholars of many races and many countries, I had not been able to discern that scientific ability and moral discipline were the peculiar property of those of blanched skin and English speech.

But this was not all. The moment that we had declared both our possession of the bomb and its efficiency by using it against an enemy, we had served notice on every country that its countinued existence and independence of policy were conditioned on its prompt possession of a similar weapon. This meant two things: that any country which was our rival or potential rival was bound to push nuclear research for the sake of its own continued independent existence, with the greatly stimulating knowledge that this research was not intrinsically in vain; and that any such country would inevitably set up an espionage system to get hold of our secrets.

This is not to say that we Americans would not be bound in self-defense to oppose such leaks and such espionage with our full effort for the sake of our very national existence; but it does mean that such considerations of legality and such demands on the moral responsibility of loyal American citizens could not be expected to have the least force beyond our frontiers. If the roles of Russia and the United States had been reversed, we should have been compelled to do exactly what they did in attempting to discover and develop such a vital secret of the other side; and we should regard as a national hero any person attached to our interests who performed an act of espionage exactly like that of Fuchs or the Rosenbergs.

I then began to evolve in my mind the general problem of secrets; not so much as a moral issue, but as a practical issue and a policy which we might hope to maintain effectively in the long run. Here I could not help considering how soldiers themselves regard secrets in the field. It is well recognized that every cipher can be broken if there is sufficient inducement to do it and if it is worth-while to work long enough; and an army in the field has one-hour ciphers, twenty-four hour ciphers, one-week ciphers, perhaps one-year ciphers, but never ciphers which are expected to last an eternity.

Under the ordinary circumstances of life, we have not been accustomed to think in terms of espionage, cheating, and the like. In particular, such ideas are foreign to the nature of the true scientist, who, as Einstein has pointed out, has as his antagonist a world which is hard to understand and interpret, but which does not maliciously and malignantly resist this interpretation. "The Lord is subtle, but he isn't plain mean."

With ordinary secrets of limited value, we do not have to live under a perpetual fear that somebody is trying to break them. If, however, we establish a secret of the supreme value and danger of the atomic bomb, it is not realistic to suppose that it will never be broken, nor that the general goodwill among scientists will exclude the existence of one or two who, either because of their opinions or their slight reistance to moral pressure, may give our secrets over to those who will endanger us.

If we . . . play with the edged tools of modern warfare, we are running not merely the danger of being cut by accident and carelessness but the practical certainty that other people will follow where we have already gone and that we shall be exposed to the same perils to which we have exposed others. Secrecy is thus at once very necessary and, in the long run, quite impossible. It is unrealistic to give over our main protection to such a fragile defense.

There were other reasons, moreover, which, on much more specific grounds, made me feel skeptical of the wisdom of the course we had been pursuing. It is true that the atomic bomb had been perfected only after Germany had been eliminated from the war, and that Japan was the only possible proving ground for the bomb as an actual deadly weapon. Nevertheless, there were many both in Japan and elsewhere in the Orient who would think that we had been willing to use a weapon of this terribleness against Japan when we might not have been willing to use it against a white enemy. I myself could not help wondering whether there might not be a certain degree of truth in this charge. In a world in which European colonialism in the Orient was rapidly coming to an end, and in which every oriental country had much reason to be aware of the moral difference which certain elements in the West were in the habit of making between white people and colored people, this weapon was pure dynamite (an obsolete metaphor now that the atomic bomb is here) as far as our future diplomatic policy was concerned. What made the situation ten times worse was that this was the sort of dynamite which Russia, our greatest antagonist if not our greatest actual enemy, was in a position to use, and would have no hesitation whatever in using.

It is the plainest history that our atomic bomb effort was international in the last degree and was made possible by a group of people who could not have been gotten together had it not been for the fact that the threat of Nazi Germany was so strongly felt over the world, and particularly by that very scholarly group who contributed the most to nuclear theory. I refer to such men as Einstein, Szilard, Fermi, and Niels Bohr. To expect in the future that a similar group could be gotten together from all the corners of the world to defend our national policy involved the continued expectation that we should always have the same moral prestige. It was therefore doubly unfortunate that we should have used the bomb on an occasion on which it might have been thought that we would not have used it against white men.

There was another matter which aroused grave suspicion in the minds of many of us. While the nuclear program did not itself involve any overwhelming part of the national military effort, it was still in and for itself an extremely expensive business. The people in charge of it had in their hands the expenditure of billions of dollars, and sooner or later, after the war, a day of reckoning was bound to come, when Congress would ask for a strict accounting and for a justification of these enormous expenditures. Under these circumstances, the position of the high administrators of nuclear research would be much stronger if they could make a legitimate or plausible claim that this research had served a major purpose in terminating the war. On the other hand, if they had come back empty-handed—with the bomb still on the docket for future wars, or even with the purely symbolic use of the bomb to declare to the Japanese our willingness to use it in actual fact if the war were to go on—their position would have been much weaker, and they would have been in serious danger of being broken by a new administration coming into power on the rebound after the war and desirous of showing up the graft and ineptitude of its predecessor.

Thus, the pressure to use the bomb, with its full killing power, was not merely great from a patriotic point of view but was quite as great from the point of view of the personal fortunes of people involved in its development. This pressure might have been unavoidable, but the possibility of this pressure, and of our being forced by personal interests into a policy that might not be to our best interest, should have been considered more seriously from the very beginning.

Of the splendid technical work that was done in the construction of the bomb there can be no question. Frankly, I can see no evidence of a similar high quality of work in the policy-making which should have accompanied this. The period between the experimental explosion at Los Alamos and the use of the bomb in deadly earnest was so short as to preclude the possibility of clear thinking. The qualms of the scientists who knew the most about what the bomb could do, and who had the clearest basis to estimate the possibilities of future bombs, were utterly ignored, and the suggestion to invite Japanese authorities to an experimental exhibition of the bomb somewhere in the South Pacific was flatly rejected.

Behind all this I sensed the desires of the gadgeteer to see the wheels go round. Moreover, the whole idea of push-button warfare has an enormous temptation for those who are confident of their power of invention and have a deep distrust of human beings. I have seen such people and have a very good idea of what makes them tick. It is unfortunate in more than one way that the war and the subsequent uneasy peace have brought them to the front.

All these and yet other ideas passed through my mind on the very day of Hiroshima. One of the strong points and at the same time one of the burdens of the creative scholar is that he must stand alone. I wished—oh how I wished!—that I could be in a position to take what was happening passively, with a sincere acceptance of the wisdom of the policy-makers and with an abdication of all personal judgment. The fact is, however, that I had no reason to believe that the judgment of these men on the larger issues of the situation was any superior to my own, whatever their technical information might be. I knew that more than one of the high officials of science had not one tenth my contact with the scientists of other countries and of other standpoints and was in nowhere nearly as good a position to assess the world reaction to the bomb. I knew, moreover, that I had been in the habit of considering the history of science and of invention from a more or less philosophic point of view, and I did not believe that those who made the decisions could do this any better than I must. The sincere scientist must back his bets and guesses, even when he is a Cassandra and no one believes him. I had behind me many years of lonely work in science where I had finally proved to be in the right. This inability to trust the Powers That Be was a source of no particular satisfaction to me, but there it was, and it had to be faced.

One of my greatest worries was the reaction of the bomb on science and on the public's attitude to the scientist. We had voluntarily accepted a measure of secrecy and had given up much of our liberty of action for the sake of the war, even though—for that very purpose, as many of us thought—more secrecy than the optimum was imposed, and this at times had hampered our internal communications more than the information-gathering service of the enemy. We had hoped that this unfamiliar self-discipline would be a temporary thing, and we had expected that after this war—as, after all, before—we should return to the free spirit of communication, intranational and international, which is the very life of science. Now we found that, whether we wished it or not, we were to be the custodians of secrets on which the whole national life might depend. At no time in the foreseeable future could we again do our research as free men. Those who had gained rank and power over us during the war were most loath to relinquish any part of the prestige they had obtained. Since many of us possessed secrets which could be captured by the enemy and could be used to our national disadvantage, we were obviously doomed to live in an atmosphere of suspicion forever after, and the police scrutiny of our political opinions which began in the war showed no signs of future remission.

The public liked the atomic bomb as little as we did, and there were many who were quick to see the signs of future danger and to develop a profound consciousness of guilt. Such a consciousness looks for a scapegoat. Who could constitute a better scapegoat than the scientists themselves? They had unquestionably developed the potentialities which had led to the bomb. The man in the street, who knew little of scientists and found them a strange and self-contained race, was quick to accuse them of a desire for the power of destruction manifested by the bomb. What made this both more plausible and more dangerous was the fact that, while the working scientists felt very little personal power and had very little desire for it, there was a group of administrative gadget workers who were quite sensible of the fact that they now had a new ace in the hole in the struggle for power.

At any rate, it was perfectly clear to me at the very beginning that we scientists were from now on to be faced by an ambivalent attitude. For the public, who regarded us as medicine men and magicians, was likely to consider us an acceptable sacrifice to the gods as other, more primitive publics do.

Part Six

A SUMMARY VIEW

Chapter 17   DECISION OF DESTINY

Several of the previous selections both explicitly and implicitly make overall judgments concerning the wisdom of the great decision. Walter Smith Schoenberger *(1920–   ) published* Decision of Destiny *in 1970, from which the following selection is taken, setting forth an overall summary-analysis of the American action in 1945. Educated at the University of Pittsburgh and the Fletcher School of Law and Diplomacy, Schoenberger has taught at Tufts University and the University of Maine, where he is now professor of political science. How fully does this summary cover the most significant aspects of the problem?**

Within its general security requirements, within its traditional approach to foreign policy, and within its uncertainty as to the existing political-military situation, the United States Government reached the decision to use the atomic bombs on Japan. But that decision was affected more, perhaps, by certain characteristics of the United States political system itself. The governmental structure rested, first, on a large and complicated administrative apparatus which had grown somewhat unpredictably and inconsistently during the war. Second, it was characterized by a somewhat irrelevant method of choosing a Vice-President. Third, it provided no suitable means of assuring that the Vice-President would be prepared to assume the office of President. And, fourth, even during a war in which the powers of the President had been used

*Walter Smith Schoenberger, *Decision of Destiny* (Athens, Ohio: Ohio University Press, 1969), pp. 295–307. Reprinted with permission of the publisher.

extensively, it provided for a legislative-executive relationship which strongly conditioned the development of its policy. Each of these characteristics was to affect the decision to drop the atomic bomb.

During World War II, governmental agencies mushroomed in Washington. Many traditional agencies like the Department of State, the Department of War, and the Department of the Navy grew to such a size that their subdivisions were scattered among a number of widely separated buildings. A number of new organizations such as the Office of Price Administration, the Office of War Information, the Office of Strategic Services, the Office of War Mobilization, and the Office of Defense Transportation, to name but a few, had been established to fill specific wartime needs, sometimes with little clear definition of their relationship to the traditional agencies.

The governmental structure that Harry S. Truman took over as President suffered many of the administrative difficulties of large size and unplanned organization. Frequently there was a breakdown in communications horizontally within the governmental structure itself and vertically from it to the President. The structure suffered from an inertia produced by the need for complex interdepartmental consultations. There was the additional problem of coordinating the activities of the many operating agencies. This was particularly so during the spring of 1945. Roosevelt at best an artist as an administrator, had never been much interested in administrative detail. He had relied on his somewhat formidable personal capacity and the advice of a few advisers to handle the diplomacy of the war; and frequently he had operated somewhat out of touch with key agencies, particularly with the Department of State. Interested in greater problems, he had left the difficulties of administration—except in the personal or political sense—to be solved by others or not at all. Now, however, Roosevelt was dead, and Truman was President. Immediately there was a jockeying for position close to the new President both by those within the administration who wished to improve their situations or promote their ideas and by those, not formerly part of the government, who now envisioned opportunities resulting from real or imagined past relationships with Truman. The President consequently operated within a general administrative confusion. But all within the government was not confusion; one agency, the Manhattan Engineer District, under able administration, continued to fulfill its function efficiently. It had developed its own built-in momentum; it was guided by expert hands.

Perhaps one of the gravest difficulties the new President faced was in obtaining adequate information upon which to base his decisions, particularly those involving foreign and military affairs. Soon after he had taken office, Truman was informed by Secretary of State Stettinius that Roosevelt had regularly received a two-page daily summary of important diplomatic developments. Truman asked Stettinius to continue the practice and to send him:

. . . an outline of the background and the present status of the principal problems confronting this government in its relations with other countries. These written reports, along with material from other departments and the Joint Chiefs of Staff . . . were immensely helpful in filling gaps in [his] information. In fact, they were indispensable as aids in dealing with many issues, and from the first [he] studied them with the greatest care.

In this way he received information from the Department of State, from the Joint Chiefs of Staff, and from certain other departments. But, quite naturally, most of this information reflected generally accepted points of view and led to a continuation of Roosevelt's policies. Information suggesting changes in direction frequently failed to reach him. Information, for instance, suggesting the changing conditions in Japan existed within the administration. It is questionable that it reached the President.

Here, of course, one is dealing in areas of probability. And yet the evidence indicates that much information concerning the conditions within which the atomic bombs were used never or, at best, seldom reached the President or those at the top who advised him.

There seems to be no doubt, for instance, that the President, Byrnes, and Stimson knew of the exchanges between Foreign Minister Togo and Sato, the Japanese Ambassador to Moscow, in which the two diplomats attempted to arrange for Russian mediation. And yet it is unclear as to whether any of the three had seen all of the messages at least until Forrestal showed them to Byrnes on July 28. It is significant that Byrnes was so new in office and so preoccupied with problems in Europe that he only reviewed these exchanges in detail at that time. Whether later Sato-Togo messages were seen by Truman and Byrnes has not been determined. At any rate, given the predisposition of the United States Government to believe in a prolonged Japanese struggle, it was reasonable, even if the messages were seen, to give greater emphasis to Togo's frequent refusal of unconditional surrender than to his search for some sort of settlement which would approximate unconditional surrender.

It also seems doubtful that the work of the Foreign Morale Analysis Division, which outlined with detailed accuracy the disillusionment and reduced morale among the Japanese civilian population, ever got beyond the Office of War Information to which it was sent. This work would have substantiated the conclusion of Naval Intelligence that the Japanese were looking for an acceptable means of surrender. And yet it is unclear as to whether such conclusions were ever transmitted beyond Forrestal to Truman. That the recommendations of many of the scientists at the Metallurgical Laboratory at the University of Chicago were sent from Stimson's office either to the Interim Committee or to Truman in time to influence their decisions seems highly doubtful. And the disposition of a variety of studies by the Office of Strategic Services, which indicated among other things the growing difficulties of the Japanese economy and the advantages of associating the Emperor with a move for peace, is unclear. No indication has been found that Truman ever saw such information. And one has the feeling that much of the information available at various levels in the government which portrayed a far more realistic view of the Japanese situation than that held at the top never reached those responsible for the decision to use the nuclear weapons. Of course, Grew's point of view regarding the Emperor was presented to the President from time to time both by the Acting Secretary of State and by Stimson. If it had been substantiated by other supporting intelligence, it might have prevailed. Again, however, one lapses into conjecture.

It seems generally conclusive, however, that considerable information relevant to the decision to use the atomic bomb never reached Truman, largely because of the nature of the United States governmental apparatus. He, himself, has commented cogently on the administrative situation within which he operated:

> Strange as it may seem, the President . . . was not completely informed as to what was taking place in the world. Messages that came to the different departments of the executive branch often were not relayed to him because some official did not think it was necessary to inform the President. The President did not see many useful cables and telegrams that came from different American representatives abroad.

Even as such information failed to reach the President in the spring and summer of 1945, General Groves was going ahead as he had been ordered, producing his new weapon for use.

In addition to certain problems of administrative size and organization the decision to use the bombs resulted, in part, from the method by which the United States nominated its Vice-Presidents and from the relationship that frequently developed between the President and the Vice-President. As was customary and politically expedient, the Vice-Presidential candidate was chosen by the Democratic convention of 1944 primarily to balance the ticket, to give it a broader appeal than it would otherwise have had, and to appease contesting factions within the party. Other more knowledgeable, more experienced candidates than Truman were ready to accept the position. It is true that the Vice-Presidency did not usually attract such hopefuls since, barring the President's death, it had frequently been a dead end for politicians. And yet in 1944, various personal estimates of Roosevelt's possibly failing health led to a spirited contest. These other candidates were not, however, thought by the party leadership to be so generally acceptable as Truman. The Senator from Missouri, therefore, became the candidate. With all regard for Mr. Truman it cannot be said that he was prepared for the Presidency, particularly for the handling of foreign affairs. His previous activities had generally involved domestic politics at the national and state levels. On becoming President he was forced to deal with a variety of complicated and delicate problems concerning foreign affairs for which he had had little experience.

His inexperience, at least in part, reflected the general relationship which usually developed between the President and Vice-President in the United States system of government. The influence and activities of the Vice-President depended almost completely on the actions of the President. In this case, Roosevelt did not consult Truman on matters of foreign or military policy and helped to create a situation where his sudden death left the handling of United States policy to an inexperienced and relatively ignorant man. It must be stated, however, that Truman made every effort to eliminate that ignorance. But burdened by a number of more immediate political problems, it is doubtful that he was able to devote much time to what to him appeared primarily a military and technological problem, the use of the atomic bombs.

The relationship between the administration and the Congress also influenced, although uncertainly, the decision to drop the bombs. Particularly sensitive to congressional disapproval if it resulted in a reduction in appropriations, the administration acted as diligently as possible to justify the expenditures it incurred. The construction of the bombs and the production of their fissionable material had been accomplished only as a result of considerable unexplained costs. The technique of obtaining appropriations on these terms had been highly irregular and had required secrecy both from officials in the adminstration and from leaders of the Congress. The political imagination of certain administrators involved in the project was reasonably staggered by the possibility that the physicists might be incorrect in their anticipations. If it had proved to be impossible to construct a bomb despite the tremendous amounts devoted to the program, the halls of Congress might very well have echoed and reechoed with angry denunciations of the war's greatest boondoggle. One need not make too much of this. It hardly seems likely that the bombs were used merely to justify an expenditure. And yet this was probably a consideration in quickly testing and using them. Their successful use turned what might have been a political liability into what was undoubtedly a great political asset. What a demonstration of administrative foresight that, as a result of conducting a large and novel program throughout the war, atomic bombs had been produced just in time to effect the surrender of Japan! The timing could hardly have been more fortuitous.

Mr. Truman, therefore, acted under a number of general and specific conditions in finally sanctioning the use of the weapons. That decision represented the influence of the system of nation-states, the United States role in that system, its government's evaluation of the Japanese and Russian imponderables, and the very nature of the government itself and the President's position within it.

Within this milieu, a number of more specific forces immediately influenced President Truman's decision. Among these were factors affecting Truman's position at the Potsdam Conference. He had just heard that an atomic weapon had been successfully exploded and that two others would be ready by early August. Although he had known nothing about the Manhattan Engineer District prior to becoming President, he now knew something of the magnitude of its plant, of the expenditure that had been made for its efforts, and of the numbers and importance of the men who had been involved. Throughout the war, stimulated by the fear of prior German success, these men had devoted a considerable part of their lives to develop an atomic weapon. At least from the time the program came under the control of the War Department, the weapon had been developed for use. All activities of the Manhattan Engineer District had aimed at building it for use. And a squadron of specially modified bombers had been prepared to carry it to Japan. Now, following this tremendous effort, bombs had been built, the planes were ready, and the targets had been chosen. All of these actions were taken within the War Department by Stimson, Marshall, or Arnold, and frequently initiated by Groves. There was no need for Truman to make positive decisions to ready the weapon. These decisions were rapidly and efficiently made for him.

Bear in mind, also, the nature and position of the President when he came to power. Relatively new to national politics and completely new to administrative responsibilities at the national level, he had been abruptly elevated from a position of some prestige and little influence to what was probably the most powerful, complicated administrative position in the world. Moderate, considerate, humble, and intelligent, he had recognized his limitations and had decided to rely on those who had worked with Roosevelt to continue Roosevelt's policies for winning the war. Roosevelt's aides were men of considerable stature, force of character, and prestige. It would have been extremely difficult for Truman to have opposed their recommendations, even if he had known what they had been doing and even if he had wanted to do so. It seems unlikely that either of these conditions existed. He had been predisposed to follow Roosevelt's policies. He had been reasonably inclined to follow the advice of the men who had worked to implement those policies. There had been, therefore, no change in the Manhattan Engineer District's general directive after Truman had become President even though the threat of Germany had soon been eliminated. The bombs, when developed, were still to be used.

Consider, next, that Truman had been advised by the Interim Committee, a group of eminent scientists and government officials, to use the weapon on a military-civilian target as soon as possible. This recommendation undoubtedly had considerable influence on Truman's ultimate decision. The Interim Committee's advice, however, must be considered in terms of the committee's character and its actions. It was true that it was an interdepartmental committee with representation from the Navy Department, from the State Department, and from the Department of War. But it operated under the Secretary of War who had hand-chosen its members. All of them except William L. Clayton from the Department of State and Ralph A. Bard from the Navy Department had been personally connected with the development of the weapon. Scientists were represented, but with the exception of Fermi, who with Szilard had been instrumental in developing the first chain reaction, those on the committee were scientists responsible for the administration of the program. Furthermore, it seems that the discussion in the committee of use of the weapons was initiated almost accidentally. The item had not appeared on its agenda and was given very little of the committee's time. Among other responsibilities it had what was considered to be a more important obligation, the development of a method to administer the program after the war had ended. The committee was in a real sense the Secretary of War's committee. It advised him to use the weapon. Inasmuch as he had come to this conclusion separately, he informed the President of both his and the committee's recommendations. More realistically, however, Stimson chose individuals for the committee who were not apt to oppose use of the weapon. Furthermore, they were advised by Marshall who maintained a conservative view as to how long the war with Japan would last and by Groves who was building the weapon. They received no advice from the more optimistic officers of the Navy or Air Force. Even as the committee sat, the War Department was going ahead with preparations for the weapon's use.

Consider also the policies which the United States had followed toward Russia and Japan in the Far East through most of the war. For years this government had sought Russian entrance into the war against Japan. Such an agreement had been negotiated at Yalta in February, 1945. Only shortly after Truman became President had doubts begun to grow concerning the need for Russian help. Despite such uncertainties, which by late July, 1945, were widely held, most of the United States delegation at Potsdam felt that Russia would enter the war whether or not the United States withdrew its request. Furthermore, a withdrawal might be looked upon by the Soviet Union as a means of evading the obligations accepted at Yalta and might provoke the unrestricted advance of Russian power beyond the limits of its concessions. It might also undercut the bargaining position of the United States vis-à-vis the Soviet Union in Europe; for already the United States was accusing Stalin, intent on solidifying his control of Eastern Europe, of violating the agreements he had made at Yalta. On the surface then the United States continued to support Russian intervention which was accepted as an inevitability; and yet it does not follow that this country desired the Russians to intervene. In massing their troops on the Siberian border, they were already fulfilling the military task assigned to them, that of neutralizing the Japanese forces in Manchuria. And yet, recognizing that a Russian move was almost inevitable, it still made sense to use the nuclear weapon in an attempt to end the war with sufficient speed in order to minimize the expansion of Soviet influence in Korea, North China, and the Japanese Islands.

Not only was Truman saddled with a practically defunct Russian policy in the Far East, but he was also restricted by the emotionally charged, well-propagandized policy of requiring Japan to surrender unconditionally. Despite the fact that even at the higher levels of the United States government some believed that Japan would capitulate on conditions favorable to the United States, the Japanese steadfastly refused to consider a forced change in their imperial system. This created a serious obstacle to a change in unconditional surrender, for the Emperor was widely considered in the United States as a symbol of expansionary Japanese militarism which the United States had committed itself to eradicate. Moreover, since Japan was considered to have started the war by the attack on Pearl Harbor, it did not satisfy a widespread desire for revenge to treat Japan more leniently than Germany which had been eliminated as a power factor in Europe. Finally, conditional surrender did not satisfy the military's desire for victory. In the opinion of many, it would provide Japan with the opportunity to rise again as a threat to the United States. Therefore, although Truman might have hoped, as did some, that clarifying unconditional surrender in the Potsdam Declaration might bring about a rapid Japanese surrender, he was unwilling to specify concessions regarding the Emperor, both because of the resultant antagonism which could be expected from the United States people and from his government, and also because of his evaluation of the position of the Emperor in the Japanese system.

Consider, additionally, the military evaluation of the state of the war against Japan. It might very well last through most of 1946. It would very likely result in considerable casualties and much expense. And it might result in the obliteration of much of what was Japan. Accepting these serious predictions, it made sense from a humanitarian point of view to use the atomic weapons now available in two swift blows which might be expected to stop the bloodshed. It was true that a considerable number of Japanese would be killed, but their lives might be reasonably sacrificed to the cause of peace.

As important, perhaps, as any of these factors was the fact that the bombs existed. Their use had long been planned. The products which had taken so much effort were now available to be tested in battle against a hated enemy representing much that was considered evil. Their use would be a demonstration of the success of the program. Their testing would be done under conditions best calculated to evaluate the impact of blast. Already a team of experts was being readied to send into Japan to evaluate their effects.

The weapons were ready; the planes and crews were prepared. Japan refused to surrender unconditionally, and the long, bloody war seemed likely to continue. The Soviet Union, increasingly intractable in Europe, was about to enter the war in the Far East where its prolonged involvement against a shrinking Japanese Empire might provide it a new and dangerous position of strength. All those who advised the President supported the Interim Committee's recommendation which favored the bomb's use. And there was Harry S. Truman, a Missouri politician, farmer, and onetime businessman, steeped in many of the traditional oversimplifications of the United States approach to international politics, a new and uncertain President, a humble man, by most accounts a moral man, a man who wanted to be a strong President. He did not have to give the order to drop the bombs; that had already been done. He could have ordered the operation stopped. To him, there was no reason to do so. The bombs were dropped.

This action by the United States has been criticized on both moral and political grounds. It is difficult to accept the reasonableness of the moral criticisms. Among these, perhaps, the most frequently asserted is that the use of bombs on urban communities where they killed indiscriminately was inhumane. And yet, the previously accepted and frequently used mass conventional bombings over Japan and Germany had caused a similar result. They had merely been less efficient. By that late period of World War II such actions were common. They were also planned for future operations against Japan. Within that frame of reference, as unfortunate as it might have been, and within the theoretical uncertainties as to the level of destruction which might be expected from the atomic bombs, it probably seemed no serious moral deviation to use the weapons. With the well-developed understanding that the productivity of a nation was directly connected with its ability to resist, and with the knowledge that particularly in Japan the pattern of productivity was spread widely among small private producers in urban communities, the rationale for mass bombing had been developed. The distinction between civilian and military targets had approached the vanishing point as war became total. Certainly the distinction was no longer understood by Truman who wrote:

> In deciding to use this bomb I wanted to make sure that it would be used as a weapon of war prescribed by the laws of war. That meant that I wanted it dropped on a military target. I had told Stimson that the bomb should be dropped as nearly as possible upon a war production center of prime military importance.

The Interim Committee suggested that the targets purposefully be dual targets including military and civilian establishments. From the expected shock to the civilian population, the Japanese Government might be led to accept unconditional surrender to avoid a reapplication of the horror. It was expected to understand the futility of resistance. Of course, the United States also had its moral argument—that the immediate destruction of lives and property would, in the long run, save lives by shortening the war. Although there may be some doubt that such would be the result, no one could prove the contrary. On the other hand, that reasoning was built on the assumption that the predicted fact which was never to happen would inevitably have been the fact if the bombs had not been dropped. This, too, was beyond demonstration.

Truman and Stimson and others involved in the decision were humane individuals. They had humanity's interests at heart in describing their actions, and yet except in a very general sense their accounts evaded the major point. Those who participated in making this decision were operating near the end of the world's greatest war neither in the interests of humanity as a whole nor of Japanese humanity specifically. They acted primarily for the humanity of the United States. It was frequently said and widely believed that for them any number of enemy dead was preferable to the death of one United States citizen. They were operating in the interests of the United States and only incidentally in the interests of humanity when the two could be served by the same action. This is not to say that their action was morally justified under existing ethical norms. It does indicate that, perhaps, quite sincerely they found moral rationalizations for their actions in terms of the national value system which they were acting to preserve.

Closely associated with this moral complaint is another criticism frequently stated that, granting the justification for the bombing of Hiroshima, there was no moral basis for so quickly attacking Nagasaki before the Japanese Government had time to react. Again this criticism overlooks the rationale under which the bombs were dropped. They were used to end the war quickly by convincing the Japanese that resistance was futile. Two were dropped in close temporal proximity to create the illusion that the United States had a stockpile of such weapons. Such action was morally justifiable since it aimed to save lives by shortening the war. The fact is, the use of the two bombs was looked upon as one operation; and only tactical considerations involved in preparing the bombs and in assuring suitable weather governed the timing of the second drop. The moral justification for the first covered the moral requirements for the second.

A third moral criticism which verges on the political asserts that the use of the atomic weapons was completely unnecessary as the Japanese Government was prepared to surrender before the bombs were dropped; and the United States Government knew it. It seems likely that Truman, Byrnes, and Stimson had heard of Japanese efforts to negotiate peace. Because of their unofficial nature, in the case of attempts through Sweden and Switzerland, and because of the ambiguity of the language of the Togo-Sato exchanges, the United States Government did not think that these efforts were either representative of the Japanese Government or indicative of Japan's willingness to accept unconditional surrender.

Certainly there was a recognizable split in the Japanese Government between the peace group and the group desiring to carry on the war. Certainly the Emperor had aligned himself unofficially with the former. And yet, to bring about the final capitulation, a catalyst was necessary to eliminate the resultant indecision by providing the Emperor with the justification for action. That catalyst may have been the atomic bombs. As [Robert] Butow has written:

> The atomic bombing of Hiroshima and Nagasaki and the Soviet Union's

declaration of war did not produce Japan's decision to surrender, for that decision—in embryo—had long been taking shape. What these events did do was to create that unusual atmosphere in which the theretofore static factor of the Emperor could be made active in such an extraordinary way as to work what was virtually a political miracle.

On the other hand, it may have been Russian intervention marking the end of Togo's efforts to obtain Russian mediation that caused Japan to surrender. It must be remarked, however, that, even if Japan had surrendered following Russian involvement and a war of perhaps greater duration, the postwar political position of the United States in the Far East might have been worsened by a possible expansion of Soviet power. Again, the decision to drop the atomic bombs was essentially political or tactical, despite the moral terms in which it has been described. Evidences of possible Japanese capitulation such as they were, were interpreted in terms of the military evaluation of the state of war, in terms of anticipated postwar political relationships, and in terms of the needs of the developing atomic bomb program and the administration's domestic situation.

The most telling criticism of United States policy toward Japan was that which objected to the inflexible interpretation of the policy of unconditional surrender. That policy was based on the military concept of complete victory. Barring total annihilation of the enemy, however, it was recognized that surrender always occurred on conditions established by the victor. The public pronouncement of such a policy to a nation as strong in its nationalism as Japan might very well prolong the war. Despite the fact that many officials, both in the military and in the government, recognized this situation, the policy had been so strongly enunciated that it proved to be difficult to modify. Any change in its interpretation, it was feared, might bring unfortunate political repercussions for the administration.

But more than this, the cause of unconditional surrender was believed in by many who wanted to eliminate Japan as a threat to United States interest in the Far East and by others who believed with some feeling that Japan was representative of evil and that the power behind that evil should be stamped out. Any modification of unconditional surrender, particularly in regard to the Emperor, was considered by many to be tantamount to a compromise with evil, to an abrogation of right principle, and to a surrender of the very object for which the United States had been fighting. There is no guarantee that the Japanese would have surrendered conditionally. And yet the evidence that exists indicates that, had the unconditional surrender formula been modified significantly, it is very likely that Japan would have surrendered, perhaps before the atomic weapons were used, on terms which would have been advantageous to the United States.

The political consequences of utilizing the atomic bombs are difficult to evaluate because this action was not the only cause of the developing postwar antagonism. Some have said that the use of the bombs, in effect, was the first act in the cold war since their purpose was to obtain for the United States a political position in the Far East to offset possible Russian threats. It seems certain that the desires to counteract the expansion of Soviet power in the Far East was an element of the motivation for using the atomic weapons. But it seems to be too simple to call their use either the first act or the cause of the cold war. For, as a matter of fact, the antagonism between the Soviet Union and the Western Powers had already begun to develop before the bombs were used. Just as the United States, in this case, was maneuvering for position in the Far East, so the Soviet Union had already obtained positions of strength in Eastern Europe. The contest to develop respective positions of strength for the postwar political struggle was quite recognizable before August of 1945. The bombs' use was only one among many actions which led to the postwar confrontation between the United States and the Soviet Union.

The current nuclear armaments race has been attributed to the demonstration of the power of the atomic weapons on Hiroshima and Nagasaki. This position, it seems, rests on the erroneous assumption that the Soviet Government had practically no knowledge of the potentialities of the weapons at that time, and that it was forced to speed up its efforts to develop comparable weapons once it recognized that the bomb was available. The evidence seems to indicate, however, that Soviet scientists had already acquired much, if not all, of the theoretical knowledge necessary for developing a weapon and that Stalin probably knew of the nature of the United States weapon before it was used. Given the tenets of the communist ideology, given the emerging conflict of interest between the Soviet Union, on the one hand, and the United States and Great Britain, on the other, it seems reasonable to believe that the Soviet Government would have exerted considerable energy to develop a similar weapon whether or not the bombs had been dropped.

Similarly the argument that the use of the bombs, insofar as this act threatened the mutual trust which existed among the Allies, undercut the chances of effective postwar international organization seems inconclusive. This approach, in effect, condemns the use of the atomic weapons for their destructive impact on a changing international political pattern which was leading to world order. It seems, however, that the United Nations had never been based on mutual trust and that it was essentially a device within which the techniques of nationalism were expected to be practiced in the interests of the states which were members of the organization. It is true that some foresaw the development of world peace through the international organization. But practicing statesmen were not generally among this group. They were intent on satisfying more immediate national aspirations. It does not seem that the promotion of a successful

United Nations would have been changed materially one way or the other had the bombs not been dropped.

Only symbolically can the use of the atomic bombs be said to have caused definable moral consequences. The morality of total war had already been sanctioned by the requirements of national security. The use of the atomic weapons symbolized the acceptance of total war and provided the precedent for their possible use by other governments. Given the insecurities inherent in the international system of states, given the apparently overriding concern of men to preserve their nations' existence, it seems that no precedent would be needed for the future use of nuclear weapons. Their magnitude presently has become so overwhelming, their ownership so distributed, that they have introduced an element of stability into relationships among states possessing such weapons. And yet this element of stability has only placed limits on the degree of international antagonism. And such limits are not absolutely restrictive. Nuclear weapons may again be used.

The decision to use the atomic bombs, then, reflected a complex of domestic and international political forces affecting the United States Government. It was based on political rather than moral grounds, although the action was described sincerely, perhaps, in moral terms. Their use symbolized, as perhaps no other act has, the bankruptcy of the nation-state system which justifies with national morality the moral abomination of total war. And yet men in nations hold most dearly their national myths. Men in nations react violently to changes in national prerogatives. And men in nations appear resolved to live in such units within the foreseeable future. The key to peace lies in establishing the basis for accommodation among the interests of the various states. It does not lie in unconditional surrender for a national enemy. It does not lie in total war and the use of nuclear weapons.

Guide to Further Reading

Since August 1945, the problem of the decision to use the atomic bomb has continued to be of widespread interest. Within a short time several of the participants in the decision gave their views on the question in personal memoirs and reminiscences. Historians as well soon began to recount and evaluate the complex events at the end of the war with Japan. As additional information has become available the many aspects of the 1945 decision have been explored very extensively.

Among the memoirs involved, those of Harry S. Truman head the list. In the first volume of *Memoirs*: *Years of Decisions* (Garden City, N.Y., 1955), he sets forth his view that the atomic bomb was a military weapon and that he never had any doubts that it should be used. His radio address of August 9, 1945, reporting on the Potsdam Conference and justifying use of the bomb to shorten the war is reprinted in Cyril Clemens (ed)., *Truman Speaks* (Webster Grove, Mo., 1946). In vol. VI of *The Second World War*: *Triumph and Tragedy* (Boston,

1953) Winston Churchill indicates that he had no doubts that it was right to drop the bomb and that use of the bomb was never an issue. Clement Attlee, who replaced Churchill at the Potsdam Conference, reveals in "The Hiroshima Choice," *The Observer*, September 6, 1959, that although he was not called upon to make a decision on the atomic bomb, he would have agreed to its use.

Elting Morison's superb biography of Henry L. Stimson, *Turmoil and Tradition* (Boston, 1960), includes an interesting section on the Secretary of War's views and decisions concerning the weapon. James F. Byrnes, who became Secretary of State in July, 1954, in *Speaking Frankly* (New York, 1947), justifies the use of the bomb as a wartime act to save lives. A fuller account of his views on the bomb, along with those of Leo Szilard, Lewis L. Strauss, Ralph Bard, and Edward Teller, are given in interviews reported in "Was A-Bomb on Japan a Mistake?" in *U.S. News & World Report*, XLIX (August 15, 1960), 62–76. In this article and in *Men and Decisions* (Garden City, N.Y., 1962), Lewis L. Strauss, an assistant to the Secretary of the Navy in 1945 and later chairman of the Atomic Energy Commission, expresses the view that the United States made a mistake in the manner in which the bomb was used. Strauss wanted a test demonstration of the bomb in a forested area of Japan, and he regrets that the United States did not show its willingness to allow Japan to retain the emperor. Joseph C. Grew, at one time Acting Secretary of State, in *Turbulent Era* (2 vols.; Boston, 1952), discusses his efforts to have some explicit public statement made by the United States that Japan could retain the emperor.

Among the discussions of the atomic bomb by American scientists who worked on the project, that of Arthur H. Compton, director of the Chicago Metallurgical Laboratory and a member of the Scientific Advisory Panel of the Interim Committee, is the most extensive. In *Atomic Quest* (New York, 1956), he presents a substantial account of atomic developments, including a discussion of his own reluctant decision that the bomb had to be used. "If the Atomic Bomb Had Not Been Used," *The Atlantic Monthly*, CLXXVIII (December, 1946), 54–56, by Karl T. Compton, provides an early justification for the decision. Vannevar Bush, wartime director of the Office of Scientific Research and Development, in *Modern Arms and Free Men* (New York, 1949), defends the use of the bomb for ending the war quickly and saving lives. Edward Teller and Leo Szilard, whose views appeared in the article in *U.S. News & World Report* mentioned above, have also written on the subject. In *The Legacy of Hiroshima* (Garden City, N.Y., 1962), Teller, who directed the development of the hydrogen bomb, reiterates his belief that it was right to develop the bomb but wrong to use it against Japan without specific warning. He suggests that a better course would have been detonation of the bomb at a high altitude over Tokyo Bay at night, followed by an ultimatum to the Japanese. Szilard, in "A Personal History of the Atomic Bomb," *The Atlantic Community Faces the Bomb*, University of Chicago Round Table No. 601, September 25, 1949, recounts his interview with Byrnes and criticizes the South Carolinian's opinions and the offhand way that Truman disclosed the existence of the new weapon to Stalin at Potsdam. Brief interviews with prominent scientists and others are given in William L. Laurence, "Would You Make the Bomb Again?" *New York Times Magazine*, August 1, 1965. This issue, which includes other articles on the bombing of Japan, was reprinted in part in John W. Finney et al., *Hiroshima Plus 20* (New York, 1965). Some of the views of J. Robert Oppenheimer, who in 1945 was director of the Los Alamos laboratory and a member of the Scientific Advisory Panel of the Interim Committee, are found in the transcript of the U.S. Atomic Energy Commission Personnel Security Board hearings of 1954, *In the Matter of J. Robert Oppenheimer* (Washington, D.C., 1954).

Military men have also written on the development and use of the atomic bomb. The most complete account is *Now It Can Be Told: The Story of the Manhattan Project* (New York, 1962) by General Leslie R. Groves, who vigorously defends the use of the bomb and shows that it was generally assumed that the bomb would be used when it became available. In "The Atom General Answers His Critics," *Saturday Evening Post*, CCXX (June 19, 1948), 15–16 ff., Groves defends the early public release of the Smyth Report (*Atomic Energy for Military Purposes*) on the development of the atomic bomb. Admiral William D. Leahy, Chief of Staff to Roosevelt and Truman, in *I Was There* (New York, 1950) states that the weapon was not necessary to end the war and that its use meant a lowering of American ethical standards. Captain Ellis M. Zacharias, in *Secret Missions* (New York, 1946), expresses his belief that the military, naval, and psychological factors were of primary importance in defeating Japan; the enemy would soon have surrendered without the utilization of the bomb and should have been given more time to move in response to the Potsdam Declaration.

Various official and semiofficial accounts deal with the atomic project and the decision to use the bomb. Henry De Wolf Smyth's *Atomic Energy for Military Purposes* (Princeton, N.J., 1945) was released with the public announcement of the new weapon, providing a general account of the scientific research and technical work that were involved in making the bomb. William L. Laurence, *Dawn Over Zero: The Story of the Atomic Bomb* (New York, 1946), is a popular account of the development of the new weapon by a *New York Times* science correspondent who was assigned to the Manhattan Project and flew on the Nagasaki mission. The official United States Air Force history, edited by Wesley Frank Craven and James Lea Cate, is *The Army Air Forces in World War II.* Vol. V: *The Pacific: Matterhorn to Nagasaki, June 1944 to August 1945*, indicates that the chief significance of the atomic bomb was in providing a face-saving excuse for the Japanese militarists. Two volumes published by the United States Strategic Bombing Survey: *Japan's Struggle to End the War*, (Washington, D.C., 1946) and the *Summary Report (Pacific War)* (Washington, D.C., 1946) indicate that the atomic bombs did not defeat Japan though "they did shorten the war and expedite the peace." The surveys conclude that Japan would undoubtedly have surrendered prior to November 1, 1945, even if an invasion had not been threatened, even if the bombs had not been used, and even if Russia had not entered the war. On the other hand, Rudolph A. Winnacker, a member of the Historical Division of the War Department, defends the dropping of the bombs on both strategic and moral grounds in "The Debate About Hiroshima," *Military Affairs*, XI (spring, 1947), 25–30. The first volume of the official history of the Atomic Energy Commission, *The New World, 1939/1946* (University Park, Pa., 1962), by Richard G. Hewlett and Oscar E. Anderson, provides a detailed account of the developmental program of the atomic bomb. J. Ehrman, *Grand Strategy*, vol. VI of *The History of the Second World War, United Kingdom Series* (London, 1956), justifies the decision to utilize the new force in terms of the situation in Japan and the power and intransigence of the Japanese militarists.

General historical accounts include Robert Jungk, *Brighter than a Thousand Suns* (New York, 1958); Fletcher Knebel and Charles W. Bailey, *No High Ground* (New York, 1960), reviewing various criticisms of the decision to use the new weapon; John Francis Purcell, *The Best-Kept Secret: The Story of the Atomic Bomb* (New York, 1963), emphasizing the engineering aspects of the project; Len Giovannitti and Fred Freed, *The Decision to Drop the Bomb* (New York, 1965), concluding that the decision was made in good faith to end the war quickly; Stephane Groueff, *Manhattan Project: The Untold Story of the Making of the Atomic Bomb* (Boston, 1967), focusing on the work of Groves. An important short scholarly analysis was made by Louis Morton in "The Decision to Use the Atomic Bomb," *Foreign Affairs*, XXXV (January, 1957), 334–353. Medford Evans provides a right-wing attack on those opposing the use of the bomb in *The Secret War for the A-Bomb* (Chicago, 1953). Nat S. Finney, "How FDR Planned to Use the A-Bomb," *Look*, XIV (March 14, 1950), 26–27, surmises as to how President Roosevelt would have utilized the new device. Michael Amrine, in *The Great Decision: The Secret History of the Atomic Bomb* (New York, 1959), argues that the bomb should not have been used without a clear warning or demonstration, and that more time should have been taken to think over the implications of the new force. Richard F. Haynes, *The Awesome Power: Harry S. Truman as Commander in Chief* (Baton Rouge, 1973) shows the tremendous growth of presidential military power and criticizes Truman for dropping the bomb on Japanese cities rather than selecting an unpopulated test area.

Some scholars have focused on the role of the scientists in the development and use of the bomb. Robert Gilpin, *American Scientists and Nuclear Policy* (Princeton, N.J., 1962) provides a brief discussion of the 1945 decision within the larger context of the emerging role of scientists in formulating governmental policy. Very important in enlarging our understanding of the role of the scientists at the Chicago laboratory is Alice Kimball Smith's article, "Behind the Decision to Use the Atomic Bomb: Chicago 1944–45," *Bulletin of the Atomic Scientists*, XIV (October, 1958), 288–312. Mrs. Smith has also written a detailed account of the activities of American scientists in dealing with the social and political aspects and with controls of atomic energy in *A Peril and a Hope: The Scientists' Movement in America: 1945–47* (Chicago, 1965). This volume includes the text of the Franck Report, which was also published in somewhat abridged form in *Bulletin of the Atomic Scientists*, I (May, 1946), 2–4, 16, as "A Report to the Secretary of War—June 1945." Fletcher Knebel and Charles W. Bailey in "The Fight Over the A-Bomb," *Look*, XXVII (August 13, 1963), 19–23, discuss the unsuccessful efforts of scientists to get their views before President Truman. Bertrand Goldschmidt, *L'Aventure Atomique: Les Aspects Politiques et Techniques* (Paris, 1962) focuses on the historical development of atomic energy. A popular dual biography, *Lawrence and Oppenheimer* (by Nuel Pharr Davis, New York, 1968), deals with the relationships of these two leading physicists, often to the disparagement of Lawrence. David H. Frisch, "Scientists and the Decision to Bomb Japan," in *Alamogordo Plus Twenty-Five Years*, ed. Richard S. Lewis and Jane Wilson with Eugene Rabinowitch (New York, 1971), reprinted from the *Bulletin of the Atomic Scientists* (December, 1970), analyzes and evaluates possible alternative courses that might have been taken to demonstrate the force of the atomic bomb. David Irving, *The German Atomic Bomb: The History of Nuclear Research in Nazi Germany* (New York, 1967), shows that the German atomic project was very limited and did not develop far since scientists rather than the military directed it and the thrust of the program tended to focus on theory rather than on technology.

The moral aspects of the decision to drop the bomb have interested most of the writers dealing with the events of 1945. Journals of religion and theology, such as the *Christian Century* and the *Catholic World*, included in the last months of 1945 considerable commentary on the destruction of Hiroshima and Nagasaki by the new weapon. Robert Maynard Hutchins, *The Atomic Bomb versus Civilization,* Human Events Pamphlets No. 1 (Washington, D.C., 1945) stresses the moral dimensions of the decision and urges that a world state and government must be adopted as the only hope for mankind in the future. Norman Cousins and Thomas K. Finletter in "A Beginning for Sanity," *Saturday Review of Literature*, XXIX (June 15, 1946), 5–9, 38–40, review the need for a sound policy control of the bomb and suggest that this new force may have been directed against the Soviet Union. Fred J. Cook, *The Warfare State* (New York, 1962) believes that the dropping of the bombs meant the enthronement of naked force; he presents a picture of self-deluded military men contrasted with far-sighted scientists: the military mind, he feels, is the worst possible for dealing with the complex problems of the nuclear age.

The diplomatic context and consequences of the use of the atomic bomb have been the concern of more historical analysis than any other aspect of the great decision. Especially since the mid-1960's various revisionist interpretations have been published placing much of the blame for the origins of the Cold War on the United States, with the dropping of the atomic bombs as a primary determinant. Antirevisionists have in turn questioned the use of evidence and the interpretive framework of the revisionists. In an early article, I. I. Rabi, the physicist, in "Playing Down the Bomb," *The Atlantic Monthly*, CLXXXIII (April, 1949), 21–23, attacks the interpretation of P. M. S. Blackett as unwarranted and confused. A. J. R. Groom, "U.S.-Allied Relations and the Atomic Bomb in the Second World War," *World Politics*, XV (October, 1962), 123–137, discusses the ambiguous relations between the United States, Great Britain, and Canada respecting the atomic developmental program. Important general accounts of the diplomatic context of atomic warfare include Gaddis Smith, *American Diplomacy during the Second World War, 1941–1945* (New York, 1965); Raymond G. O'Connor, *Diplomacy for Victory: FDR and Unconditional Surrender* (New York, 1971); John Lewis Gaddis, *The United States and the Origins of the Cold War, 1941–1947* (New York, 1972); and Lisle A. Rose, *Dubious Victory: The United States and the End of World War II* (Kent, Ohio, 1973). An early revisionist work, D. F. Fleming, *The Cold War and Its Origins* (2 vols.; London, 1961), suggests that the use of the atomic bomb set a regrettable precedent and marked the end of the wartime alliance and the start of the postwar struggle for world balance of power. David Horowitz, *The Free World Colossus: A Critique of American Foreign Policy in the Cold War* (New York, 1965; rev. ed., 1971) sees the development and use of the atomic bomb as a crucial factor leading to the Cold War. The critical response to the revisionist interpretation of Gar Alperovitz in *Atomic Diplomacy* (New York, 1965) was considerable. Among the more important discussions of this work are Christopher Lasch, "The Explosion That Froze the World," *Nation*, CCI (Sept. 6, 1965), 123–24; Athan Theoharis, "Atomic Diplomacy," *New University Thought*, V (May, June, 1967), 12, 73–77; Martin J. Sherwin, "The Atomic Bomb as History: An Essay Review," *Wisconsin Magazine of History*, L (winter, 1969–70), 128–134, which also, in reviewing other books, deals with the role of scientists in policy formulation; and Robert James Maddox, "*Atomic Diplomacy*: A Study in Creative Writing," *The Journal of American History*, LIX (March, 1973), 925–934, with Alperovitz' reply, 1062–1067. Other revisionist writings include Gar Alperovitz, *Cold War Essays* (New York, 1970); Barton J. Bernstein, "American Foreign Policy and the Origins of the Cold War," in Barton J. Bernstein, ed., *Politics and Policies of the Truman Administration* (Chicago, 1970), 15–77; Barton J. Bernstein, "The Atomic Bomb and American Foreign Policy, 1941–1945: An Historiographical Controversy," *Peace and Change*, II (spring, 1974), 1–16; Charles L. Mee, Jr., *Meeting at Potsdam* (New York, 1974); and Barton J. Bernstein, "Roosevelt, Truman, and the Atomic

Bomb, 941–1945: A Reinterpretation," *Political Science Quarterly*, XC (spring, 1975), 23–69. Critiques of revisionist interpretations include Charles S. Maier, "Revisionism and the Interpretation of Cold War Origins," *Perspective sin American History*, IV (1970), 313–347; Henry Pachter, "Revisionist Historians and the Cold War," in Irving Howe, ed., *Beyond the New Left* (New York, 1970), 166–191; and Robert James Maddox, *The New Left and the Origins of the Cold War* (Princeton, 1973). Warren F. Kimball, "The Cold War Warmed Over," *American Historical Review*, LXXIX (October, 1974), 1119–1136, provides an extended critique of the Maddox book along with discussion of works by Joyce and Gabriel Kolko and John Lewis Gaddis. Joseph I. Lieberman, *The Scorpion and the Tarantula: The Struggle to Control Atomic Weapons, 1945–1949* (Boston, 1970) details the history of the movement to bring about international control of atomic weapons. The same general topic is covered from a revisionist viewpoint in Barton J. Bernstein, "The Quest for Security: American Foreign Policy and International Control of Atomic Energy, 1942–1946," *The Journal of American History*, LX (March, 1974), 1003–1044. Martin J. Sherwin, *A World Destroyed: The Atomic Bomb and the Ground Alliance* (New York, 1975) utilizes recently declassified documents focusing on the Roosevelt atomic policies.

Finally, another group of writers have dealt with the situation in Japan in 1945. The most comprehensive account of Japanese maneuvers toward the final surrender is that of Robert J. C. Butow, *Japan's Decision to Surrender* (Stanford, Calif., 1954). Toshikazu Kase, *Journey to the Missouri* (New Haven, Conn., 1950), published in England as *Eclipse of the Rising Sun* (London, 1951), is an account of Japan's side of the surrender negotiations by a former member of the Japanese Foreign Office. Shigenori Togo, the foreign minister of Japan at the end of the war, has written his views of the events of this period in *The Cause of Japan* (New York, 1956). Both William J. Coughlin, "The Great *Mokusatsu* Mistake," *Harper's*, CCVI (March, 1953), 31–40, and Kazuo Kawai, "Mokusatu, Japan's Response to the Potsdam Declaration," *Pacific Historical Review*, XIX (November, 1950), 409–414, are concerned with the problem of the Japanese reception of the Potsdam Declaration. William Craig, *The Fall of Japan* (New York, 1967) and Lester Brooks, *Behind Japan's Surrender: The Secret Struggle that Ended an Empire* (New York, 1968) provide general accounts of the final days of the war and the surrender negotiations. Harold Stein, "The Rationale of Japanese Surrender," *World Politics*, XV (October 1962), pp. 138–150, in a review of Herbert Feis, *Japan Subdued*, discusses facets of Japanese governmental behavior relating to the surrender issue. Laurens van der Post, *The Prisoner and the Bomb* (New York, 1970) argues that the United States was right to drop the bomb to forestall a bloody invasion and the possible slaughter of prisoners of war; atomic destruction gave the Japanese an excuse to surrender without great loss of face. Joseph Laurance Marx, *Nagasaki: The Necessary Bomb?* (New York, 1971) focuses on the events in Japan in 1945 and the use of the second atomic bomb against Nagasaki. The second bomb is also the focus of Bernstein, "Doomsday II: After Hiroshima Was Nagasaki Necessary?" *New York Times Magazine* (July 27, 1975), 7 ff.